MW00335220

# TEACHING EFFECTIVE SOURCE USE

# TEACHING EFFECTIVE SOURCE USE

## Classroom Approaches That Work

Jennifer A. Mott-Smith

Zuzana Tomaš

Ilka Kostka

UNIVERSITY OF MICHIGAN PRESS

ANN ARBOR

Copyright © by the University of Michigan 2017
All rights reserved
Published in the United States of America
The University of Michigan Press
Manufactured in the United States of America

♾ Printed on acid-free paper

ISBN-13: 978-0-472-03689-9

2020   2019   2018   2017          4   3   2   1

No part of this publication may be reproduced, stored in a retrieval system, or transmitted in any form or by any means, electronic, mechanical, or otherwise, without the written permission of the publisher.

We dedicate this book to our students,
who have put their trust in us and taught us much
over the years and who continue to inspire us
to improve our teaching.

## Acknowledgments

We'd like to thank everyone who helped in the writing of this book, including the student and published writers whose writing we used; our editor, Kelly Sippell, who helped us conceive the form the book would take; and our families, who supported us throughout the process. Thank you.

# Contents

# Chapter 7  Bringing It All Together: Teaching the Dimensions of Source Use

# Introduction

## Why We Wrote This Book

TEACHING EFFECTIVE SOURCE USE is a comprehensive and practical resource for teachers working with student writers, particularly second language (L2) writers. We undertook this project because, although there has been an explosion of research and theorizing about source use over the past twenty years, many of the insights gained from this work have not yet made their way into classrooms. Indeed, a 2010 survey found that writing instructors were not satisfied with the available teaching materials and pointed to the need for more comprehensive, high-quality instructional materials that teachers can use to support L2 writers' writing from sources (Tomaš, 2010). A recent review of L2 writing textbooks published since then also revealed minimal attention to source use. Perhaps because of the lack of good materials, the approaches of some instructors is to spend classroom time focusing on the development of decontextualized sentence-level skills (practicing paraphrasing one sentence at a time, for example), to offer warnings against misuse of sources, and to rely on software to detect plagiarism when grading. While such approaches may be useful at times, we believe that they need to be situated within a much more comprehensive approach that emphasizes not the mechanics of source use but its meaning.

We have written this book for all educators who help student writers with source-based writing assignments. Developed for teachers working with L2 writers, many of the lessons have proven useful for native (L1) speakers as well. The book can be used in a variety of contexts, including college-level ESL writing courses, Intensive English Program writing courses, high school ESL classes, and EFL programs in international contexts. It can also be used by instructors teaching in Writing across the Curriculum, Writing in the Disciplines, and graduate L2 teacher training programs; by consultants and tutors in university writing centers; and by library faculty working with students on research projects. The book can be used to develop a lesson to meet an immediate need, but our primary vision is for teachers to use the book to develop lessons on source use for an entire course.

# A Multidimensional Approach

Our approach to source use has five dimensions that provide multiple vantage points from which to address the goal of teaching effective source use:

1. *The concept dimension* defines keywords and values that undergird Western academic source use.

2. *The discourse dimension* addresses the ways in which sources are used within discourse communities.

3. *The sentence dimension* addresses the skills necessary to paraphrase, summarize, and quote effectively.

4. *The process dimension* covers strategies for effective source use employed during the entire reading-thinking-writing process.

5. *The response dimension* emphasizes learning to give, receive, and apply feedback on source use.

The dimensions allow us to conceptualize different perspectives on source use that teachers can take. They are not discrete but overlapping, and many of our lessons incorporate ideas from more than one dimension. Our multidimensional approach not only helps student writers avoid plagiarism but guides them to articulate their source-based ideas more effectively and with a more authoritative voice. We do not provide lessons that focus on minutiae, such as the use of ellipsis to omit words from a quote, because we believe that such things are details and should be addressed as questions about them arise rather than in formal class lessons. There are also many resources available that address these types of details. Instead, we present lessons that focus on meaning because we believe that they empower students to become strong academic writers.

## Terminology

Our multidimensional approach is non-punitive. Throughout the book, we use terminology that avoids judgment. Because the term *plagiarism* carries ethical connotations, we prefer to use *textual reuse*, which is descriptive and allows for an open discussion of the decisions writers make as they construct their texts. When we discuss the conventional view of plagiarism, we prefer the term *prototypical plagiarism* (Pecorari, 2003) because it flags the fact that the construct of plagiarism is problematic. We use the term *attribution* to refer to the various formal ways in which writers give credit to their sources, including quotation marks, citations, and a reference page. When attribution does not meet the standards of the context, we prefer to call it *unconventional attribution* rather than *inadequate attribution*, as the former term is less judgmental.

We also prefer the term *attempted paraphrase* (Keck, 2006) to *unacceptable paraphrase* because it emphasizes the effort of the student writer rather than inadequacy. Finally, we use the terms *source use* and *referencing* as umbrellas for all of these terms. *Effective source use* refers to source use that is rhetorically persuasive and/or establishes authority and that is well-integrated linguistically. *Conventional source use* refers to source use that follows the rules relevant to the context.

## Using This Book

We suggest that readers begin with the first chapter, *"Plagiarism" Hysteria: Taking a Stance against the Cat-and-Mouse Game*, to become familiar with the ideas and assumptions that frame our approach. This chapter discusses the ways that plagiarism has traditionally been cast in ethical terms and argues that this frame is not conducive to student writers' mastering of effective source use. We stress that teachers should recognize the diverse behaviors that have been included under the umbrella of plagiarism, understand the historic roots of plagiarism as a cultural construct, and appreciate the diversity of plagiarism standards and judgments made by different individuals and in different disciplines. Further, we challenge the stereotyping of L2 writers as plagiarizers and explore three approaches in the literature to understanding L2 writers' source use: culture, language, and identity.

Following this introductory chapter, we lay out our approach to teaching effective source use over five chapters, each of which addresses one of the five dimensions. These five chapters may be read out of order. Each is structured similarly, beginning with a discussion of the theory and research that informs the dimension, followed by presentation of lessons for the classroom. Each chapter ends with a summary of take-away points.

Chapter 2, *The Concept Dimension*, addresses the cultural ideas that students need to understand in order to use references effectively and conventionally. These ideas include authority, voice, originality, knowledge transformation, ownership, discourse community, common knowledge, plagiarism, and copyright. We argue that it is necessary to teach L2 writers how to be original and how to establish authority in writing. We believe that it is important to discuss why textual reuse can engender such strong negative reactions in some contexts while being allowed, even expected, in others.

In Chapter 3, *The Discourse Dimension*, we focus on teaching source use from the perspective of establishing authority and making room for one's ideas within a discourse community. We discuss both text-level source use decisions and the larger disciplinary discourses that shape these decisions. We explore the rhetorical functions of references, connect the notions of stance and engagement to referencing, and briefly discuss disciplinary differences in referencing.

Then in Chapter 4, *The Sentence Dimension*, we move from discourse- and text-level issues to sentence-level issues. We explore patchwriting in detail and encourage teachers to explore the topic together with students as a way to open a dialogue about how L2 writers construct texts. In addition, we discuss the need to teach L2 writers how to distinguish their voices from those of their source texts in order to learn to paraphrase and quote conventionally. We discuss what makes paraphrasing and summarizing difficult, including the formulaic nature of language and the fact that paraphrasing often involves critiquing an idea or combining it with others in addition to restating it accurately. We also discuss what makes quoting difficult, focusing on how to incorporate quotes smoothly in one's writing.

In Chapter 5, *The Process Dimension*, we look at the use of sources over the entire reading-thinking-writing process so that teachers can scaffold and assess the subprocesses that students are often left to accomplish on their own. We present strategies for avoiding procrastination, selecting sources, reading, keeping track of sources, and integrating ideas from source texts into a paper.

Chapter 6, *The Response Dimension*, discusses the importance of ongoing, formative response as a way to practice applying the rules of effective source use. Because it is important to support students so that they can understand and know how to apply teacher feedback, we discuss response as a dialogue between teacher and student that can give teachers insight into student theories of source use. We discuss self-assessment and peer response as ways to develop the metalanguage of source use and independence in writing.

In the final chapter, *Bringing It All Together*, we show how three experienced writing instructors (the co-authors of this book) incorporate lessons from each of the five dimensions into their writing courses. Specifically, Jennifer describes her first-year college composition course for L2 writers; Zuzana describes her research paper writing course for third- and fourth-year undergraduate L2 writers; and Ilka describes a graduate writing course for L2 writers.

To help teachers quickly access the lessons described in the various chapters of the book, a Lessons Chart that gives an overview appears in Appendix 1.

Appendix 2 includes a list of texts and videos at a range of levels for use in the classroom. Appendix 3 shows writing samples that we have used to illustrate our discussions of lessons and that can be used to develop your own lessons. Appendix 4 features three types of idea organizers: a graphic organizer, an outline, and a chart.

## A Note on Source Use in the Context of Academic Writing

We would like to acknowledge that teaching source use is only one part of the work of teaching writing. We certainly do not want to imply that other issues that arise when teaching writing, such as creating space for students to pursue their own ideas, expand their analytical thinking abilities, and develop their writing processes, should be replaced by the rhetorical or genre concerns that are part of referencing. However, referencing is a fundamental way that academic writers provide support, construct authority, and establish significance, so learning to reference is important to the growth of students as academic writers. Regardless of the context in which you work, we hope that this book helps you gain insights into the complexities and nuances of source use and leaves instructors feeling informed and confident to deal with this component of academic writing. We also hope that the lessons included here help instructors build confident and skilled academic writers who have authoritative voices and can weave sources into their writing conventionally, effectively, and meaningfully.

# 1

# "Plagiarism" Hysteria:
## Taking a Stance against the Cat-and-Mouse Game

---

**What best describes the rightness or wrongness of plagiarism?**

A.   It is always wrong because it is theft and fraud.

B.   Plagiarism is not a right or wrong kind of thing.

C.   In some situations, it is OK.

D.   There is nothing wrong with it.

–(Turnitin, n.d.)

---

THE THREE OF US RECENTLY COMPLETED AN ONLINE QUIZ designed to test knowledge of "plagiarism." None of us scored full points. One of the questions that we got "wrong" was the one shown. One of us checked answer C, and two selected answer B. Even though we each worked separately on the quiz, we share perspectives: for example, we knew that a sentence considered "plagiarized" by an English professor might be acceptable to a biology professor and a sentence cut-and-pasted into a work document would be acceptable if the genre were based on a boilerplate. We also knew it is acceptable to reuse text for satire or homage. And, as L2 writing teachers, we knew that students sometimes reuse text unknowingly and other times deliberately to practice unfamiliar language, and that such reuse entails language learning benefits. Despite our reasoning, however, the "right" answer was A: so-called plagiarism is "always wrong."

## The Cat-and-Mouse Game

The "always wrong" answer reflects the fact that prototypical plagiarism is generally understood as an ethical issue, as a matter of honesty and fairness. So, when a writer uses another writer's idea without clear attribution, most people believe that it is a dishonest representation of the writer's work and that reusing it is unfair to the unattributed writer. Delving a little deeper, we can see that this understanding is predicated on another value: materialism. Unattributed words and ideas are seen as *stolen*, and they can be stolen because they can be *owned*. Thus, in this view, words and ideas are commodified. This hegemonic view is reflected in the plagiarism policies of many Western universities. This materialistic view contrasts sharply with non-materialistic views of discourse in other academic communities in which ideas belong to everyone. This view also contrasts with the views of teachers who recognize many other reasons for non-attributed textual copying than those that are acknowledged in Western institutional policies and of teachers who are resistant to the punitive system (Benesch, 2016) or feel caught in it.

In the ethical view, writer intent is important. The assumption is that the "plagiarizing" writer intended to present someone else's work as his/her own. As Pecorari (2013) convincingly argued, even institutional policies that judge "plagiarism" objectively through textual comparison nevertheless are embedded in the language of ethics and hinge on student intent. And, although teachers may know that there are myriad reasons for reusing source text without attribution, they may still feel that students are trying to get away with something when they do not cite. Teachers may feel deceived, disappointed, foolish, and/or angry, and become obsessed with finding the uncited source text.

Why do we teachers become so obsessed? In an insightful analysis of the *discourse of ethics* surrounding Western discussions of source use, Valentine (2006) explained that the ethical frame "situates students within a binary of honest or dishonest" (p. 90). Once a student has been suspected of "plagiarizing," the instructor discounts the honest work the student did on the writing task and henceforth expects the student to re-demonstrate honesty and the ability to do compositional work. In other words, the instructor comes to see the student not as a person who constructed the text in an unconventional way, but as a cheater who will continue to cheat. Thus, instructors sometimes shift their focus from teaching students to avoid copying text and neglecting to attribute ideas to policing and punishing them when they do these things. They end up playing a cat-and-mouse game, chasing down potentially copied sources in an attempt to "catch" students and, ironically, often come to resent this work.

From the perspectives of many L2 writing students, the cat-and-mouse game is unpleasant as well. It may be confusing and alienating, particularly if they are accused of "plagiarism" but do not believe they have done anything wrong. L2 writers' understandings are often, naturally enough, based on prior schooling experiences; some have used copying in the past and it was not considered cheating. Depending on the context, such practices may be perfectly logical. For example, if the purpose of a writing task is not to compose a paper that offers a new idea but to demonstrate that one has read a set of assigned texts, then it makes sense to reuse words and ideas; citations would then become a form of busy work since the student knows that the teacher knows where the words and ideas came from. For many L2 writing students, therefore, punishment for textual reuse may seem arbitrary and unfair, and it may lead to disengagement and resistance.

## Removing the Ethical Frame from Discussions of Source Use

Removing the ethical frame from the discussion of source use provides a way out of the cat-and-mouse game and opens up opportunities for meaningful teaching about effective source use. There are several steps involved in removing this frame, including:

- acknowledging that there are many different behaviors that are called "plagiarism"
- changing our terminology
- recognizing that what we call "plagiarism" is not a universal and that it has historic roots
- accepting that standards for referencing vary widely.

*Plagiarism* is a confusing term because it refers to a broad range of behaviors, including some that are deceitful and some that are not. The distinction between deceitful and non-deceitful behaviors is important for teachers because the two behaviors demand different responses. Deceitful behavior (e.g., hiring someone to write a paper) is of course "always wrong" and may deserve punishment. Non-deceitful behavior, which typically stems from a student not knowing that something is problematic or lacking the ability to avoid it, on the other hand, should be approached with a pedagogical response.

As authors, we recognize three common forms of non-deceitful textual reuse. The first is *unconventional attribution*, where student writers may not realize that both in-text citations and a reference page are required, that ideas as well as words must be cited, or that when re-quoting they need to cite both the author of the quote and the author of the article in which they read the quote. While it is relatively easy to explain conventional citing behavior, students may need a great deal of practice before they do it consistently and accurately.

Another form of unconventional attribution involves the *reuse of an organizing structure* (e.g., using the same points in the same sequence as a source to support a similar argument). In this case, teachers often object to it not only because it violates their attribution expectations, but also because they believe that students have not done enough of their own thinking. This is a harder teaching problem to address since it involves teaching students a range of writing skills, including how to construct arguments, choose supporting points or quotes, and conduct research.

A third common, non-deceitful form of textual reuse is *patchwriting*, a term coined by Howard (1992) to refer to the mixing of words in a text such that a phrase drawn from one source is juxtaposed with a phrase drawn from another, with some of the writer's own wording interspersed. Patchwriting may take the form of unattributed quotes, "near copies" (Campbell, 1990; Keck, 2006), or so-called "unacceptable paraphrases." Patchwriting is widely known in the field of L2 writing as a way for student writers to practice and acquire academic discourse. While many teachers and scholars discuss the ways in which we can move students from patchwriting to more independent word use, others have begun to suggest that patchwriting itself may be beneficial and used to promote L2 writing fluency.

After acknowledging that there are many behaviors that fall under the umbrella of prototypical plagiarism, teachers should use more accurate terminology when discussing source use. Numerous studies since the 1990s have shown that much source use, particularly by L2 writers, is not deceitful (Abasi, Akbari, & Graves, 2006; Abasi & Akbari, 2008; Angélil-Carter, 2000; Campbell, 1990; Currie, 1998; Flowerdew & Li, 2007; Pecorari 2003, 2006; Petrić, 2012; Starfield, 2002) and, as a result, new terms have been introduced. For instance, Currie (1998) referred to the "apparent plagiarism" of an L2 writer, and Pecorari (2003) introduced the terms *prototypical* and *non-prototypical plagiarism* to refer to deceitful and non-deceitful plagiarism, respectively. Similarly, Chandrasoma, Thompson and Pennycook (2004) used the terms *transgressive* and *non-transgressive intertextuality*.

We believe that it is important for teachers to contribute to removing the ethical frame from discussions of textual reuse by changing the language that they use. This is not an easy task, however. It involves careful analysis of various terms. For instance, the term *textual borrowing* is acceptable in that it is non-punitive, but we nevertheless prefer not to use it because the notion of *borrowing* is based on the commodification of ideas and is thus inaccurate: A borrowed item cannot be used by the borrower and by its owner at the same time, but an idea can be. Changing terminology also involves developing strategies for avoiding punitive words.

In writing this book, for instance, to avoid using *plagiarism*, we have employed a preferred term (*prototypical plagiarism*), substituted conceptually different terms (*textual reuse*) or other words (e.g., writing "referencing standards" rather than "plagiarism standards"), specified behaviors (e.g., patchwriting, citing), distanced ourselves from the usage by means of quotation marks ("plagiarism"), accepted the use of the word in some phrases (*plagiarism policy, accusations of plagiarism*), and omitted the word where possible. While changing language may temporarily render teachers' discourse a bit awkward, we believe that it is worth it in the long run.

A third important step in removing the ethical frame, particularly for Western-raised or Western-trained teachers, is to place "plagiarism" in historical context. Unattributed textual reuse was not always considered deceitful in the English-speaking world. Before the 18th century, imitation was a common and acceptable way to write. In some contexts, writers welcomed copying as a way to spread their ideas to a wider audience. During the Romantic Period (which began at the end of the 18th century and continued through the mid-19th century), the notion of authorship changed. Authorship came to be seen as the pursuit of a divinely inspired person, working alone to produce original texts. (See Angélil-Carter, 2000; Blum, 2009; Howard, 1999; Lunsford & Ede, 1994; Sutherland-Smith, 2008; Woodmansee, 1994, for discussions of the development of modern constructions of the *author*.) With this new image of the author, the role of imitator was reduced to that of "plagiarizer," and as the Other of the author, the plagiarizer came to be seen as not doing any genuine work and therefore as immoral (Howard, 1999).

Knowing this history helps us see that "plagiarism" is not a universal. In addition, recognizing that the construction of "plagiarizer" depends on the Romantic construction of the *author* opens an opportunity to question our beliefs about textual reuse and collaboration because many writers, writing scholars, and instructors already doubt the idea that writers produce brand new ideas completely on their own. For example, studying collaboration in writing, Lunsford and Ede (1994) forcefully concluded, "After a lengthy research project and eight years of study, we feel confident in saying that the traditional model of solitary authorship is more myth than reality" (p. 418). In a similar vein, it is not uncommon to find writers describing their own processes in ways that challenge Romantic understandings of originality: "The principle that 'originality' is more about a kind of transformation of existing ideas than the invention of the absolutely new is one that I can relate to as an artist and author" (Tan, 2001, p. 4). Once we recognize the extent to which writers borrow ideas from other people and texts, it creates room for us to allow, and perhaps even encourage, our students to do the same.

Finally, a fourth step in removing the ethical frame from discussions of source use involves recognizing the diversity of referencing standards and judgments within Western institutions. Instructors who have served on a university committee charged with drafting a plagiarism policy have likely encountered the differences of opinion of their colleagues, both in terms of how "plagiarism" should be defined and what textual practices constitute it. This lack of agreement has been explained by researchers and theorists in several ways: disciplinary differences in referencing conventions; genre differences, particularly in the workplace genres that many of us now find ourselves teaching (e.g., the business memo); and individual variation. The differences are so profound and so little understood that two leaders in the field of textual reuse, Diane Pecorari (2015) and Bojana Petrić (2015), recently called for more research into gatekeepers' judgments about source use. Our point here is that, if such profound differences exist, they belie a strict, moralizing approach to textual reuse, and as teachers, we need to take into account the lack of agreement on how sources ought to be used.

To summarize, we believe that teachers can contribute to better policies for and better teaching of effective source use by removing the ethical frame. Doing so involves distinguishing between the different behaviors called "plagiarism," revising our terminology to be pedagogically rather than punitively oriented, historicizing "plagiarism" as a cultural construct, and recognizing the variation in referencing standards and judgments.

## CONSIDER

What are your responses to these two quotes? What are the implications of each for writing teachers?

"Learning a distaste for plagiarism is part of learning academic values and orientations, part of the process of academic acculturation." (Pecorari, 2013, p. 39)

"Patchwriting belongs not in a category with cheating on exams and purchasing term papers, but in a category with the ancient tradition of learning through apprenticeship and mimicry." (Howard, 1999, p. xviii)

# L2 Student Writers in an Age of "Plagiarism" Hysteria

It is of particular concern to us that L2 writers are singled out as "plagiarizers" in both scholarship and the popular press. For example, one scholar working in Australia wrote, "Concerns about plagiarism are on the increase within many areas of the global university system, especially in the context of the increasing number of international students that now form a key aspect of so many university programmes" (Song-Turner, 2008, p. 39). An article from Minnesota Public Radio echoes this sentiment, noting that "the frequency [of prototypical plagiarism] is rising alongside statewide international enrollment, which jumped almost 15 percent from fall 2009 to fall 2012," concluding, disturbingly, with a list of "Minnesota colleges and universities with the largest international student populations" (Farhang, 2014). These representations are concerning because they stereotype international students as "plagiarizers," and these stereotypes may influence teachers' perceptions of them and their writing.

At the same time, the current college generation is seen as to be tending toward a level of textual reuse that has heretofore been considered unconventional. Around the world, these students are thought to be digital natives who can skillfully exploit the internet to construct their papers. In a scholarly study done in Australia, Sutherland-Smith (2008) linked the internet to prototypical plagiarism through the argument that the technology makes copying easy; and both she and Marshall and Garry (2006), in a study from New Zealand, linked plagiarism and the internet through the argument that students think it is okay <u>not</u> to cite internet sources. In a U.S. study, Blum (2009) made an even more complex argument, tying the development of the subjectivity of the current college generation to the use of the internet and arguing that this generation does not buy into the logic of citation. Blum painted a picture of college students who tend to doubt that traditional notions of originality are possible and for whom originality lies in pastiche (i.e., in selecting and recombining things). (See also Pecorari, 2013.) These students value sociability, sharing, and collaboration and find a shared identity in borrowing texts in social situations; textual ownership and attribution are not part of these practices.

The advent of the internet has led to a cultural shift in the way people construct texts, and Blum's study helps us begin to make sense of this profound change. At the same time, however, the reaction to millennials' use of the internet has been one of "hysteria" (Howard, 2007) over the presumed loss of morals of the younger generation and is based on the assumption that "plagiarism" is a breach in ethics. It is important to recognize, therefore, that we have no idea how prevalent deceitful plagiarism actually is. There are many reasons why we do not have this information: For example, it is not possible to ascertain whether all cases have been counted, studies may be invalid because the participants themselves have differing understandings of "plagiarism" or because of the difficulties of self-report (e.g., students tell researchers what they think they want to hear), and studies may not be comparable due to differing definitions of "plagiarism" (Pecorari, 2013). But most important, these studies cannot reveal a loss in integrity among college students because they do not systematically distinguish between deceitful and non-deceitful plagiarism. To the extent that studies confound cheating with other behaviors labelled "plagiarism" that arise from a lack of knowledge or skills, we cannot know the extent of the ethical problem.

## Issues in L2 Writers' Source Use

Much scholarship on L2 writers has set aside the issue of ethics and offered other explanations of textual reuse. Because many of these explanations are based in the assumption that L2 source use is ineffective, we would like to emphasize that there are many L2 writers (including one of the authors of this book) who do not struggle with source use. These explanations may be divided into three categories: culture and past schooling experiences, English language proficiency, and issues of identity.

Sometimes students from a given country or culture are seen as typical "plagiarizers" due to the learning practices of their cultures. Chinese learning culture, for example, is known to make use of memorization and models in writing instruction. These learning practices are then connected to more abstract cultural forms, such as the Confucian tradition (Shi, 2006) or the Chinese literary tradition (Cai, 1999). They are also connected to the textual practices of student writers, namely, the avoidance of explicit attribution (Shi, 2006) or the avoidance of a strong authorial voice (Ramanathan & Atkinson, 1999; Scollon, 1994), and thus are seen as leading to unconventional source use. Teachers working with Chinese students may themselves have observed similar learning and textual practices among their students. For instance, they may know of an app called Youdao, which not only provides translations, but also a sentence of the day, in Chinese and English, for the purpose of teaching so-called "beautiful sentences." Teachers may be concerned that their students may copy these sentences in their writing.

Such cultural arguments are problematic, however, in that they often stem from a deficit analysis of students' cultural experience or knowledge. Cultural analyses often create or are based on stereotypes that form teachers' expectations of their students. It is one thing to acknowledge a learning culture by saying that Chinese student writers often choose not to emphasize an individual authorial voice in the text, but it is quite another to assume that an individual Chinese student writer will make this choice or that she or he does not, in fact, have a voice. Cultural stereotypes also eclipse the differences within a culture. There is ample evidence that prototypical plagiarism is a controversial issue in China just as it is in the United States (see Hu & Sun, 2015; Huang & Han, 2008; Liu, 2005; Zhu, 2008). However, even our Chinese students may not know this, and we may too readily accept their claims that "plagiarism is okay where we come from." Cultural analyses also tend to ignore similarities between learning cultures such as Americans' use of memorization. As one U.S. creative writing teacher aptly put it, reflecting on her own textual construction and that of Mark Twain, "Unconscious plagiarism is the cost of paying attention to language" (Toor, 2011). The challenge for teachers is to recognize cultural differences that help us meet our students' needs, while at the same time not letting our beliefs about a given culture create our expectations for, or explanations of, the performance of individual students.

In addition to cultural explanations, L2 writers are sometimes assumed to be prototypical plagiarizers due to their lack of English proficiency. This is because limited vocabulary size, mastery of syntax, and reading ability are known to affect the ability to produce effective paraphrases and summaries. In addition, reading ability affects the ability to enter the scholarly conversation of a discourse community. Beginning readers often struggle to understand the multiple ways in which authors represent sources in their texts, using them sometimes to support their argument and other times to show an opposing argument, for instance. Without this understanding, they cannot follow the line of argument or relate the argument to their own ideas in their writing.

Reading ability is further tied to familiarity with a large number of English texts. For example, Prior (2001) looked at what goes into reading the phrase *guardians of truth*. According to Prior, interpreting the phrase "requires not a dictionary, but an experienced history of texts, particularly of how 'truth' and its 'guardians' have been represented in certain academic and public texts, a history that helps identify the tone or key of this phrase as [for example,] parodic" (p. 63). Because L2 writers may not have been exposed to as many English texts as students who grew up in an English-speaking environment, they are likely to be less familiar with the complex intertextuality undergirding many usages and may miss important meanings and connotations. While writing instructors cannot supply a lifetime worth of reading of English texts, it is important for them to work consistently with students on reading skills, analyzing the texts that will become the sources for the students' writing assignments.

As we focus on language issues, however, it is important to remain aware that we, as instructors, play the pivotal role in determining which students are considered "plagiarizers." Research has shown that student texts that are judged sophisticated or authoritative are less likely to be judged to contain "plagiarism" (Angélil-Carter, 2000; Williams, 2015). In a study by Starfield (2002), for instance, a student whose text contained citations but did not demonstrate authority was found to have "plagiarized," while a student who had not cited properly but whose text showed good control of the topic was given a high grade by the same teacher. It is important for teachers to respond to student writing in ways that make room for student writers to develop authority and do not shut them down for their approaches to using sources. We should also be careful not to judge L2 writers unfairly based on English proficiency. It is not surprising that L2 writers have more difficulty than native English speakers in producing smooth paraphrases and matching the level of sophistication of the source text language (Campbell, 1990; Folse, 2008), and we should keep in mind that "students writing in a language that is not their first are more vulnerable to false assumptions about the kind of language that they are capable of, and perhaps also the kinds of ideas they are expected to produce" (Angélil-Carter, 2000, p. 79).

Finally, student writers may also face complex issues of power and identity that affect their ability or willingness to use sources in academic ways. For some, there may be a conflict between their writing identity and the use of English. This may be particularly true for students from post-colonial societies with complex historic and economic relationships with Inner Circle English-speaking countries. Looking at students in Hong Kong, for example, Pennycook (1996) argued that "many [students] seem to feel that they have no ownership over English—it remains an alien language—and thus to write 'in their own words' is not something that can be done in English" (p. 225).

For other L2 writers, there may be a conflict between their identity and academic writing more broadly. Much research has discussed how discursive conflicts affect both writing and English language classrooms (see, e.g., Canagarajah, 1997, 2001, 2002; Lu, 1987; Pratt, 1991), and these conflicts, of course, affect the teaching and learning of effective source use as well. Simply put, when the discourse of the school excludes or seems to exclude the knowledge and lived experiences of students, students may resist learning. A study conducted in South Africa by Angélil-Carter (2000) showed how such conflicts play out around source use. For some students, the requirement to use sources made it extremely hard for them to develop their ideas and demonstrate their authority in writing, as they felt that teachers discounted their own knowledge, which could not necessarily be cited. While we have no easy fix for these complex and interrelated issues of language, identity, and power, we believe that it is important for teachers to find ways to let students use their own knowledge and claim their own authority as they learn conventional source use. We also believe that it is important to let conflicting discourses collide; by letting such conflicts play out, students learn to negotiate them.

While most of this book is predicated on the assumption that we need to teach L2 writers how to use sources effectively and conventionally, we also want to acknowledge the important work of questioning the need to do so. Benesch (1999, 2001) has provided a means for us and our students to challenge this goal in her development of the concept of *rights analysis*. Rights analysis is "a conceptual framework for questions about power and resistance, such as: What are the explicit and implicit regulations in a particular setting? How do students respond to these regulations? How are decisions about permitted and unpermitted behaviors made?" (Benesch, 2001, p. 62). In Benesch's formulation, students work together to answer these questions in order to understand how power has worked to bring about a given institutional goal, such as the goal of having everyone use sources in a certain way. We recognize that rights analysis is an important balance to the imposition of conventional source use.

## Revisiting the Wrongness of "Plagiarism"

Surely the only way we can answer the question we began with ("What best describes the rightness or wrongness of plagiarism?") is with our own write-in response, which might go something like this: First of all, it depends on what behaviors you are referring to when you say "plagiarism," and second, it depends on what discipline you are in and what genre you are considering. Furthermore, both historic analysis and our experience teaching student writers has shown us that what has traditionally been called "plagiarism" often involves no deceit, and thus cannot be understood as "wrong." Differences in learning cultures and language proficiency, as well as identity and power, play important roles in L2 student writers' textual reuse, all of which further complicate the issue. Furthermore, as writing instructors, we recognize that framing a writing issue as one of right and wrong does not forward the cause of learning. In order to help student writers learn to use sources effectively, we must take a stance against the ethical frame around prototypical plagiarism and the hysteria that it gives rise to. Therefore, there is no simple answer to this question.

# Take-Away Points

- Textual reuse (a.k.a. "plagiarism") is most often understood as an ethical issue, and when it is framed in this way, it has a negative impact on learning. Thus, removing the ethical frame is extremely important.

- There are many different behaviors that are called "plagiarism," but many of them are not in fact deceitful.

- Teachers need to use language that distinguishes between deceitful and non-deceitful types of textual reuse and respond to these behaviors differently.

- What we call "plagiarism" is not a universal concept and has historic roots in the Romantic era.

- Standards of textual reuse vary widely across disciplines, genres, and individuals.

- It is commonly thought that deceitful source use is a growing problem connected with the internet; however, actual rates of *deceitful* source use are not known and are virtually impossible to ascertain.

- Culture is often seen as an explanation for the unconventional source use of L2 writers, but such explanations are problematic in that they often stem from a deficit analysis of students' cultural experience or knowledge. These views create and/or are based on stereotypes.

- English language proficiency—including reading, paraphrasing, and vocabulary skills—has been connected to effective source use and should be addressed by teachers.

- Teachers should be careful not to shut down L2 student writers' development by being too strict or punitive about source use.

- Teachers should recognize the complex identity issues that some L2 writers experience in learning academic English and conventional source use; they should be intentional about letting students use their own knowledge even if doing so conflicts with conventional referencing standards.

# 2

# The Concept Dimension:
## Exploring the Cultural Constructs Surrounding the Terms *Originality* and *Plagiarism*

---

"How can I say something original when everything's already been said?"

"Why do you expect me to know more than these experts?"

"Why is citing such a big deal?"

"Do I have to cite this author when I had this idea before I read it?"

"Do I have to cite if I can't remember where I learned this from?"

–Questions from L2 students in a U.S. college composition course

---

OFTEN WHEN L2 WRITERS FIRST ENCOUNTER teachers' expectations for original writing and attributed source use, they ask questions such as those listed—questions that reveal the complexity of the cultural constructs of *originality* and *plagiarism*. As teachers, we may find such questions exasperating, and that may be in large part because they are not easy to answer. These questions raise issues of authority, ownership, writer status, and the roles of learning and memory, issues that are intimately connected to source use and that complicate simple ethical understandings of it. The goal of this chapter is to discuss the concepts that need to be taught for students to achieve an understanding of Western academic approaches to source use. First, we address authority, voice, originality, and transformed knowledge; then we move on to exploring the topics of ownership, community membership, and common knowledge. The chapter concludes with a discussion of plagiarism and copyright.

## CONSIDER

The previous paragraph contains no citations because we deleted them. Were you surprised by this? How would the use of citations have changed the paragraph? If a student submitted that paragraph as part of a paper, would the lack of citations raise red flags? Why or why not?

# What We Know from Research and Theory

## Authority: Voice, Originality, and Transformed Knowledge

As noted in Chapter 1, scholarship on source use has determined that the ability of a writer to establish textual authority is key to avoiding charges of proto-typical plagiarism (Angélil-Carter, 2000; Fountain & Fitzgerald, 2008; Starfield, 2002). That is, when teachers feel that students have control of a topic, they tend to give the paper a higher grade and do not enforce attribution rules that are as strict (Angélil-Carter, 2000; Starfield, 2002). It therefore makes sense to develop ways to teach the skills of establishing textual authority (Abasi, Akbari & Graves, 2006; Pecorari, 2015). In doing so, there are three important concepts to address: authorial voice, originality, and transformed knowledge.

When we say *authorial voice*, we are talking about the impression a reader makes of an author's identity as she or he reads the text (Matsuda, 2001; Matsuda & Tardy, 2007). In the schooling context, we are of course talking about the impression a teacher makes of a student's identity. This impression is influenced by the student's writerly decisions (although it may also be unfairly influenced by identity factors as well, as stated in Chapter 1). Teachers may, for example, form an unfavorable impression of students' authority based on the fact that the students do not engage the positions of other authors directly; students, on the other hand, may find it inappropriate to engage directly because doing so places them on the same level as or above published authors. Teachers may also form an unfavorable impression if they suspect copying, while students may prefer copying to rephrasing as a sign of respect to the source texts (Abasi, Akbari & Graves, 2006). Thus, in order to help student writers develop a voice that strikes teachers as authoritative, it is important to tell students that a strong authorial voice is valued and that it involves directly engaging with the positions of others as well as writing in one's own words. It is also important to explain that establishing authorial voice involves using references and first-person pronouns, topics discussed in Chapter 3.

Textual authority is also established through originality. One reason that understanding originality may be difficult for student writers is that teachers are often not explicit or specific about their expectations for originality. We have encountered teachers in our institutions who impose expectations for originality when grading that do not match up with the stated requirements of their assignments. In the following explanation from Briggs (2003), it is apparent that the expectations of originality on typical writing assignments in the Humanities are not consistent with the Romantic definition:

> . . . what's really expected of these students is some demonstration of an ability to sift through a body of published ideas and to piece together a selection of discussions and arguments relevant to the topic, with the aim of reaching a conclusion of some kind. Some sort of originality is expected here, of course; crucially, though, what is expected is not so much an originality of ideas or argument, produced by so-called "free" thought, but an originality that is generated as an effect of a particular set of research and referencing techniques as they are put to use in a specific context. (p. 21)

We believe that it is essential that teachers specify their originality expectations. For instance, if tasks are designed to ask students to combine ideas from several source texts rather than develop their own original ideas (in a Romantic sense), teachers should explain to them that the originality of the task lies primarily in reorganization and synthesis. Or, if a task asks students to apply a theory to an example, teachers should explain that that application can be seen as a type of originality. Other forms of originality might include reporting new data, comparing a text to an experience, and/or bringing an idea from one discourse community into another.

In our experience, L2 writers are particularly well-positioned to capitalize on this last form, as they may have culturally different ideas that appear new to teachers. This idea is supported by Leki (1995), who identified the use of cultural knowledge as a coping strategy used by international students in the U.S. Leki described a Taiwanese student whose "term paper in Behavioral Geography became a comparison of Taiwanese and U.S. shopping habits [and whose] term paper in World History became a comparison of ancient Chinese and Greek education" (p. 242). Helping L2 writers realize that their diverse backgrounds provide them with the cultural capital that many of their native-speaking counterparts may not have not only helps them establish textual authority but also may make them feel empowered by demonstrating that they are an asset to their academic institution.

Teachers often see the original aspect of a writing assignment as the line of argument that students develop after drawing from several sources of information. For some L2 writers, however, it may be difficult to fulfill the requirements of conventional source use while at the same time developing their own line of argument (see, e.g., Thompson's 2005 discussion of Tony, and Angélil-Carter's 2000 discussion of Tshediso). There may be a number of contributing reasons for this difficulty: Students may feel that only published knowledge is valued and their knowledge is not, or they may read published knowledge as facts to be reported rather than as positions to be analyzed, critiqued, and juxtaposed. Thus students may need practice bringing together their knowledge with that of scholars in an environment that supports the students' voices.

We also believe that teacher expectations of originality should allow room for students to be students, particularly in pre-college and early college contexts. That is, it makes sense to expect students to write about ideas that are new to them, though not necessarily new to scholars more broadly; this is what writing-to-learn means. Students should be encouraged to think through ideas and interpret them for themselves. In such cases, "the new element is likely to be the student's own understanding" (Pecorari, 2013, p. 72).

Finally, a key point in understanding originality and establishing textual authority is recognizing the extent to which knowledge is transformed during the reading-thinking-writing process. This type of knowledge transformation involves producing texts anchored in other sources but shaped by the writer's own interpretations, intentions, and organizational logic. (For more information, see Bereiter & Scardamalia, 1987.) Research has shown that it can be difficult for L2 writers to distinguish where the ideas of source texts leave off and one's own ideas begin (Shi, 2006). As one student in Shi's (2011) study explained, "I just take a whole bunch of stuff, think about it for a while and then come up with my own ideas. There is a lot of gray area in describing what I think of as my own because it came from someone else's ideas originally" (p. 316). Moreover, this difficulty in distinguishing where source text ideas end and one's own ideas begin has been found to contribute to ineffective paraphrasing (Pecorari, 2013) and unconventional citing decisions (Shi, 2011). Thus, we believe that examining examples of knowledge transformation with students can help them learn to identify the line between copying and transformation, which in turn will help them discover how they can be "original" in their writing and when to cite.

## Ownership, Community Membership, and Common Knowledge

Transformed knowledge, of course, is considered to be the writer's "own" even though it may be entangled in a cobweb of intertextuality. Ownership is an important concept for effective source use because when a writer is seen as owning an idea, attribution is not required. The concept of ownership is complicated by the fact that it is typically related to membership status in a discourse community. For instance, when a composition or L2 writing scholar uses the term *discourse community*, a term widely used in these fields, it is not always cited. If, however, a college student used this term in a paper, some teachers would be surprised if it were not attributed. This is because student writers are often seen by faculty as outside the discourse community when they are taking a course outside their major (e.g., a biologist writing about poetry), when they are still developing their knowledge of their field (e.g., a student biologist learning biology), or when they come from social backgrounds that have traditionally been seen as outside the academy. As members of the discourse community in which the term *discourse community* is *common knowledge*, scholars of writing own the term; in contrast, a student who has not established such membership does not yet have such ownership and is therefore expected to cite. L2 writers are often seen as having less ownership of English than L1 writers so it is possible that they may be expected to cite even more, though researchers have yet to investigate this. (For an overview of some of the issues surrounding L2 students and the ownership of English, see Norton, 1997.)

Thus, differing standards of referencing exist for writers of different status; student writers are often expected to attribute more than "expert" writers and are punished more severely when they do not (Howard, 1999). An important question arises here: If teachers want to teach student writers to cite like scholars, at what point in their learning process do they have, and are they seen as having, ownership of the ideas they are writing about? On this question, research studies have shown disagreement. For instance, Shi (2011) found that teachers, as well as students, had differing opinions about whether learned knowledge required attribution:

> Some believe that memorized knowledge needs to be unpacked to distinguish one's own ideas, others' ideas, and one's agreement with others' ideas; whereas others argue that mingling other people's ideas is a natural process of developing one's own ideas so it is difficult to define when ideas start to become one's own. (pp. 328–329)

Shi's (2010, 2011) work also provides insight into the reasoning of those students who claimed ownership of knowledge they had learned. For example, one student explained, "If I learnt it in the past and understand it, I think it's my knowledge" (Shi, 2011, p. 326). Another student took the point further, explaining that she "found it ridiculous that some professors would require a citation for such knowledge she had internalized. She reflected on her resistance which took the form of making up fake references to save time looking for the original one" (p. 325).

In making attribution decisions, student writers are often confused in cases in which they believe an idea is their own but discover that it has already been published by someone else. One study showed that students worried that such an idea would be considered cheating (Petrić, 2004), while another study showed that students considered it to be okay since such ideas are common knowledge (Angélil-Carter, 2000). In addition, L2 writers often do not cite information that is common knowledge within the discourse community of the classroom; specifically, they have been found not to cite lectures or textbooks (Shi, 2010), information for which the teacher knows the source (Shi, 2011), or ideas established through frequent use in class (Chandrasoma, Thompson, & Pennycook, 2004). Some student writers believe that the entire internet is common knowledge and need not be cited. Because of the complexity of making decisions about common knowledge and the choice to attribute, we believe that it is important for teachers to discuss the concepts of discourse community and ownership with students and examine instances of reused ideas in order to develop the skills writers need to make attribution decisions.

## "Plagiarism" and Copyright

Many studies have shown that L2 writers are not clear about what "plagiarism" is (Currie, 1998; Moon, 2002; Shi, 2006; Sutherland-Smith, 2005). Thus, if instructors want students to avoid "plagiarism," it makes sense to teach them what it is. As shown in Chapter 1, studies reveal that there is little agreement among teachers as to what constitutes "plagiarism" (Borg, 2009; Flint, Clegg, & Macdonald, 2006; Lei & Hu, 2014; Pecorari & Shaw, 2012; Roig, 2001; Sutherland-Smith, 2005). For instance, in a study of eight instructors at Swedish universities, Pecorari and Shaw (2012) found that their participants "had diverse and conflicting views on what constitutes appropriate and inappropriate intertextuality; and that they again were different in terms of the sorts of factors which they weighed up in coming to their judgments" (p. 152). While it may not be possible to teach students to avoid "plagiarism" according to a universal definition, it is possible to expose them to multiple ways that academics think and talk about it.

One way that Westerners think about "plagiarism" is as theft. This metaphor comes from the similarity between *prototypical plagiarism* and *copyright infringement*. While the two concepts have common connections in their relation to the Romantic notion of the solitary, divinely inspired author, copyright infringement nevertheless differs from student copying in important ways. For instance, copyright is a matter of law, whereas student copying is not. Second, copyright concerns published texts, whereas student copying typically concerns unpublished ones. And third, copyright is primarily about ownership and typically financial profit, whereas student copying is about ethics and the demonstration of writing skills.

In the classroom, rather than emphasizing the similarity between "plagiarism" and theft by speaking about "stealing ideas or words," it may be helpful to discuss the differences between them. In our experience, some L2 student writers feel that the contextual differences are so obvious that they do not see how the crime metaphor can be applied to the schooling context. They believe, for instance, that the concept of ownership of ideas makes sense only when an idea is taken from a published text (Shi, 2006). Furthermore, student writers may not recognize their textual practices as "plagiarism" when a crime analogy is used. As Pecorari (2001) explained: "Students who view copying or closely modeling as good writing strategies may not connect the dire warnings of an illegal activity with their own work and may simply disregard the warnings" (p. 243).

Another reason student writers may not be clear about what "plagiarism" is is that they may have encountered contradictions in source use requirements. This may occur when different instructors impose different attribution requirements and may lead to confusion or disengagement (Angélil-Carter, 2000). Contradictory requirements may be due to different conventions for different genres or disciplines. For example, many genres—such as business memos, newspaper articles, medical diagnoses making use of the *Diagnostic and Statistical Manual of Mental Disorders (DSM)* (McCarthy, 1991, as cited by Angélil-Carter, 2000), and legal briefs making use of the work of clerks (Posner, 2007, as cited in Williams, 2010)—do not require attribution. (Disciplinary differences are discussed further in Chapter 3.) In addition, both homage and satire (whether an allusion within a text or the entire text) reuse ideas and words without attribution.

Finally, students may be confused if they notice that teachers do not always follow their own referencing rules. For instance, students may notice that some textbooks contain no references (Posner, 2007, as cited in Williams, 2010), that teachers reuse course texts (Pennycook, 1996) and one another's syllabi (Kaufman, 1999, as cited in Price, 2002) without attribution, and that teachers use inadequate attribution in their PowerPoint presentations (Conzett, Martin, & Mitchell, 2010). They may also notice that plagiarism policies themselves are often copied both by teachers cutting and pasting them into their syllabi (Abasi & Akbari, 2008) and by institutions copying them from other institutions (Pecorari, 2013; Price, 2002). Because students notice these things, we believe that it is important to engage them in discussions of these contradictions.

## Connecting to the Classroom

Six lessons related to concept dimension are presented. A chart providing an overview of these lessons, and the lessons in the other chapters, appears in Appendix 1. Having students examine the concepts surrounding *originality* and *plagiarism* ensures they understand them, involves students in discussions in which they are free to challenge the concepts, and helps them to develop the writing abilities they need to be original and avoid unconventional reuse of source texts. For students who need a basic introduction to prototypical plagiarism, teachers can lead a discussion of the concepts discussed in this chapter, as well as the different types of textual reuse (patchwriting, unconventional attribution, cheating) discussed in Chapter 1. *The Chronicle of Higher Education* also has many articles and blog entries on "plagiarism" available online without charge; the language level of the articles is well-suited to first-year college students. In addition, we have listed several texts and videos in Appendix 2: Teaching Materials. We also believe that it is important to approach originality not only from the perspective of what it entails, but also from the perspective of how writers access their own creativity. Teachers can address this perspective by asking students to freewrite and by sharing with them writers' descriptions of their creative processes.

# Lesson 1:
# Developing Something to Say

**Focus**: Authority and originality

**Description**: Students develop a line of argument on a controversial topic, drawing from their own experiences and two source texts.

**Rationale**: Students may not understand what teachers mean by "originality" in the context of writing from sources. Furthermore, they may not have had experience developing their own arguments or combining their own ideas with those of source texts. This lesson, therefore, introduces them to these important skills of source-based writing.

**Students**: Intermediate to Advanced L2s; L1s

**Preparation**: Provide students with copies of the plagiarism policy of your institution and Howard's (1995) "proposed policy on plagiarism," which is part of the *College English* article, "Plagiarisms, authorships, and the academic death penalty." As homework, ask them to read both texts, using active note-taking strategies (see Chapter 5, Lesson 4). The students should take notes that capture the main points of each text. Provide scaffolding questions such as: What specific behaviors are considered punishable in each policy? How is *plagiarism* defined? What sections does the policy have? The students should also take notes on their own responses to the texts. Scaffold this process by asking students to copy out a quote (using quotation marks and a page number citation) and either freewrite about their own related emotions and experiences or build supporting or counterarguments.

**Procedure**:

1. Ask students to freewrite on their personal connections to plagiarism and share what they wrote in small groups.

2. Ask students to work in small groups to compare the main ideas of the two texts and to discuss their ideas about which aspects of which policy they prefer.

3. Bring students back together as a class and model a "new" idea—namely, an idea that you have that does not occur in either text. For instance, the Howard policy does not explore the differences between the ramifications of being found "guilty" of prototypical plagiarism for international students and domestic ones. Encourage the students to generate other "new" ideas from their own knowledge and experience.

4. Assign a writing task. There are a variety of approaches students could take:

- Compare the two positions, commenting on the good and bad aspects of each and using illustrations from their own experiences.

- Write a letter to a friend discussing the topic, describing the differing positions that they have read about and commenting on them.

- Critique one position, using ideas from the other and their own experiences.

- Create their own position, based on ideas drawn from both positions and their own experiences.

5. Ask students to read one another's writing and give feedback on which aspects of the papers they see as "original."

**Adaptations**: Choose two texts that reveal basic disagreements about a different controversial topic that your students have some experience with.

# Lesson 2:
# That's What I Do!
# Relating to Other Writers' Source Use

**Focus**: Source use—different approaches

**Description**: Students read L2 student writer remarks about their source use and discuss the remarks in a non-judgmental context.

**Rationale**: L2 writers have often experienced different ways of using source texts and constructing authority. This lesson, therefore, provides an opportunity for them to discuss and value these different approaches while at the same time providing an opening for the discussion of Western academic approaches to textual reuse.

**Students**: All levels of L2s

**Preparation**: Make a handout with several quotes from this list:

- ❑ "At certain stage you are at the border between imitation and plagiarism . . . . First, it's pretty much imitation. The sentences are exactly the same . . . . It's the very first step of developing your own writing style . . . . And after some time, you change a lot and add in your personal style" (as quoted in Shi, 2006, p. 275).

- ❑ ". . . I don't have the vocabulary to express my own style . . . . After I read an article, I tend to use exactly these words that were in the article because I think they sound better than mine" (as quoted in Shi, 2006, p. 273).

- ❑ "I consider it important to memorize sentences to write better. . . . If the English teacher required me to write a long English essay . . . . I would turn to famous sayings and sentences derived from famous writers and essays on the same topic. I would imitate what other people say and use their sentences in my essays. I would at most change a single word but I would not change the main frame or structure . . . . I would use famous sayings, proverbs, and quotable phrases quite often, . . . for I consider they are essential in writing. . ." (Ho, 1998, p. 234, as quoted in Ramanathan & Atkinson, 1999, pp. 54–55).

- ❑ "If you write an assignment from different references, I think it's not plagiarism. It's just like the mosaic" (as quoted in Shi, 2006, pp. 274–275)

- ❑ "What I've started doing now is to use the prescribed works [assigned texts] only, that's what I've attempted to do particularly with my latest essays . . . . I'm trying to do so because when you come up with your own examples and your own ideas then it is assumed [by the teacher] that you are plagiarizing—simply because there is no referencing. Somehow it is assumed that whatever you know that is tangible and constructive you must have read it somewhere. It is impossible that you might have heard it or you might have thought it on your own" (as quoted in Angélil-Carter, 2000, p. 74).

- ❑ ". . . when I was reading as a preparation for an assignment or an essay, I would read maybe four readings, and then in my mind I would compile them into one whole, to make a coherent and logical argument, and then I write maybe four or eight pages, as one whole thing. So if I had to mention say Leftwich [the name of an author], immediately my logical flow is interrupted . . ." (as quoted in Angélil-Carter, 2000, p. 88).

**Procedure**:

1. Give students the handout with the quotes, and let them free-write about one quote that catches their eye.

2. Form groups among students who wrote about the same quote. Ask groups to discuss the quote and report back to the class on the issues that came up in their discussions.

3. Ask students to examine their own source use on a writing task that they have already completed. In writing, ask them to describe their source use and explain their citing decisions, drawing on the quotes for comparison or contrast.

**Adaptations**: Select one quote that seems particularly apt for your students, assign a freewrite, and then discuss afterward. Or, set up the quotes on google docs or a discussion board on a course website as a way for students to share their thoughts.

# Lesson 3:
# When Is Attribution a Must?

**Focus**: Attribution—genre differences

**Description**: Students read texts looking for ideas that may have come from other texts and note whether or not they are attributed; they then develop explanations for why the information is or is not attributed and draw conclusions about whether the source is credible for academic writing.

**Rationale**: We often simply tell our students to cite whenever they reuse the ideas and words of another author. However, not all genres require attribution. This lesson, therefore, has students examine citing differences in texts of different genres.

**Students**: High-Beginner to Advanced L2s; L1s

**Preparation**: Prepare several sample texts that use attribution and several that do not. For attributed ideas, use a student paper, a published academic article, or a Wikipedia article. For unattributed ideas, use texts from the schooling context—e.g., a textbook chapter, PowerPoint notes from a lecture, a plagiarism policy statement, or a university website—as well as some from non-academic contexts, such as a website of a non-profit organization, a work memo, or a news article. Also, ask students to bring in some texts of these types as well.

**Procedure**:

1. Examine the sample texts as a class. Note the genre of each and whether or not attribution is used. Explain that some genres require attribution whereas others do not.

2. Ask students to work with the texts that they brought in. They should read the text and highlight sentences that contain ideas that they think the author may have gotten from somewhere else, noting whether or not the ideas are attributed. Scaffold the work by providing a set of questions:

   ■ What genre is your text? (textbook chapter, scholarly article, Wikipedia article, website of a non-profit organization, website of a company, website of a private individual, work memo, news article, etc.)

   ■ Copy three sentences from your text that you believe contain information drawn from other texts.

   ■ What makes you think that this information comes directly from other texts?

   ■ For each sentence, is there a citation? (The citation might be in the sentence itself or nearby in the surrounding text.)

   ■ Why do you think there is, or is not, a citation?

3. Ask students to share their findings with the class so that all the students learn about the various genres examined by others.

4. As a class, discuss which of the compiled texts can be viewed as credible academic sources. (See also Chapter 5, Lesson 1, Can I Trust This Text? Evaluating the Credibility of Sources.)

**Adaptations**: This lesson can be used as preparation for a later research paper assignment. Students locate texts on their research topic by entering a keyword into Google and then into Google Scholar. Then they bring in the top two articles found in each for comparison.

# Lesson 4:
# Discussing Reasons to Cite:
# Attribution and Common Knowledge

**Focus**: Attribution—common knowledge

**Description**: Students read sentences from student papers that contain unattributed ideas and the explanations the students gave for not citing and consider whether they agree with the stated explanations or not.

**Rationale**: Students and teachers may make differing decisions as to whether a given idea is common knowledge and requires attribution or not. This lesson, therefore, engages students in a discussion of reasoning around citing decisions and helps them develop their theories of attribution.

**Students**: Intermediate to Advanced L2s; L1s

**Preparation**: Make a handout with these quotes from Shi, 2011, pp. 316–317:

a. Student paper: "However, spontaneous mutation occurs more frequently than induced because spontaneous mutations can occur simply due to natural radiation, and during replication in DNA." (From a Biology 100-level paper titled "One type of spontaneous mutations is point mutation")

   Student explanation: "I learnt it some time ago (in high school). There is no need to give references for information or knowledge learnt in the past."

b. Student paper: "New York and films have had a working relationship since the first film was shot in the city in 1896." (From a Film 100-level paper titled "Martin Scorsese vs. Woody Allen: Presentations of New York city on film")

   Student explanation: "I did not cite the reference because it's kind of information or fact, not an opinion.

c.  Student paper: "It is not entirely clear why the United States did not choose to remove Mr. Hussein from power when they had the opportunity to after the success of Operation Desert Storm, apart from the fact that Colin Powell, then the commanding general of the coalition troops, stressed that they should not enter Baghdad for that purpose." (From a Political Science 300-level paper titled "Realism vs. domestic politics and the case for war against Iraq")

Student explanation: "I just take a whole bunch of stuff, think about it for a while and then come up with my own ideas. There is a lot of gray area in describing what I think of as my own because it came from someone else's ideas originally."

d.  Student paper: "The Realist perspective emphasizes that a causal determinant of the theory is whether or not the theory fits the situation in the real world." (From a Political Science 300-level paper titled "Realism vs. domestic politics and the case for war against Iraq")

Student explanation: "This is from lecture notes [handouts] by the instructor. I didn't think that it warranted a citation."

e.  Student paper: "Some of these allergic reactions include skin rash, edema (swelling of tissue), bronchospasm (constriction of the airways), and shock. These side effects are not only present for the penicillin- like antibiotics. These side effects also present for antibiotics like cephalosporin and tetracycline." (From an English 100-level paper titled "The Danger of the abuse of antibiotics and its safe alternative herbs")

Student explanation: "That's general information so I do not need to cite."

f.  Student paper: "Because streptomycin leads to disruption during translation, protein is not being made, and as a result, deaths occur in bacteria. Since streptomycin can significantly affect the population of the bacteria, in order for the bacteria to survive, they must have resistance to this antibiotic." (From a Biology 100-level paper titled "One type of spontaneous mutations is point mutation")

Student explanation: "I did not indicate the source because I couldn't remember where I read it. Probably it's in one of these journal articles."

(Used with permission of NCTE.)

**Procedure**:

1. Put students in small groups; they should read the handout that has sentences from student papers containing reused ideas, together with the students' explanations for not citing them. Ask the groups to decide whether they would have included a citation for the sentence and whether they agree with the student writer's reason for not including one.

2. Reconvene as a class to debrief. Address the following citation issues that are raised by the examples: whether it is necessary to cite knowledge learned in school, facts as well as opinions, transformed knowledge, class materials such as lecture notes, common knowledge, and information whose source they may have forgotten. Also, discuss the construct of *common knowledge* and be sure to consider how common knowledge changes according to community and whether the student writer is seen as an authoritative member of the relevant community.

3. If necessary, provide the students with guidance as to which explanations are likely to be accepted by the teachers at their institution, which might be contested, and which would probably be rejected. For example, accepted explanations might include that it is not prototypical plagiarism if the ideas and/or words are accompanied by citations and the words are quoted, or if the ideas are considered common knowledge. Contested explanations might include the claim that it is not prototypical plagiarism if the writer did not intend to deceive anybody, or if the writer used an idea that a classmate brought up in class. Rejected explanations might include that it is not prototypical plagiarism if the writer copied words without using quotes and a citation because the writer could not yet express the new ideas in their own words, or if the writer reused the organizing structure of someone else's argument but wrote it in their own words.

**Adaptations**: As a follow-up, have the students read a source text and a text based on it that contains no citations. Ask them to compare the two texts, identify sentences they believe require attribution, and generate arguments for why attribution is necessary.

# Lesson 5:
# Differing Attitudes toward Textual Reuse

**Focus**: "Plagiarism"—what is it?

**Description**: Students read statements about "plagiarism" made by people with differing attitudes toward it; then they use their imaginations to develop characters around several of the statements and write dialogues between the characters.

**Rationale**: It is important to engage students in discussions that distill different lines of reasoning around the contradictions of textual reuse. This lesson, therefore, highlights these differences and allows students to take positions temporarily to better understand them.

**Students**: Intermediate to Advanced L2s; L1s

**Preparation**: The students should read some texts about plagiarism and originality before doing this lesson. A list of such texts appears in Appendix 2. For the lesson, make a handout with these quotes:

> College Teacher: "I don't want my own words coming bouncing back to me in student work. I expect they will listen in lectures and go away and do their own reading to make their own meanings. I don't expect to see the meanings I have made from my own experiences and understandings come back to me in their work" (quoted in Sutherland-Smith, 2008, p. 145).

> Professor: "It amuses me in the classroom when I hear students quoting me back to myself . . . when I hear my own words and ideas come flying back at me, I try to take it as the sincerest form of flattery" (Toor, 2011).

> Blogger: "Why do students plagiarize?
> - Because of the pressure of grades.
> - Because they fear that they can't write well.
> - Because digital tools make it so easy . . . .
> - Because they . . . are lazy or mercenary or panicky.
> - Because they think they can get away with it.

> For teachers, plagiarism is a toilsome task. Suspecting it and investigating it and confronting a student with it and filing a charge with a conduct committee and attending the hearing is unpleasant and time-consuming.

> Teachers have to hold firm, though, and they must devise tactics up front to discourage the practice." (Bauerlein, 2011)

Professor: "If we put less energy into catching cheaters and more into teaching writing and critical thinking, we should achieve the very objective of academic integrity: students more invested in their learning *and therefore* less inclined to cheat and plagiarize" (Zwagerman, 2008, p. 702, original emphasis).

PhD candidate in Engineering: "[I] did not use quotation marks around direct quotes because he didn't realize [I] needed to for this type of assignment. [I] assumed the professor would know that these were taken from other sources. . . . that was the point of the assignment: to show the professor [my] familiarity with these sources" (Valentine, 2006, pp. 99–100).

Undergraduate student majoring in Communication: "If he or she [the teacher] knows the source, and we've all discussed it many times, why should it be necessary to tell him or her what it is?" (quoted in Chandrasoma, Thompson, & Pennycook, 2004, pp. 182–183).

Professor: "Plagiarism is outrageous, because it undermines the whole purpose of education itself: Instead of becoming more of an individual thinker, the plagiarist denies the self and the possibility of learning. Someone who will not, or cannot, distinguish his or her ideas from those of others offends the most basic principles of learning" (White, 1993, p. A44, quoted in Howard, 1999, p. 24).

Undergraduate student in the Arts division: "I think the reason they didn't cite anything is laziness" (Shi, 2011, p. 332).

Undergraduate student in Business and Law class: "This plagiarism is being strange to me because how can we learn if not to write things out of the book. I don't really understand when we should write the cites next to the words we reference. I mean, should we be doing this all the time for every sentence or just some of the times. If just some of the times, then when is right and when in wrong? How should we just *know* these things? (emphasis in the original)" (as quoted in Sutherland-Smith, 2008, p. 178).

**Procedure**:

1. Ask students to brainstorm about how student writers use references in their writing. They may say that students use references to provide them with ideas that are better than their own; or students use the language of the source text if they find it difficult to express the ideas in their own sentences.

2. Explain that scholars use sources for a variety of reasons, including to provide support, to demonstrate how much they have read, to provide a basis to build on, and to bring a text they like to a wider audience. Introduce the idea that some unattributed source use is acceptable among scholars; examples include homage, in which a writer honors the source text, and satire, in which the writer makes fun of the source text for a purpose.

3. Ask students to read through the quotes on the handout and choose two or three to work with. Tell them that their task is to develop characters based on the quotes. The students will need to use their imaginations to provide information not supplied by the quote. You may want to use a set of questions such as the following to scaffold the student work:

   - What is the attitude of this person toward textual reuse?
   - What motivation(s) does this person think students have for reusing text without attribution?
   - Given this person's understanding of textual reuse and student motivations, what response to textual reuse would they want a teacher to have?

4. Ask students to write a dialogue between the characters they have developed. Students may use the quotes on the handout, putting them in their characters' mouths (properly cited, of course!). They may also draw discussion ideas from the readings on plagiarism and originality that they have done. Sample 1 in Appendix 3 is a student paper written in response to this assignment.

**Adaptations**: Students can perform their dialogues as role plays for the class. Ask the students who are watching to answer the three scaffolding questions above for each character. You could also have the students video record the role plays using their phones or computers and then create a remix video that could be used as a conversation starter the following term. (Of course, only those students who agree to have their footage shared publicly should be included in the remix video.)

# Lesson 6:
# Facing Charges of "Plagiarism"

**Focus**: "Plagiarism"—facing accusations.

**Description**: Students learn the definition of "plagiarism" and the process for adjudicating it as laid out in their institution's policy. Then, they analyze a case of textual similarity and apply the policy to the case by writing either a letter of appeal defending the student or a paper stating the case against him or her.

**Rationale**: Student writers may find themselves facing charges of prototypical plagiarism that have severe consequences for their continued education, but they may not understand why they are being charged, be familiar with how such cases are adjudicated in their institutions, or know how to defend themselves. In this lesson, therefore, students study institutional definitions of, and adjudication procedures for, "plagiarism," think strategically about arguments to make when accused of "plagiarism," and develop language for making these arguments.

**Students**: High-Intermediate to Advanced L2s; L1s

**Preparation**: Provide students with access to your institution's plagiarism policy. Prepare a handout with the following cases that are actual student writings. (Bold indicates words in the student writing that are the same as words in the source text. Teacher and student remarks are composites.)

## 1. Case 1

Student writing: The writer said that **Marin is waiting for a car to stop, a star to fall** which I think the writer use metaphor in this sentence, **a car** and **a star** are all refers to a man who can change her life. Marin **is waiting for a car to stop**, and I think the reason why the writer use a car to refers a man is that Marin is waiting for a man who can take her away from her currently life like a car can take her to everywhere she wants to go. the man which Marin waiting for can also allow Marin to live every life she wants to live. From this sentence that Marin is **dancing by herself under the streetlight**, **is singing the same song somewhere**, I think Marin is lonely in the bottom of her hearts.

Source: Marin, under the streetlight, dancing by herself, is singing the same song somewhere. I know. Is waiting for a car to stop, a star to fall, someone to changer her life. (Source: Cisneros, 1984)

Teacher remarks: The assignment was to choose a quote from the book and analyze it. The student did that, but she used Cisneros' exact words with no attribution whatsoever.

Student remarks: The assignment was to choose a quote from the book and analyze it. We were supposed to explain both the surface and the deeper meaning. That's what I did.

## 2. *Case 2*

Student writing: **A value is a belief, a mission, or a philosophy that is meaningful. Whether we are consciously aware of them or not, every individual has a core set of personal values. Values can range from the commonplace, such as the belief in hard work and punctuality, to the more psychological, such as self-reliance, concern for others, and harmony of purpose**. Values are related to the norms of a culture, but they are more general and abstract than norms.

In Roberston's (1994) "Values," it is said that "Freedom. the freedom of the individual is regarded as one of the most important values in American life; Americans believe devoutly that they are and should remain 'free'," I believe that freedom is important to every American. It is an essential of personal values. So the value has able to impact a country's culture, which goes to democracy.

Source: A value is a belief, a mission, or a philosophy that is meaningful. Whether we are consciously aware of them or not, every individual has a core set of personal values. Values can range from the commonplace, such as the belief in hard work and punctuality, to the more psychological, such as self-reliance, concern for others, and harmony of purpose. (Source: Gulla, 2010)

Teacher remarks: The first three sentences, or most of the introduction to this paper, are copied verbatim from the internet. Besides being uncited, the copied words bring in ideas that are not relevant to the ensuing discussion, e.g., the idea that a value can be a "mission" or "philosophy," and that there are "commonplace" and "more psychological" values. The student does not mention these ideas again in the paper.

Student remarks: I thought it would be a good idea to introduce the general topic with a good definition. This definition is available on the internet, so it's general knowledge.

## 3. *Case 3*

Student writing: **When I was still in the beginning years of middle school, I remember seeing my dad to the most moving and meaningful thing I've ever seen anyone do. We were in Burlington picking my sister up from college at her apartment. It was cold and snowing and less than a week from Christmas. We had just left the warm and toasty interior of her apartment and returned to the freezing car. We were about to pull out of the lot, when my dad turned around and pulled toward the dumpster. . . .**

Source: When I was still in the beginning years of middle school, I remember seeing my dad to the most moving and meaningful thing I've ever seen anyone do. We were in Burlington picking my sister up from college at her apartment. It was cold and snowing and less than a week from Christmas. We had just left the warm and toasty interior of her apartment and returned to the freezing car. We were about to pull out of the lot, when my dad turned around and pulled toward the dumpster.... . (Source: www.coursehero.com/file/10109892/Rheotric-II-Stereotypes-Essay/)

Teacher remarks: This plagiarism is particularly annoying because the student borrowed someone else's voice to write a personal, first-person account. I was so confused as I was reading initially: Did my international student really go to middle school in Burlington? Then I realized, of course not! I could not pull up all of the Coursehero paper without paying for it, so I'm not sure how much more of the essay is copied, but it looks like it's the whole paper. The student does discuss the course texts further on, but I simply don't trust him anymore. I can't accept this paper.

Student explanation: It was the end of the semester and I didn't have much time to write this paper. The teacher said we could write about an experience with a homeless person so long as we used references to the reading texts. So, I used this experience from the internet paper, and connected it to quotes from our class readings.

## 4. Case 4

Student writing: Verbal communication is communication, which is operated by means of speaking in other words; verbal communication is based on language. On the other hand, non-verbal communication is communication, which convey meaning through behaviors, facial expressions, eye contacts and body languages etc. **Culture plays an important role in non-verbal communication, and it is one aspect that helps to influence how learning activities are organized. In many cultures, for example, there is often an emphasis on non-verbal communication, which acts as a valued means by which children learn. In this sense, learning is not dependent on verbal communication; rather, it is non-verbal communication which serves as a primary means of not only organizing interpersonal interactions, but conveying cultural values, and children learn how to participate in this system from a young age.** In other words, each culture has different meaning in certain behavior. Meaning of non-verbal communication based on culture too.

Source: Culture plays an important role in non-verbal communication, and it is one aspect that helps to influence how learning activities are organized. In many Indigenous American Communities, for example, there is often an emphasis on non-verbal communication, which acts as a valued means by which children learn. In this sense, learning is not dependent on verbal communication; rather, it is non-verbal communication which serves as a primary means of not only organizing interpersonal interactions, but conveying cultural values, and children learn how to participate in this system from a young age. (Source: Wikipedia: http://en.wikipedia.org/wiki/Nonverbal_communication)

Teacher remarks: A whole section was taken from Wikipedia and reused verbatim without quotation marks in the student's paper. This is not the only problematic section in the paper so I doubt that this is a matter of simply forgetting to cite. Not to mention that I was very clear when I discouraged my students from using Wikipedia as a source in the paper.

Student remarks: I forgot to put quotes around this section; the draft was due in the final week of the semester so I think I was just rushing and not paying close attention. But I followed the rules—I introduced the quote and I also explained it afterwards. Why am I being punished just for forgetting?

**Procedure**:

1. Present this quote, which is from a professor, to the students:

   "Faculty members. . .remain in the front lines of a war against plagiarism. What is at stake? Truth and honor. What is the cost? Our time grading and looking up the plagiarized papers, our belief in the integrity of our students, and their learning" (Moore, 2002).

   As a class, discuss the key ideas (e.g., ownership of ideas, student honor, faculty time, faculty trust of students, student learning) the professor identifies as being at stake when it comes to prototypical plagiarism.

2. Ask the students to read the institutional plagiarism policy and locate its definition of "plagiarism." Depending on the wording of the policy, you may also want to bring the students' attention to related terms such as *cheating*, *fabrication*, *falsification*, and *collusion*. Discuss the definitions and answer student questions about them.

3. Working together as a class, outline the process that is followed from the moment "plagiarism" is suspected by a teacher through to resolution. Draw a visual representation of the process on the board or on an overhead projector, indicating points at which it may be considered resolved (for example, the teacher may resolve the situation after discussing it with the student and before anyone else knows about it, the teacher may resolve the situation after putting a letter in the student's record, an institutional review board may resolve the issue by putting the student on probation). Also, indicate the student's role at each point (the student is expected to attend a conference called by the teacher, the student is expected to show up at a hearing of the institutional review board), and at what points the student can appeal.

4. Put students in small groups to analyze the cases, one case per group. Groups should compare the student text to the source text in terms of both the wording and the meaning and consider the remarks made by the student and by the teacher. Here are some questions that you can use to scaffold the groups' analyses:

   a. What type of textual reuse is this (unconventional attribution, no attribution, patchwriting)?

   b. How much copying is there (a few words, a few sentences, a few paragraphs, or virtually the whole thing)?

   c. Does the textual reuse appear to be deceitful or non-deceitful?

   d. Do the remarks of the teacher and student indicate a disagreement or misunderstanding? If so, what do you need to know to resolve it?

   e. Does the textual reuse warrant punishment, according to the institutional policy?

   f. Does the textual reuse warrant punishment in your opinion?

5. Ask the groups to generate defenses of the textual reuse/similarity and write a formal appeals letter incorporating them. (You may need to show the class how to format a formal letter.) Or, if the students find the reuse indefensible, ask them to write a memo in which they describe the misstep and apply the policy to the case.

6. Ask students to share their letters and papers either in class or on Google Docs, where they can post comments using comment boxes.

**Adaptations**: Ask the students to role-play and act out the appearance of the student writers before the plagiarism review board.

## Take-Away Points

- Teaching concepts helps student writers learn to use sources effectively and hold their own in discussions of source use.

- Authority, voice, originality, knowledge transformation, ownership, common knowledge, "plagiarism," and copyright are cultural constructs that are not universal but differ by context.

- It is important to teach ways to establish authority in writing, including how to establish authorial voice, be original, and demonstrate transformation of knowledge.

- Instructors should be explicit about what counts as originality in their classes (e.g., constructing an argument by recombining ideas from other texts).

- Instructors should discuss with students what is meant by knowledge transformation, examine examples of it, and practice it.

- It's helpful to discuss the terms *discourse community* and *ownership* and to come to an understanding of what constitutes common knowledge in your classroom.

- Important contextual differences between "plagiarism" (student copying) and copyright infringement should be discussed with students.

- Teachers need to address how context affects referencing standards so that students understand why different teachers have different expectations for source use.

# 3

# The Discourse Dimension:

## Teaching How Writers Use References to Situate Themselves in a Discourse Community

---

"I feel frustrated teaching referencing. Students seem to get it at the sentence-level, like when we practice paraphrasing, but then they can't use their sources well in a paper."

— Jamila, an ESL teacher in U.S. Intensive English Program

---

JAMILA'S FRUSTRATION WITH TEACHING EFFECTIVE WRITING from sources echoes many interactions we have had with writing teachers over the years. Perhaps because the teaching of referencing often focuses on sentence-level concerns such as citing, paraphrasing, and summarizing, many L2 writers do not have the rhetorical awareness necessary to use sources effectively in longer pieces of writing such as research papers. For this reason, we believe in the importance of teaching source use *at the discourse-level*. When we say *discourse*, we are referring both to the text-level source use decisions that a writer makes to communicate to an intended audience and to the larger disciplinary discourses that affect these decisions. As student writers learn to make effective text-level decisions, they increasingly establish their authority and membership in their academic discourse community. To be able to make such decisions, writers need to understand the rhetorical functions of referencing, how to situate themselves relative to claims (i.e., indicate *stance*), and how to engage readers. This chapter addresses each of these issues and concludes by discussing the variations in source use expectations across disciplinary discourse communities. Familiarizing writers with these aspects of source use helps them understand that successful writers do not cite simply to avoid prototypical plagiarism, but rather, to participate in an academic conversation.

---

### CONSIDER

Review the excerpts about contrastive rhetoric in Lesson 3 (see pages 48–51) where each writer used a reference to the same source, Kaplan's (1966) seminal article. What makes their uses of the source different one from the other? What is each writer's position toward the information in the source, and how can you tell?

---

## What We Know from Research and Theory

### Using References to Establish a Framework of Ideas and Authority

Scholars write to make a contribution to their field. As shown in Chapter 2, the writing of scholars involves a process of *knowledge transformation*, in which new texts are anchored in sources but shaped by the writer's own organizational logic, interpretations, and conceptual contributions. Scholars use references to sources (i.e., quotations, paraphrases, citations, and summaries) to create a framework for their claims, and that framework gives the current work its relevance and importance (Hyland, 2004, citing Myers, 1990, and Berkenkotter & Huckin, 1995) within the community. These frameworks function in a variety of ways, including:

- providing a specific context for the current contribution (Hyland, 2004) by highlighting ideas deemed relevant or important by the writer.

- capturing a chronological evaluation of the topic (Dong, 1996; Harwood, 2009).

- explaining and clarifying differences among opposing ideas or theories (Harwood, 2009; Hunt, 2002).

- letting experienced community members know who the writer's allies are (Harwood, 2009; Hyland, 2002).

- creating and/or justifying a research niche (Harwood, 2009; Swales, 1990).

- supplying support for claims in order to persuade (Gilbert, 1977; Dubois, 1988, as cited in Hyland, 2004; Harwood, 2009).

The use of references not only makes the text relevant but also establishes the authority of the writer by telling experienced community members that the writer is informed (Harwood, 2009; Hyland, 2002) and by associating their work with that of well-respected scholars (Gilbert, 1977, as cited in White, 2004; Hyland, 2002). Furthermore, the use of references can help establish other aspects of the author's voice: (1) by citing and building on the work of other scholars, writers can construct the impression that they are respectful (Garfield, 1965, as cited in White, 2004; Robillard, 2006): (2) by acknowledging that an idea is not their own, they construct the impression of modesty (Harwood, 2009); (3) by recognizing the good aspects of a source that they then go on to critique, they construct an impression of fairness (Harwood, 2009); and, most basically, (4) by giving credit where it is due, they construct an impression of honesty.

The term *rhetorical function* refers to both the ways in which references create a framework for an author's ideas and the ways in which they establish an author's persona. Research has shown that many academic L2 writers are aware of at least some of the rhetorical aspects of referencing (Shi, 2010, 2011) and that those who use a variety of rhetorical functions produce texts that are judged more positively by teachers (Petrić, 2007). In looking at the master's theses of L2 writers, Petrić found that it was a wider range of rhetorical functions, and not a greater number of sources, that made the writing more effective and thus more highly rated. In fact, the lower-rated theses in her study included more citations, but these citations were used primarily to attribute an idea to its source without a clear rhetorical function. Furthermore, a study by Hirvela (2016) found that understanding the rhetorical functions of sources was necessary for students to be able to synthesize the ideas they were reading about. These studies show how important it is to learn the rhetorical functions of references. When the function is not clear, quotes and paraphrases may seem unmoored or even incomprehensible, and a literature review may be nothing more than a list of summaries.

Effective source use involves not only understanding the rhetorical functions of references and repurposing source ideas for integration into one's own writing, but also smooth linguistic integration of them. Student writers need to learn how to blend their ideas with ideas from source texts through skillful textual modifications (Borg, 2000; Petrić, 2012) in order to "erase the trail" of patchwriting (Howard, 1999, p. 7). The ability to do such blending overcomes the production of "choppy" texts that switch back and forth between a less sophisticated writer voice and more sophisticated source voices. While we take up language issues further in Chapter 4, we introduce the "smooth" integration of references here because it involves writing whole paragraphs and arguments and not only isolated sentences. Focusing on the functions of references at the text level provides opportunities for students to improve the flow of their writing.

## Connecting References to One's Own Beliefs and the Engagement of Readers

While we may think of academic writing as impersonal, it is more personal than we sometimes acknowledge. Western academic writers incorporate attitude, evaluation, and reader engagement into their writing, and often in sentences that contain references. At the same time, they are careful not to be overly personal; for instance, they tend to avoid words that exaggerate or are overly passionate.

Ken Hyland's (2011, 2015) work on stance and engagement provides ample illustrations of the ways in which academic writers incorporate these personal aspects into their source use. *Stance* refers to the writer's attitude toward the source text and includes the writer's belief in a particular claim under discussion, his or her emotional response to the claim, and his or her presence in the text. *Boosters* and *hedges* are two ways to reveal stance. Boosters eliminate alternatives (e.g., *obviously, as we know, definitely*), while hedges withhold commitment and open up a space for the reader to dispute the claim (e.g., *it may be that, possibly*). Interestingly, both may function to establish solidarity with the reader. Both boosters and hedges are incorporated into sentences that reuse source text, as when we write, "Obviously, Hyland's (2011) work is central to our understanding of source use" (booster) or "It may be that Hyland's (2011) work is central to our understanding of source use" (hedge).

Student writing often contains overzealous boosters and lacks appropriate hedges. Boosters can be off-putting to readers if, for instance, the text claims that something is obvious, but it is not obvious to the reader. At the same time, a lack of hedges may result in sentences that are not literally true, as when we say *The media always treats that issue negatively* but we mean *The media often depicts that issue negatively*. Since academic readers expect claims to be literally true, students need to be made aware that colloquial expressions may be imprecise and exaggeration is not valued.

A lack of hedges may also result in sentences that misrepresent a source text. For instance, at the top of this chapter, we quoted a teacher who said, "I feel frustrated teaching referencing. Students seem to get it at the sentence-level, like when we practice paraphrasing, but then they can't use their sources well in a paper." If we were to write about this teacher, we might write, *Jamila does not seem to know how to approach the teaching of referencing at the discourse level.* Here, *seem to* is a hedge. If we made the claim that *Jamila does not know how to approach the teaching of referencing at the discourse level*, we would be opening ourselves up to attack and we may in fact be wrong. Academic readers expect claims to be qualified, and hedges are the way to do this. Because research has shown that less experienced L2 writers struggle with hedging effectively (e.g., Hinkel, 2005) and because ineffective use of both boosters and hedges may leave the impression that a writer is not engaged in critical thinking, it is important for instructors to help student writers learn to use boosters and hedges effectively.

In addition to boosters and hedges, *attitude markers* are a third way to reveal stance, as they reveal the writer's affect. Attitude markers include adjectives (*surprising*), adverbs (*unfortunately*), phrases (*we hope that*), and reporting verbs. Reporting verbs often reveal whether or not the writer reusing the information agrees with that information, disagrees with it, or remains neutral. For example, if an author writes, "Hyland *acknowledged* that…," it can be inferred that the author believes Hyland's statement is true. On the other hand, the verbs *assume* or *claim* may be taken to imply disagreement. In addition, reporting verbs may also reflect the stance of the source author (Pecorari, 2013), or more precisely, the writer's understanding of the stance of the source author. So when we read "Hyland *argued*," we know that Hyland believed that he was presenting a hypothesis and not accepted fact, and when we read "Hyland *remarked*," we know that Hyland did not believe the point was central to his argument. Reporting verbs may also indicate the strength of conviction of the writer or source author, as in "Hyland *speculated*," which indicates less conviction than "Hyland *made clear*."

Hyland has also discussed *self-mention* as a way of indicating stance. Self-mention refers primarily to the use of first-person pronouns. While we acknowledge that first-person pronouns are not as common in the hard sciences, they are used in social science and humanities disciplines as well as in many student genres to establish authorial presence. Depending on how they are used, they establish authority to varying degrees. For instance, they may point to the writer as a guide through the text (*Let us now consider…*), as the architect of the essay (*First, I consider…then, I…*), as an opinion holder (*I believe that Howard is right when she argues that…*), and as an originator (*Our argument is that…*) (Tang & John, 1999). Both opinion holder and originator are particularly relevant to referencing, and originator is important for knowledge transformation because it allows writers to delineate the differences between their own work and that of other authors. However, research has shown that L2 writers use *I* less frequently than scholars (Hyland, 2015) and that they relied more on indirect ways of attributing information (e.g., *it is believed that…*) or failed to attribute information completely (Moore, 1997; Shi, 2004). Thus, it is important for L2 writers to study the ways in which more experienced writers directly refer to themselves as well as to their sources.

While stance reveals the writer's attitude toward the content of their own text, engagement refers to how writers rhetorically recognize their readers (Hyland, 2011, 2015). *Engagement* includes reader mention (e.g., *you, we*); direct questions, which invite collusion; and directives (e.g., *Assume that, Let's, must, should*), which construct the text as a dialogue. A common example of a directive in a reference is the citation that a writer gives to point readers to further reading (*See also; For a detailed analysis, see…*); such citations serve the function of what Harwood (2009) calls "signposting," or providing a source to less informed readers or readers who want to know more (p. 501). These features of source-based academic writing make it clear that referencing is not only about avoiding prototypical plagiarism, but also, and primarily, about participating in an academic conversation.

## Differences in Source Use across Disciplinary Discourse Communities

There is an emerging consensus that important differences in referencing expectations exist across disciplines. Specifically, there are well-known differences between humanities and social sciences, on the one hand, and science and engineering on the other. Hyland's (1999, 2000, 2011) influential work has compared academic writing in philosophy, sociology, marketing, applied linguistics, biology, electronic engineering, mechanical engineering, and physics. Hyland found that humanities and social science texts tended to use more citations overall and, specifically, more writer-fronted citations than those in the sciences and engineering. *Writer-fronted citations* highlight the source author by putting the author's name at the beginning of the sentence; they have also been called *integral citations* by Swales (1990). Humanities and social science texts also used more quotes and stance markers than science and engineering texts. In addition, reporting verbs that referred to *verbal expression* (*discuss, hypothesize*) were used more in humanities and social science texts, whereas reporting verbs that referred to the *research process* (*observe, discover*) were more common in science and engineering.

These differences align with differences in epistemology. The avoidance of writer-fronted citations and the absence of stance markers in the hard sciences has been connected to a tradition of objectivity, whereas the abundance of them in the social sciences is tied to a tradition of recognized interpretation (Hyland, 2004). In addition, the use of research process verbs in the hard sciences reflects an understanding of the research process as objective and replicable, whereas the varied use of reporting verbs in the social sciences helps establish a shared context with readers in disciplines with more varied research agendas (Hyland, 2004). One implication of these differences for writing teachers is that, in the sciences, students are often expected to treat ideas from source texts as facts, whereas in social sciences and humanities they are expected to treat them as claims.

In addition to these disciplinary differences, Hyland's research has also revealed some commonalities. For instance, *information-fronted citations*—those that omit the author's name from the sentence and put it in a note (also called *non-integral citations* by Swales, 1990)—were common in all disciplines except philosophy. All disciplines also used reporting verbs that expressed the writer's agreement with the claim or that withheld evaluation (though only the social science texts used reporting verbs that indicated disagreement, e.g., *fails to*). Hyland's (2004) data also show that some verbs such as *suggest, propose,* and *show* were among the most frequently used verbs in disciplines in all three areas (humanities, social sciences, and hard sciences).

As shown in Chapter 2, it is important to discuss differing expectations for source use in different contexts to keep students from becoming confused or disengaged. Here, we argue that exploring disciplinary differences and their connections to epistemology is also important. Teachers may want to approach this differently at different levels. In first-year writing courses, for instance, teachers may want to keep the focus on aspects of source use that are common across disciplines (e.g., the use of affirming and neutral reporting verbs, information-fronted citations, and summary), while only beginning the discussion of disciplinary source use. One relatively simple place to start would be to explain that writer-fronted citations are rare in hard science texts (Hyland, 2000), and that writer- and information-fronted citations function differently, with writer-fronted citations indicating the writer's stance toward the information, and information-fronted citations allowing the information to stand more objectively.

Another topic for first-year writing courses might be disciplinary differences in the reuse of words. Research has shown that attribution expectations seem to differ across disciplines. Shi (2011, 2012) found, for example, that students and instructors in the humanities and social sciences tended to judge copied words as problematic, while those in the sciences did not. These findings reinforce those of Flowerdew and Li (2007), who found considerable language reuse in published science texts and speculated that originality of findings was more important than originality of language in that community. Hyland (2004) found no uses of quotes in the hard science and engineering disciplines that he studied, suggesting that writers in these disciplines may not use attributed quotes. In terms of teaching, there is not yet enough research evidence to declare definitively how writers reuse words in the sciences, but we think that this is an important discussion to have with students because of the concern that students who follow one teacher's guidelines might be accused of prototypical plagiarism by another.

In more advanced courses, such as Writing in the Disciplines or graduate courses, teachers may find it useful to delve more deeply into disciplinary differences. Since there is not yet enough research to make coherent generalizations about the rhetorical constraints of each discipline, perhaps the best way to approach this is through observation and analysis. For instance, students may benefit from systematically observing the ways in which scholars in their disciplines use sources and considering the ways in which the forms align with knowledge construction. In addition, through observation they can develop knowledge of the cited authors that have become symbols of a *core concept* in the field (White, 2004). In TESOL, for example, *Bourdieu* has become a standard citation when discussing class difference; the name evokes the concept of *cultural capital* without naming it.

Finally, we would like to add that, even if addressing disciplinary differences is beyond the scope of the course goals, it is important for teachers to realize that their own source use expectations may carry a disciplinary bias that they need to make transparent.

## Connecting to the Classroom

Students need to understand the role that source use plays in establishing both their authority as writers and a framework for their ideas within a discourse community. In order to help them develop these skills, it is important to assign writing tasks that have authentic audiences and purposes and to provide student writers with the opportunity to use sources for sophisticated rhetorical functions. Writing assignments designed for knowledge display are not as useful in this regard because student writers reproduce ideas primarily to demonstrate that they have done the required reading and they use citations primarily to avoid prototypical plagiarism. In addition to completing authentic writing tasks, students benefit from analyzing models of source use. Without an understanding of the rhetorical functions of sources, stance and engagement markers, and the ways in which source use is tied to epistemology, it is hard to establish membership in an academic discourse community or write with authority. The lessons presented are designed to develop these understandings and skills.

# Lesson 1:
## What Does Our Class Believe?
## Writing in a Mini-Discourse Community

**Focus:** Referencing—introduction

**Description:** Students write paragraphs summarizing data from a survey taken by their classmates. They use provided language to smoothly capture generalizations, contrasts, and similarities. They also include their own ideas and quote and cite their classmates.

**Rationale:** To L2 writers, conversing within an academic discourse community may seem like an esoteric notion, and working references smoothly into a paragraph may be difficult. This lesson, therefore, places referencing in the known community of the classroom.

**Students:** High-Beginner to Advanced L2s

**Preparation:** Write a short (2–5 question) online survey using Google Forms or Survey Monkey on a topic that students feel strongly about. Also, prepare a handout with some language to scaffold the writing of paragraphs presenting survey results and quotations. You could include language that focuses students on capturing the main position of the class with phrases such as:

- ❑ It is accepted that. . . .
- ❑ It is clear that. . . .
- ❑ Most of my peers stated that. . . .
- ❑ They argued convincingly that. . . .
- ❑ As students/immigrants/young adults/etc., we believe that. . . .
- ❑ definitely

You could also include language to help students develop smooth language to express contrasting opinions:

- ❑ *While many of my colleagues argued that. . ., others argued that this was not the case.*
- ❑ *Whereas . . . was emphasized, others claimed that. . . .*
- ❑ *Many students stressed. . . . However, others suggested that. . . .*
- ❑ *While some argued that. . . , it should be stressed that the majority argued that. . . .*

You could also include language to help students express similar opinions:

- ❑ *Similarly,*
- ❑ *Wang (2017), too, argued that. . . .*

You may want to provide language that shows the students how to bring in their own views:

- ❏ *I agree with Al Shehri (2017) that. . . .*
- ❏ *Although many of my colleagues felt that, I believe that. . . .*

Finally, you may want to provide quote frames:

- ❏ *<u>Last name</u> (<u>date</u>) argued/claimed/said/explained/noted/ suggested that, "<u>quote</u>."*
- ❏ *According to <u>last name</u> (<u>date</u>), "<u>quote</u>."*

**Procedure**:

1. Ask students to take the survey.

2. Display the results using a projector. Introduce the idea of *discourse community*, and explain that students should think of the class as a discourse community and the survey results as a representation of the beliefs of the discourse community. The students' job is to write a paragraph that captures these beliefs.

3. In small groups, ask students to spend five minutes discussing the results of the survey. They should note patterns that they can report on.

4. Students should interview two other students about their views on the topic. They should record what their classmates say along with the speakers' last names and the date.

5. Ask students to write paragraphs that capture an overview of the survey results, using the language that you provide on the handout and including an illustrative quote from one of their interviews.

**Adaptations:** Ask students to design their own survey, collect data, and write a description of the results in paragraph form.

# Lesson 2:
# Whose Idea Was This?

**Focus:** Referencing—conversation in academic writing

**Description:** Students highlight the ideas from different authors in different colors in a piece of academic writing in order to visualize academic writing as a conversation; they then evaluate the source use.

**Rationale:** Students may not realize the extent to which scholarly writing is a conversation. This lesson, therefore, helps them see the extent to which academic writers use references to other sources.

**Students:** Intermediate to Advanced L2s

**Preparation:** Choose a piece of academic writing that contains references. If you want to model effective source use in a student genre, choose a paper written by a former student or Sample 2, 3, or 4 (Version A) from Appendix 3.

**Procedure**:

1. Ask students to read the text. Make sure they understand it.

2. Ask students to highlight the sentences that contain ideas from cited texts (cited paraphrases, quotes, and summaries). They may do this on paper using colored markers or in Word (for a student paper) or Adobe (for a published .pdf article), using a different color for each cited author.

3. Put students in groups to respond to these questions:

   ■ About how much of the article appears to be the author's own ideas? (Compare the highlighted parts to the unhigh-lighted parts; think in percentages.)

   ■ Were you surprised by how much of the article was based on other sources?

   ■ How many different sources did the writer use?

   ■ Did the writer use these sources evenly, or are some sources used more than others?

   ■ Do you think the writer overused any sources? What makes you say so?

**Adaptations:** In advanced classes in which you want to teach the genre of research reports, use a published study in which the sections (e.g., literature review, methods, results, implications) are indicated by subheadings. Ask students: Is the level of source use consistent across the different sections? If not, why do you think the authors used sources more in certain sections and less in others? You can also ask students to dig deeper into the rhetorical functions of specific references, using the lists on pages 38 and 48.

# Lesson 3:
# What's the Point of Referencing Anyway?

**Focus:** Referencing—rhetorical functions

**Description:** Students read several excerpted texts that refer to the same source and identify the rhetorical functions used in each.

**Rationale:** Some student writers may know that references are used for support and to avoid charges of "plagiarism," but they may not realize the extent to which scholars use references to realize other intentions. This lesson, therefore, highlights the rhetorical functions of referencing so that students can become better readers and writers of texts.

**Students:** Advanced L2s; L1s

**Preparation:** Collect several social science or humanities texts containing references to the same source. Introductions, literature reviews, or theoretical sections of scholarly articles work well. Since it is important that the students understand the topic well, they should read the source text and discuss the topic prior to doing the lesson. Also, they should read the papers that referenced the source, if possible. Prepare a handout with background information on the texts you are using, the excerpts containing references, and a list of rhetorical functions.

If you want to teach a unit on contrastive rhetoric, you can use Kaplan's (1966) article, "Cultural thought patterns in intercultural education," in which he argued that different languages have different ways of organizing a text. Excerpts from several texts that refer to Kaplan's seminal article are provided here. If you use these excerpts, this list of rhetorical functions works well: (1) providing a base for the current article to build on; (2) establishing the writer's authority by aligning with a known expert; (3) rebutting claims; (4) summarizing an earlier work for objective discussion; (5) and offering a critique. If you want to supply the students with a longer list of rhetorical functions, you can add more from the list on page 38.

## *Texts referring to Kaplan (1966), in order of publication:*

a. In "Contrastive rhetoric: Japanese and English," Hinds (1983) sought to reinforce Kaplan's understanding of "Oriental" organizing structure and refine it at the same time. He wrote:

> Kaplan's article has stood essentially alone in the field, despite the fact that it points the way to a major area of inquiry in the fields of second language acquisition, textual analysis, and educational applications of linguistic research. In order to advance our understanding of contrastive rhetoric beyond the insights already provided by Kaplan, it is necessary to understand the flaws in the original research design. These flaws can then be prevented in subsequent studies. Thus, even at this late date, it is appropriate to make critical comments about the analyses presented in Kaplan's article. (Hinds, 1983, p. 185)

b. In 1987, Kaplan coedited the book *Writing across languages: Analysis of L2 Text* with Ulla Connor. The book sought to capture current research on contrastive analysis; it contained a chapter by Hinds. Kaplan wrote the first chapter, beginning it this way:

> ...[In] 'Cultural Thought Patterns in Intercultural Education' (1966), . . . I tried to represent. . . the notion that the rhetorical structure of languages differs. It is probably true that, in the first blush of discovery, I overstated both the difference and my case. In the years since the article first appeared, I have been accused of reductionism–of trying to reduce the whole of linguistics to this single issue. It was not my intent then, and it is not my intent now, to claim more for the notion than it deserves. Nevertheless, I have become gradually more convinced that there is some validity to the notion. (Kaplan, 1987, p. 9)

c. In 2004, Casanave wrote a book entitled *Controversies in second language writing* and dedicated a chapter to the controversies surrounding contrastive rhetoric. At the beginning of the chapter, she wrote:

> Contrastive rhetoric (CR) as a field of study began with the publication of Robert Kaplan's 1966 article in *Language Learning*. Kaplan assumed a kind of linguistic relativity, specifically that the rhetorical aspects of each language are unique to each language and culture. In second and foreign language education, this assumption implies that differences between the discourse-level features of a learner's first and second language cause difficulties for L2 learners who are trying to acquire discourse-level patterns in their second languages. In other words, inherent in the CR project is the assumption of negative transfer from L1 to L2. Understanding such differences, so the claim goes, can help scholars and teachers explain some of the problems that L2 learners have in organizing their writing in ways that seem acceptable to native speakers. (Casanave, 2004, p. 27)

d. In the same book, slightly later in the chapter, Casanave went on to develop her discussion of controversies surrounding the Kaplan article:

> To begin at the beginning of the CR controversy, we need to go back to Robert Kaplan's (1966) original CR article, which these days is still often cited but less often read. I found this article to be a very strange piece of writing. I don't know if I am the only reader who reacted this way, but in spite of the fact that Kaplan discussed the linear nature of English expository prose (or more broadly, "English communication"), I did not find the piece to be particularly linear. (Casanave, 2004, p. 27)

**Procedure**:

1. Review with the students what they learned from reading Kaplan (1966). In this famous article, Kaplan proposes that not only do languages vary in their sentence structure, but they also vary in their rhetorical structure. The article is known as the "doodles" article because it contains visual line representations of

"English" (a straight line), "Semitic" (a zigzag), "Oriental" (a spiral), "Romance" (a jagged line), and "Russian" (a slightly different jagged line) languages (p. 15). The main claim rests on the notion that cultures determine rhetorical organization, a connection that is problematic since it stereotypes L2 writers as writing in certain predetermined ways and seems to foreclose on the possibility that some L1 writing skills might usefully transfer to L2 tasks. The article is also problematic as a research study; Kaplan draws his conclusions about L2 rhetorics not from analysis of texts in those languages, but rather from texts written in English by L2 student writers. Moreover, he does not describe his methods of analysis. It can also be pointed out that his conclusion, that teachers need to teach English rhetoric to foreign students, does not recognize the value of letting student writers both create new organizing patterns and re-create genres to meet rhetorical needs.

2. Hand out the excerpts containing references to Kaplan and the list of rhetorical functions. Explain to the students that they will read four excerpts from articles that refer to Kaplan (1966). Although they were published over a long period of time, the excerpts are engaged in a continuing conversation about the Kaplan article. The students should read the excerpts in chronological order, examining how each writer represents Kaplan's article and determining the rhetorical function of the reference.

3. Guide the students through an analysis of the first excerpt. Begin by reading the entire excerpt, and then go back and read one sentence at a time, describing what the writer does in each sentence. The sentence by sentence description may go as follows: Hinds comments that the Kaplan article "has stood essentially alone in the field," which can be read both as a recognition that it was seminal and as a lament that more work has not been done. Hinds indicates that he has a plan to advance the work that Kaplan started, from which we can infer that he supports the project of contrastive rhetoric. His plans include addressing the article's "flaws," and his choice of this word suggests that the problems are minor, and indeed, he suggests that they can be corrected. With the final sentence ("it is appropriate to make critical comments about the analyses"), Hinds seems to be defending his critique, as if it is hard for him to critique the article that stands alone. After a careful reading of the excerpt, determine the function of the reference: Hinds' reference to Kaplan functions to provide a base or springboard for Hinds' own work. Hinds is building on Kaplan and also establishing his own authority by aligning himself with Kaplan and critiquing him in a respectful way.

4.  Ask students to work in groups to analyze the remaining excerpts in the same way:

- **Sentence-by-sentence description of Kaplan (1987):** Kaplan restates his position ("that the rhetorical structure of languages differs") and then cedes some ground to his detractors in a move to rebut their argument ("probably true that, in the first blush of discovery, I overstated…"). In this sentence he also frames his error as overstatement. He goes on to say that his detractors accuse him of "reductionism," which he denies. He then reaffirms his original idea, with the added implication that he now has even more evidence to support it.

  Function of the reference: Kaplan's reference to his earlier work functions to reassert his position and rebut arguments made against him.

- **Sentence-by-sentence description of Casanave (2004), first excerpt:** Casanave traces the birth of the field of contrastive rhetoric to Kaplan's article. She characterizes his approach as "linguistic relativity" and then summarizes the article. In so doing, she updates some of his language (using "discourse-level features" as a synonym for "rhetorical aspects"), but generally stays close to Kaplan's ideas.

  Function of the reference: Casanave's reference to Kaplan functions to introduce the discussion of contrastive rhetoric in an objective way.

- **Sentence-by-sentence description of Casanave (2004), second excerpt:** Casanave traces the beginning of the controversies about contrastive rhetoric back to Kaplan's article. She notes that the article is often cited but not often read, implying that it is out-of-date, or that writers who cite it may themselves not have analyzed it properly; in other words, there may be misinformation out there that, we can infer, she is now going to correct. She then gives her own reading of the article, signaled by the use of *I*. For Casanave, there is a disconnect between Kaplan's claim that English rhetoric is linear and the fact that his article is not linear.

  Function of the reference: Her reference to Kaplan functions to critique the article for its lack of self-awareness, implying that its main claims might not be true.

5.  Reconvene as a class in order to go over the work of the small groups.

**Adaptations:** Ask students to read exerpts from student papers from a previous term that contain references to the same set of readings. The student papers may not be in dialogue with one another as scholars in the same field often are, but they will use references to the same sources for different functions. They will also provide models of effective references written by student writers.

# Lesson 4:
# Reporting Verbs: Does the Writer Agree?

**Focus:** Vocabulary—reporting verbs

**Description:** Students read sample sentences and determine the writer's stance toward the cited idea based on the choice of reporting verb and contextual cues; then they develop three lists of reporting verbs: verbs that indicate agreement, those that indicate doubt, and those that vary according to context. They use the lists to revise reporting verbs in their own writing.

**Rationale:** Student writers often do not use a large array of reporting verbs or understand the differences in stance that different verbs imply. Therefore, this lesson introduces them to a number of common reporting verbs.

**Students:** Intermediate to Advanced L2s

**Preparation:** Prepare a handout with sentences containing reporting verbs. You may want to write paraphrases of texts the students have already read, using verbs from the provided list. This list includes verbs that are of immediate use to student writers; however, it is not exhaustive, as teaching too many verbs at once may overwhelm students. For verbs that vary depending on context, it makes sense to include two sample sentences, one that suggests agreement and the other that suggests doubt. You may also use the sample sentences provided, which are completely made-up (meaning, the cited sources are not real).

## Reporting Verbs List

Verbs that suggest **agreement:** *acknowledge, be aware, bear in mind, demonstrate, grasp, make clear, note, prove, show, understand.*

Verbs that suggest **doubt:** *allege, assert, assume, believe, claim, insist, presume, speculate.*

Verbs that **vary** depending on context: *argue, conclude, find, hypothesize, report, suggest.*

## Sample sentences:

a. Smith (2014) **presumed** that the local government would not respond to global warming. However, a 2010 report from the town council outlined its concerns over the economic impacts of hotter temperatures.

b. Al Hamoud (2007) **concluded** that more attention needs to be paid to the disappearance of Monarch butterflies across North America. For those of us who have not seen one since childhood, this seems like a reasonable conclusion.

c. Wang (2006) **demonstrated** that the global temperature has risen by two degrees over the last three years.

d. Contreras and Brown (2001) **asserted** that children of working parents are more motivated than children from middle-class families. However, their results have not been replicated.

e. Lomda (2003) **found** that a daily dosage of ecyprotin is beneficial in preventing flu.

f. Mishkin (2000) **showed** that preschool children who are read to learn to read faster.

g. Maley (1999) **insisted** that professional athletes are respected no less than scientists or artists, but as we all know, athletes are not necessarily considered smart or educated.

h. Keriotis (2012) **claimed** that women would not make good soldiers, but two recently completed Ranger training with the U.S. Army, fulfilling the same rigorous requirements as the men.

i. Handa and Kuromoto (2010) **argued** that, while women have many career opportunities in the U.S., sexism still exists. This can be seen in the fact that women earn 77 cents for every dollar that men make.

j. Huynh (2006) **made clear** that landmines remain an issue in Cambodia.

k. Barteau (2015) **argued** that the ebola virus is spreading through sexual contact. However, it seems much more likely that it is spreading mostly through the butchering of infected animals for meat and funeral practices whereby people wash the dead by hand (Stankić, 2015).

l. Khouri (2000) **found** that international students experience difficulty throughout their time abroad. However, most studies since have **concluded** that the most difficult period is the first semester, after which adaptation occurs and some difficulties are alleviated.

m. Cherokee (2006) **speculated** that people with children are more likely to have pets than people without. However, there is little data to support her claim.

n. While Takács (1999) **concluded** that children of gay parents grow up just as happy as children of straight parents, Malevich's more recent data **show** that this is not always the case.

**Procedure**:

1. On the board, write a model sentence that includes a reporting verb and teach the term *reporting verb*. Explain that some verbs indicate that the writer agrees with the claim, while others indicate disagreement or uncertainty, and still others may vary according to context; the point of this lesson is to figure out which is which.

2. Hand out the sample sentences. Ask students to use contextual cues and their vocabulary knowledge to decide whether the writer agrees with the claim of the cited author or not for each sentence. The students should make three lists of reporting verbs: those that suggest agreement, those that suggest doubt, and those that differ by context.

3. Ask students to compare their answers with a partner.

4. Hand out an answer sheet and give the partners time to check their answers. Respond to any questions the students may have.

5. Ask students to reread one of their own papers, highlighting the reporting verbs. Then, ask them to revise the verbs, choosing verbs from their lists to accurately reflect stance and bring more variety to their writing.

**Adaptations:** If you want your students to learn more actively, rather than providing them with sample sentences on a handout, type up the sentences on one sheet, cut it up, and give one sentence to each student. You can then draw three columns on the board and have the students attach their sentences to the board in the appropriate column. Alternatively, you can create a multiple choice "test" in Survey Monkey, Google Survey, or using the Kahoot mobile app. For each sentence, students can choose a) writer agrees or b) writer doubts. Also, you may want to provide an open-ended survey question or textbox for students to explain their reasoning, as this will allow you to formatively assess the students' current understandings.

For more advanced classes, have the students find an academic article in their field, highlight the reporting verbs in it, and write a short analysis (100–200 words) of the author's use of reporting verbs. These questions can be provided to guide their analysis:

❑ What reporting verbs does the author use most often?

❑ In which part(s) of the article are these verbs used?

❑ Does the author use any reporting verbs that you do not know? Record the sentences with reporting verbs that are new to you. Give the dictionary definitions of the reporting verbs; then decide whether the verbs indicated the author's agreement or disagreement.

❑ What types of reporting verbs does the author use? Make three lists: for verbs that suggest agreement, those that suggest doubt, and those that vary.

❑ In addition to verbs, does the author use any type of words to indicate agreement or disagreement with the source (e.g., adverbs such as *clearly, wrongly, mistakenly*)?

# Lesson 5:
# How Much Will Readers Accept?
# Avoiding Overgeneralizations and Unfair Claims

**Focus:** Hedging

**Description:** Students read a text and compare it with claims based on it. They determine whether the claims are fair or not and whether they are overgeneralizations or not. They are introduced to hedges as a way of fixing unfair and overgeneralized claims.

**Rationale:** Students sometimes use overgeneralizations and unfair claims about authors' positions. This lesson helps students learn how to recognize such claims and hedge them.

**Students:** Intermediate L2s

**Preparation:** Prepare a handout that lists words students often used when making overgeneralizations and/or unfair claims. On the handout, supply alternative vocabulary for making more acceptable, qualified statements:

| Overgeneralizing or Unfair Words | Hedged Words |
|---|---|
| *all, every* | *many, most, virtually all* |
| *everyone* | *many people* |
| *always* | *often* |
| *It is clear that…*<br>*It is true that…* | *It may be that…*<br>*It seems likely that...* |
| *is, are*<br>(in unmarked overgeneralizations such as *Asian people are good at math.*) | *may be* |
| *believes* | *seems to believe* |

Also, prepare a handout with a reading and some sample claims based on the reading, some of which are overgeneralizations or unfair claims, and others of which are acceptable claims that model hedges. We suggest using this excerpt from *Fast Food Nation* by Eric Schlosser (2001):

> The 1960s were the heyday of artificial flavors in the United States. The synthetic versions of flavor compounds were not subtle, but they did not have to be, given the nature of most processed food. For the past 20 years food processors have tried hard to use only "natural flavors" in their products. According to the FDA, these must be derived entirely from natural sources–from herbs, spices, fruits, vegetables, beef,

chicken, yeast, bark, roots, etc. Consumers prefer to see natural flavors on a label, out of a belief that they are healthier. The distinction between artificial and natural flavors can be somewhat arbitrary and absurd, based more on how the flavor has been made than on what it actually contains. "A natural flavor," says Terry Acree, a professor of food science at Cornell University, "is a flavor that's been derived with an out-of-date technology." Natural flavors and artificial flavors sometimes contain exactly the same chemicals, produced through different methods. Amyl acetate, for example, provides the dominant note of banana flavor. When you distill it from bananas with a solvent, amyl acetate is a natural flavor. When you produce it by mixing vinegar with amyl alcohol, adding sulfuric acid as a catalyst, amyl acetate is an artificial flavor. Either way it smells and tastes the same. The phrase "natural flavor" is now listed among the ingredients of everything from Stonyfield Farm Organic Strawberry Yogurt to Taco Bell Hot Taco Sauce.

A natural flavor is not necessarily healthier or purer than an artificial one. When almond flavor (benzaldehyde) is derived from natural sources, such as peach and apricot pits, it contains traces of hydrogen cyanide, a deadly poison. Benzaldehyde derived through a different process—by mixing oil of clove and the banana flavor, amyl acetate—does not contain any cyanide. Nevertheless, it is legally considered an artificial flavor and sells at a much lower price. Natural and artificial flavors are now manufactured at the same chemical plants, places that few people would associate with Mother Nature. Calling any of these flavors "natural" requires a flexible attitude toward the English language and a fair amount of irony. (Schlosser, 2001, pp. 126–127)

## Claims

A. Schlosser (2001) explains that natural flavors are better than artificial ones because they are better for you.

B. Schlosser (2001) believes that natural and artificial flavors are both unhealthy, and that we should never eat foods containing them.

C. Schlosser (2001) points out that natural flavors are present in many of the foods we eat.

D. Schlosser (2001) believes that natural flavors are produced by old-fashioned technology, and we should embrace artificial flavors because they are the wave of the future.

E. Schlosser (2001) argues that the distinction between artificial and natural flavors may not hold up to scrutiny.

F. Schlosser (2001) reveals that natural flavors are poisonous.

G. Schlosser (2001) believes that many natural flavors are just as artificial as artificial ones.

**Procedure**:

1.  Go over the reading with students to make sure that they understand it.

2.  Hand out the sample claims to students. Tell them that their job is to determine whether each claim is an accurate representation of Schlosser's position or not.

3.  To give students an idea of how to proceed, discuss several claims together as a class. Begin by looking at Claim A as an example of an unfair claim. Ask students to read the claim and locate the sentence(s) in the text most closely related to it:

    ■ **Claim A, related sentence:** "Consumers prefer to see natural flavors on a label, out of a belief that they are healthier" (Schlosser, 2001, p. 126).

    Ask students to identify the difference between the sentences. Point out that Schlosser's sentence was about consumers' beliefs, whereas the claim makes it look like the consumers' beliefs are Schlosser's. Suggest a way to make the sentence fair: Schlosser (2001) explains that *some people believe that natural flavors are better than artificial ones because they are healthier*. Draw the students' attention to the fact that, in the text, Schlosser represents not only his own position, but also positions of food processors, the FDA, consumers, and Terry Acree. Explain that, when writing, it is important to differentiate between the positions of an author and the positions of the people he or she refers to in the text.

4.  Go through the same process with Claim B as an example of overgeneralization. Read Claim B with the students and ask them to locate the sentence(s) in the text most closely related to it:

    ■ **Claim B, related sentences:** "A natural flavor is not necessarily healthier or purer than an artificial one. When almond flavor (benzaldehyde) is derived from natural sources, such as peach and apricot pits, it contains traces of hydrogen cyanide, a deadly poison" (Schlosser, 2001, p. 127).

    Ask students what the difference between the sentences is. Point out that, while Schlosser gives an example of one natural flavor that is not healthy, he does not generalize about how healthy either natural or artificial flavors are. Neither does he make any recommendations for what people should eat. Explain that, when writing, it is important not to overgeneralize the points made in a source text.

5.  Go through the same process as a class with Claim C as an example of a hedged, fair claim. Read Claim C with the students and ask them to locate the sentence(s) in the text most closely related to it:

    ■ **Claim C, related sentence:** "The phrase 'natural flavor' is now listed among the ingredients of everything from Stonyfield Farm Organic Strawberry Yogurt to Taco Bell Hot Taco Sauce" (Schlosser, 2001, p. 127).

    Ask students what the difference between the sentences is. Discuss the specificity of the source and the lack of specificity of the reference.

6.  Ask students to work in pairs to determine whether the remaining claims accurately represent Schlosser's text or not. When the students have come up with their answers, go over the claims as a class:

    ■ **Claim D, related sentence:** "A natural flavor," says Terry Acree, a professor of food science at Cornell University, "is a flavor that's been derived with an out-of-date technology" (Schlosser, 2001, p. 126).

    <u>Determination</u>: Unfair because it takes Acree's position and ascribes it to Schlosser. Moreover, it adds the idea that we should embrace artificial flavors, an idea that does not appear in the text.

    ■ **Claim E, related sentences:** "The distinction between artificial and natural flavors can be somewhat arbitrary and absurd, based more on how the flavor has been made than on what it actually contains. . . . Natural flavors and artificial flavors sometimes contain exactly the same chemicals. . ." (Schlosser, 2001, p. 126).

    <u>Determination</u>: Fair. This seems to be the main point of the passage, and it is reinforced throughout. The hedge *may not* reflects Schlosser's use of the hedges *can be* and *sometimes*.

    ■ **Claim F, related sentence:** "When almond flavor (benzaldehyde) is derived from natural sources, such as peach and apricot pits, it contains traces of hydrogen cyanide, a deadly poison" (Schlosser, 2001, p. 127).

    <u>Determination</u>: Overgeneralization because Schlosser gives only one example of a poisonous natural flavor and does not make a generalized claim that natural flavors are poisonous.

- **Claim G, related sentences:** "Natural and artificial flavors are now manufactured at the same chemical plants, places that few people would associate with Mother Nature. Calling any of these flavors 'natural' requires a flexible attitude toward the English language and a fair amount of irony" (Schlosser, 2001, p. 127).

  <u>Determination:</u> Fair inference. The use of *many* is a hedge that leaves room for some natural flavors actually being natural.

7. Discuss the differences between *all, many,* and *most,* explaining that it is better not to make generalizations that don't allow for exceptions. Show the students an example:

   - *All natural flavors are poisonous.*—A weak claim because just one counterexample demonstrates that it is false. It asks the readers to accept too much.

   - *Many natural flavors are poisonous.*—A stronger claim because it is not made false by just one counterexample.

   - *Most natural flavors are poisonous.*—A claim that is persuasive only if there are statistics that show that a majority of natural flavors are poisonous and they are cited.

   - *Natural flavors are poisonous.*—An ambiguous claim because it could mean either that all natural flavors are poisonous or that some natural flavors are poisonous; it is possible to use this phrasing if the writer explains what is meant.

8. Give students the handout with the lists of overgeneralizing/unfair words and hedged words. Tell them that it is important not to overstate claims because readers will stop believing them, and explain that using the hedged words will help them avoid making overstatements.

**Adaptations:** Ask students to apply what they learned in this lesson to a paper that they already wrote and then reread the paper to identify problematic claims. For overgeneralizations, they can highlight occurrences of *all, every, everyone, always, never, no one, nothing* and similar words, and expressions of certainty such as *it is obvious that, it is clear that, obviously, definitely, it is true that.* Then they should decide whether the sentences they identified are in fact an overgeneralizations. If they are, they should revise them, using the hedges where appropriate. For unfair claims about source texts, students can skim for sentences with references. Then, assuming that you are working with a text that the whole class has read, students can work in pairs to decide whether the representation of the source text is accurate or not. If they deem it inaccurate, they should revise it.

# Lesson 6:
## Exploring Academic Uses of *I*

**Focus:** Authority—first-person pronouns

**Description:** Students locate the first-person pronouns in a published text, categorize the uses, and learn that *I* can be used to establish authority and ownership of ideas.

**Rationale:** While scholars, particularly in social science and humanities disciplines, use *I* to establish textual authority and differentiate the ideas they claim as their own from those of others, many students are confused about whether they can use it or not. This lesson, therefore, gives students an in-depth look at the use of first-person pronouns so that they can make better decisions about when to use them in their writing.

**Students:** Intermediate to Advanced L2s; L1s

**Preparation:** Choose a reading text containing a number of first-person pronouns. Also, prepare examples of first-person pronouns from both student and published writing. For a piece of student writing, you could use Sample 2 in Appendix 3 or one of your own students' papers. For a piece of published writing, the two excerpts about contrastive rhetoric from Casanave (2004) used in Lesson 3 work well. Although they appear only a few pages away from each other in the same book, both are about Kaplan's seminal article, and both indicate some doubt about Kaplan's claims, they differ in their use of *I*. In the first, Casanave indicated that there may be other sides to the issue without the use of the first person: "Understanding such differences, *so the claim goes*, can help scholars and teachers explain some of the problems that L2 learners have in organizing their writing . . ." (p. 27, emphasis added). In the second, by contrast, she indicated her doubt more personally: "In spite of the fact that Kaplan discussed the linear nature of English expository prose . . ., I did not find the piece to be particularly linear" (p. 31). With the use of *I* in the second excerpt, Casanave demonstrates her authority to hold her own opinion, even as she casts doubt on it herself: "I don't know if I am the only reader who reacted this way..." (p. 31).

Make a handout with the six uses for first-person pronouns identified by Tang and John (1999, pp. S27–S29). The uses, with examples and explanations, are listed in order from the usage with the weakest authorial presence to the strongest.

## 1. Representative

*With the world map we have today, . . .*

The representative **we** includes all people. The usage is not specific to the writer and therefore has no authorial presence.

## 2. Guide through the Essay

*From the data in Table 1, we can see that . . . .*

*Let us consider . . . .*

The guide **we** is used to steer the reader to a certain part of the text or point to be made. This usage includes the author and the reader, joining the two in a common thought process. It often uses verbs such as **see, note, observe.**

## 3. Architect of the Essay

*First I consider . . ., and then I go on to discuss . . . .*

The architect **I** (or **we** for multiple authors) explains the structure of the text. While it is similar to the guide, Tang and John separate the two, seeing this usage as having slightly more authorial presence than the guide.

## 4. Recounter of the Research Process

*I audiorecorded the interviews and transcribed them.*

The recounter of the research process **I** (or **we** for multiple authors) tells what the author did before writing, particularly during the research process. It often uses past tense verbs such as **worked, read, interviewed, collected.**

## 5. Opinion-Holder

*I agree with Zamel that . . . .*

The opinion-holder **I** (or **we** for multiple authors) agrees, disagrees, and expresses interest. As a holder of a position, this usage carries a considerable amount of authorial presence.

## 6. Originator

*Our main argument is that the first-person pronoun in academic writing is not a homogeneous entity* (Tang & John, 1999, p. S23).

The originator **I** (or **we** for multiple authors) states a new idea and claims authority or ownership of it. This usage has a very strong authorial presence because it shows that the writer knows she has the right and ability to originate ideas.

**Procedure**:

1. Lay the groundwork for this lesson by taking a moment to review the various forms of the first-person pronoun with your students (*I, my, me, mine, we, our, us, ours*) and eliciting the students' thoughts about whether it's a good idea to use *I* in an essay. Explain that both *I* and *we* are frequently used in academic writing, particularly by scholars in humanities and social science disciplines and in many student genres.

2. Give the examples of the use of *I* in a student-written and a published text. Discuss the choices the writers made, their possible motivations, and their different effects to demonstrate that academic writers do not avoid using the first-person singular pronoun but make choices about when and how to use it.

3. Give students the handout with Tang & John's six uses of first-person pronouns. Discuss which categories the uses of *I* in the sample texts you used fall into.

4. Put students in small groups to identify and categorize the first-person pronouns in the reading text you chose. If the pronoun is plural, ask students to determine whom it refers to (e.g., reader and the writer, writer and someone else mentioned in the text, all people in the discourse community, human beings in general, Americans) as well.

5. Reconvene as a class so students can share their findings. Ask them about their use of the first-person pronouns when writing in other languages. Also, clarify your own expectations for use of first-person pronouns. In our experience, some students overuse the first person when expressing opinion, so we explain that it is not necessary to add *I think* to a sentence such as: "Casanave's analysis is quite thorough." We also have students who avoid all uses of *I*, so we explain that using *I* is a clear way to distinguish their opinion from that of the author of the text they are discussing.

**Adaptations:** If the text you choose has many plural pronouns that function as *guide*, then this can lead to a discussion of the many words and phrases that construct the text as a dialogue between author and reader, such as rhetorical questions (*Why have we become so obsessed with smartphones?*) and imperatives (*Note, Consider, Bear in mind, Let's, See also, See Table 1*). Bringing such usages to the students' attention helps them understand academic writing as a conversation within a discourse community.

If you want to focus on disciplinary differences in the use of the first person, choose several articles from different disciplines, rather than having all the students look at the same one. Assign a different article to each small group, and ask them to count the total number of uses of first-person singular and first-person plural pronouns, and then type each one according to the six usage categories. Ask groups to compare their findings by creating a comparison chart on the board.

# Lesson 7:
# What Am I Supposed to Do?
# Differences in Referencing
# Expectations across Disciplines

**Focus:** Referencing—disciplinary differences

**Description:** Students read samples of academic writing from different disciplines and contrast the referencing by examining citation type, reporting verbs, and use of quotes.

**Rationale:** Disciplinary differences in referencing can confuse students and cause them to give up on learning about referencing, although understanding these differences can facilitate their performance in their major courses and in graduate school. This lesson, therefore, gives students an opportunity to compare referencing across writing samples from different disciplines so that they can see that the differences are systematic.

**Students:** Advanced L2s; L1s

**Preparation:** Choose sample texts that reveal disciplinary differences in referencing. They may be published articles or student papers that were edited to conform to established referencing conventions. In Appendix 3, we provide two samples of student writing that make a good contrast (see Samples 2 and 3). The samples selected will, of course, shape the direction of the lesson: some may provide clear examples of differences in citation format, while others present clear examples of how quotations are used (or not), for instance.

**Procedure:**

1. Explain that there are different style guides for source use used in different disciplines and in different classes; an instructor in Education may expect students to use APA, whereas an English instructor may require MLA. In addition, introduce the students to some of the most recognizable differences in citation style between disciplines. For instance, focus on information-fronted and writer-fronted citation, involving the students in a discussion about how the text flows differently when cited sentences begin with the author's name versus when they do not.

2. Hand out the sample texts and ask students to highlight the sentences that contain references.

3. Put students in small groups to respond to scaffolding questions about the highlighted sentences in each text. They should arrange their answers in a chart for easy comparison of the texts.

   - Are the citations in-text, footnotes, or endnotes?
   - What information is included in the citation?
   - Are the cited sentences information-fronted or writer-fronted?
   - What reporting verbs are used? What tense are they in? Is the voice active or passive?
   - Does the citation mark a quotation, paraphrase, or summary?
   - Are quotations used?
   - Are claims hedged? What words are used to hedge?
   - Are boosters used? What words are used to boost?

4. Reconvene as a class to discuss the similarities and differences that the students observed. Remind your students that not all differences in source use are due to discipline, but may also be due to differences in genre or author preference.

**Adaptations:** Depending on the goals of your class, you can take this lesson in a variety of directions. If you want to review reporting verbs, for example, extend the scaffolding questions about reporting verbs to have students determine whether they indicate agreement or disagreement with the claim. Or, you could look at how the writers in different disciplines position themselves differently vis-à-vis the information that they cite. Using Samples 2 and 3 in Appendix 3, you could show that the first writer used the sources to set up her own contrasting claim, while the second writer used the source ideas as facts, which, presumably, she agreed with.

# Take-Away Points

- Effective source use involves much more than giving credit to sources; it involves a conversation between members of a discourse community.

- Using references creates a framework for a writer's claims and helps establish authority and voice.

- Teaching students to use references for a variety of rhetorical functions connected to their lines of argument is essential to effective academic writing.

- Students need to practice incorporating references into paragraphs to improve the flow of their writing.

- Instructors should teach students how to judge when claims are overzealous or overgeneralized, and teach them to use boosters, hedges, and attitude markers that are appropriate for writing in an academic register.

- It is helpful to expand students' knowledge of reporting verbs.

- Showing students how to establish authority by using first-person pronouns and how to engage readers directly in conversation is important.

- Referencing conventions differ by discipline, reflecting the ways that different disciplines construct knowledge.

# 4

# The Sentence Dimension:
## Addressing Patchwriting, Paraphrasing, Summarizing, and Quoting

---

"I'm trying to teach quote and paraphrase, but what I get is a mix of the two: a few words from the source, a couple from the student, and a few more from the source. You just can't sort it out! And you can't correct it: it's not a proper paraphrase, but you couldn't quote it, either. I don't know what to tell the student to do with it."

*–Anneke, an EFL instructor at a Japanese university*

---

EXPERIENCED ACADEMIC WRITERS are used to incorporating the words and ideas of others into their writing. They do so in ways that allow the text to flow, marking their use of sources for the readers or making their incorporation so complete that they go unnoticed. In addition, experienced academic writers readily use quotation marks, in-text citations, and phrases (e.g., *According to…*, *We agree that…*) as boundary markers for their paraphrases, summaries, and quotes, even though they may not be fully conscious of how they do it. When student writers reuse words and ideas, on the other hand, the source use tends to be noticed because references are usually not incorporated smoothly. Student writers patchwrite, mixing their own words with those from source texts, so their use of other material is not categorizable as a paraphrase, a summary, or a quote.

This chapter examines referencing at this level, first looking at patchwriting in order to both understand it better and consider its use in the classroom. Then, we consider the linguistic challenges—including vocabulary, formulaic language, and sentence structure—that L2 writers face when paraphrasing and summarizing. Last, we discuss the linguistic incorporation of paraphrases, summaries, and quotes. We aim to go beyond more simplistic explanations of quotes ("If it's copied, then it's a quote") and paraphrases ("If it's in your own words, it's a paraphrase") and beyond the usual advice to "write in your own words."

---

### CONSIDER

Many ESL instructors believe that it is useful to encourage students to copy sentence frames and academic vocabulary into their notebooks for use later. Others believe that this makes it difficult for students to know when it's okay to reuse someone's words and when it's not. What do you think?

---

## What We Know from Research and Theory

### Patchwriting and Copying: Learning English by Reusing Text

Considerable scholarship has established that much of what is considered to be prototypical plagiarism actually helps students develop their academic English (Angélil-Carter, 2000; Chandrasoma, Thompson & Pennycook, 2004; Currie, 1998; Flowerdew & Li, 2007; Li & Casanave, 2012; Pecorari, 2003; Pennycook, 1996; Petrić, 2012). This work has largely been based on the work of Rebecca Moore Howard (1992), who introduced the term *patchwriting*. For Howard (1999), patchwriting is "a move toward membership in a discourse community, a means of learning unfamiliar language and ideas. Far from indicating a lack of respect for a course text, their [students'] patchwriting is a gesture of reverence" (p. 7).

Patchwriting comes in a number of different forms. Let us consider an example:

Source text (excerpt from Dean, 2014):

Usually people will do anything to avoid being bored, as it's such an aversive experience.

Patchwriting:

Often people do whatever they can to avoid boredom, as it's such an unpleasant experience.

Patchwriting of this type, which mixes source language and student language in the same sentence, can be considered a *near copy*. In a near copy, some of the words of the source are copied, and either some of the vocabulary is swapped out or the sentence structure is changed (Campbell, 1990). According to Campbell (1990), near copies are best understood as a type of paraphrase because students use them in ways that are similar to their use of more effective paraphrases and summaries. Keck (2006) also interpreted near copies in this way. With this type of patchwriting, it seems likely that students are not reusing source words with deceitful intent, but rather, are producing imperfect paraphrases.

Here is another example of patchwriting, which comes from the introductory paragraph of an uncorrected student paper:

> Jamaica Kincaid—author was so successful when he makes figure Lucy who has the same name as his novel. Lucy is a main figure in this novel who directs to tell about her life when she wants to move out her family and get a more perfect life. <u>Lucy offers sharp, perceptive commentary on American culture under the eye of a girl who is growing up</u>. Through character—Lucy, author want to tell with reader the growing up of a person in the changes of time and life's environment. <u>The author gives her the authority of the keen, often satiric observer of her new world, where she is free to sever ties to her past and to face determinedly the blank canvas of her future</u>. And, Lucy has got too much experiences and aware in that future.

In this example, a student writer used whole sentences from the source (underlined), intermingling them with sentences of their own. The difference between the two is striking. The source sentences remain unchanged and therefore appear less like paraphrases and more like *unattributed quotations*.

Some studies have shown that students consciously use such patchwriting as a learning strategy. For instance, Pennycook (1996) reported that one student he interviewed felt that there were "useful things to be learned from reusing the structures and words from others' texts" (p. 225). It seems likely that student writers who copy in this way may be applying language learning strategies to their writing. English teachers sometimes recommend recording useful words, set phrases, and sentence frames in notebooks for future use; they teach grammar by asking students to use specific sentence patterns but substitute vocabulary; and they show students how to use essay templates to score well on the written part of the TOEFL® (He & Shi, 2008; Mott-Smith, 2013). Each of these learning strategies reminds us that language learning and language use constantly involve reuse of language and that drawing lines around some types of source use and calling it inappropriate or cheating may strike some L2 writers as arbitrary.

Howard (1999) has pushed even further to consider the possibility that a student text that appears to be entirely copied may be a kind of patchwriting. She explained, "If students are working in discourse so foreign that the only voice available is the one that they are reading, the eclectic 'patching' that is such a natural, normal resource for composing becomes limited to the text at hand" (p. 146). Our point is not that teachers should accept completely copied papers but to argue that teachers should consider the nature of patchwriting in its various forms and be open to the possibility that patchwriting is part of the process of learning to write or, indeed, part of the process of writing itself.

Students often patchwrite because they believe—based on past writing instruction that encouraged the blending of their voices with the voices of their source texts and did not require attribution (Mott-Smith, 2011)—that patchwriting produces a better paper or that papers in which voices are blended are graded more favorably (Bloch, 2012). Studies have shown that some students patchwrite because they want to capture some of the academic register, effective wording, or authority of the source text (Campbell, 1990; Chandrasoma, Thompson, & Pennycook, 2004; Hirvela & Du, 2013; Pennycook, 1996) or bring linguistic variety to their writing (Campbell, 1990; Petrić, 2012).

Recently, there have been calls for further research into patchwriting as a teaching strategy (Pecorari, 2015; Petrić, 2015). Such research may establish not only that it is appropriate for L2 writers to patchwrite, but that it is beneficial. We believe that rather than punishing students for patchwriting, it makes sense to commend them for their attempts while guiding them toward smoother and conventionally marked ways of incorporating sources. It is also useful for teachers and students to discuss patchwriting together, both preemptively and in response to their written work, to come to a better understanding of writing and language learning processes.

## Paraphrasing and Formulaic Language

Teaching the ability to paraphrase effectively is a complex process involving the ability to substitute alternative vocabulary and syntactical structures. Research has shown that some L2 writers find it difficult to produce good paraphrases due to a lack of language proficiency (Campbell, 1990; Johns & Mayes, 1990), while others are concerned about their ability to accurately represent the meaning of the source text (Petrić, 2012; Shi, 2010). Some L2 writers even prefer near copies to more acceptable paraphrases, thinking that the latter stray too far from the original meaning (Keck, 2010). For these reasons, it is important both to improve students' language skills and to discuss sample paraphrases ranging from effective to ineffective.

## CONSIDER

An intermediate-level L2 student who is writing a paper on humor across cultures wants to rephrase this quote from a book. What decisions and challenges will the student likely grapple with? How would you rephrase the quote?

"Laughter and humor have been hailed as 'good for the body' because they restore homeostasis, stabilize blood pressure, oxygenate the blood, massage the vital organs, stimulate circulation, facilitate digestion, relax the system, and produce a feeling of well-being (Spencer, 1860; Darwin,1872; Hecker, 1873; Dearborn, 1900; McDougal, 1922; Menon, 1931)." (Keith-Spiegel, 1972, p. 5)

Writers need to have a broad knowledge of words in order to be able to make the lexical substitutions necessary for effective paraphrases and summaries. If they do not, they may end up copying or patchwriting (cf., Howard & Davies, 2009). Let's examine the vocabulary in the quote in the Consider box. A lexical analysis conducted using Lextutor (n.d.) revealed that 10.26 percent of the words come from Coxhead's (2000) academic word list (e.g., *restore, stabilize*) and 23.08 percent are so-called "off-words," meaning complex non-academic words or discipline-specific terms (e.g., *digestion, oxygenate*). This means that an intermediate-level learner attempting to rephrase this quote in his or her own words is likely to struggle with the meaning of about one-third of the words in the source text. In addition, the quote includes several collocations (words that are commonly used together). An inexperienced L2 writer who follows the advice to use synonyms when rephrasing a collocation such as *stimulate circulation* may turn to a dictionary to look for a substitute for *stimulate*, only to be confronted with a list of words that are inappropriate for an academic text on this particular topic. For instance, words such as *amp (up), brace, energize, enliven, fire, ginger (up), invigorate, jazz (up), juice up, jump-start, liven (up),* and *pep (up)* would not be fitting choices to replace the word *stimulate* (Merriam Webster, 2017). Thus, instructors need to encourage L2 writers to learn collocations in addition to basic vocabulary to avoid receiving papers that talk about humor as beneficial for "jazzing up circulation!"

Effective paraphrasing also involves the ability to produce sentences that are different in structure from those of the source text. The quote in the Consider box is quite challenging not only in terms of vocabulary, but also in terms of structure. It is a complex sentence with two clauses: a main clause and a dependent clause that are connected with the subordinating conjunction *because*. The sentence also uses the passive voice (*have been hailed*). To paraphrase this sentence, students need not only to be able to follow this sentence structure, but they need to be able to generate alternative structures that preserve meaning as well. Thus, how difficult it is to paraphrase depends on both the linguistic complexity of the source text and the writer's level of language proficiency.

What is less explored than the substitution of lexical items and syntactical structures is the role that familiarity with formulaic language plays in effective source use. Pecorari and Shaw (2012) explained that "the pervasive nature of formulaic language means that texts written in the same language not only share a common pool of words, they share a stock of phrases, multiword units, and of patterns with open slots with limited possibilities for completion" (p. 157). Thus, formulaic language may include idioms (e.g., *go hand in hand*), collocations (e.g., *limited resources*), multiword vocabulary (e.g., *blood pressure*), and other formulaic phrases (e.g., *the purpose of this study is to…*). The existence of formulaic language means that there are not actually limitless possibilities for reformulating a sentence "in one's own words." To paraphrase effectively, student writers need to know which language can be reused without attribution in academic writing. Hinkel (2016) argued for the importance of ensuring that students learn formulaic synonyms to improve their academic language. (See Hinkel, 2016, for a six-page list of formulaic expressions, many of which students can employ in source-based assignments.)

Formulaic phrases are often used by academic writers to accomplish certain tasks, called *moves*. These moves include those that are essential to building an argument, such as introducing the topic (*In this paper, I will discuss…*), stating one's thesis (*I will argue that…*), bringing in a new supporting point (*Now let us consider…*), and concluding (*In this paper, I have argued that…*). There are also a number of moves involved with referencing, which, in Chapter 3, we referred to as the rhetorical functions of referencing. These include showing contrasting views in the literature (*Although scholars generally agree that…, others have argued that…*), building on another's work (*Drawing on X's analysis, we argue that…*), and creating a space for a study (*Few studies, however, have looked at...*). It is helpful to teach student writers both the moves and the formulaic phrases associated with them. Unlike idioms, collocations, and multiword vocabulary, formulaic phrases have a number of versions (*In this paper/chapter/article, I will discuss/argue/explore…, This paper/chapter/article discusses/argues/explores . . .*). Students can be encouraged to use set phrases as is or make adaptations to them to fit their writing. They can check whether phrases are idiomatic or not by entering them in quotation marks into Google Scholar (see Swales & Feak, 2012, pp. 206–207) or by searching for them in a corpus such as the Corpus of Contemporary American English (COCA).

It has been argued, and we agree, that the use of formulaic phrases is not prototypical plagiarism because the textual similarity is based not on copying, but rather on linguistic expectations of a common topic or genre (Pecorari, 2013). However, L2 writers who do not know a lot of formulaic language may in fact be learning it from source texts and copying it into their own writing. We believe that this behavior is not problematic because it involves the process of language learning. If this is a problem, however, then the solution is to teach students more formulaic phrases since, as with other vocabulary, the greater the number the students command, the less likely it is that they will directly copy from a source text.

## Incorporation of Paraphrases, Summaries, and Quotes

Sometimes the linguistic complexity of paraphrasing keeps teachers from focusing on the other important issue—the incorporation of references into one's own writing. Incorporation involves choosing how much information about the source text to include in one's writing. Summaries are often introduced with a sentence that includes a fair amount of information (title, author, date, genre, overview of the topic): *"On Dumpster Diving" by Lars Eighner (1993) is an autobiographical essay about what it is like to be homeless.* Such sentences are commonly used in research papers and other text-based writing that student writers are assigned. By contrast, paraphrases and quotes are often used with only the author and date (and page number if required by the style guide) in the sentence. This may be because additional information about the source text has been given before. For paraphrases, both information-fronted and writer-fronted citations are common:

- *When homeless or very poor people first start to eat food from dumpsters, they feel ashamed (Eighner, 1993).* [paraphrase with an information-fronted citation]
- *According to Eighner (1993), when homeless or very poor people first start to eat food from dumpsters, they feel ashamed.* [paraphrase with a writer-fronted citation]

For quotations, information-fronted citations are less common, and teachers often explain this by saying that a sentence should not begin with a quotation (unless it's an epigraph). Writer-fronted citations are the norm in disciplines that use quotes:

> Drawing from his own experience, Eighner (1993) explained, "At first the new scavenger is filled with disgust and self-loathing" (p. 117).
> [quote with a writer-fronted citation]

However, sometimes the use of a pronoun compels the use of a citation formatted in the information-fronted way, even though the sentence structure remains that of a writer-fronted citation:

> Eighner described the process of learning to eat food from the trash, including the emotional adaptation that one has to make to eat in this way. He explained, "At first the new scavenger is filled with disgust and self-loathing" (Eighner, 1993, p. 117).

Many attribution conventions require writers to include embedded citations. When it comes to integrating this information smoothly into a sentence, paraphrasing presents more of a difficulty than quoting. This is because when writers quote, they simply copy the citation from the source text as part of the quote. For example, using the sample sentence previously introduced, we can write:

> Keith-Spiegel (1972) wrote: "Laughter and humor have been hailed as 'good for the body' because they restore homeostasis, stabilize blood pressure, oxygenate the blood, massage the vital organs, stimulate circulation, facilitate digestion, relax the system, and produce a feeling of well-being (Spencer, 1860; Darwin, 1872; Hecker, 1873; Dearborn, 1900; McDougal, 1922; Menon, 1931)" (p. 5).

However, in order to paraphrase, it is necessary to work the embedded citation into the sentence:

> Citing Spencer (1860), Darwin (1872), Hecker (1873), Dearborn (1900), McDougal (1922), and Menon (1931), Keith-Spiegel (1972) explained that laughter has good physical and psychological effects.

Alternatively, we could integrate the embedded citation into our own citation:

> *Laughter has good physical and psychological effects (Spencer, 1860;*
> *Darwin, 1872; Hecker, 1873; Dearborn, 1900; McDougal, 1922; Menon,*
> *1931, as cited in Keith-Spiegel, 1972).*

Both of these methods of incorporation present a high level of difficulty for many student writers.

Integrating quotes and paraphrases also involves indicating where the ideas of another author begin and end. This is often accomplished with *boundary markers*. Boundary markers that indicate the beginning of ideas from a source text include the phrase *According to…* or an author + reporting verb combination. Quotes are also commonly introduced with an independent clause and a colon:

> *Eighner (1993) described the process of learning to eat food from the*
> *trash, including the emotional adaptation that one has to make to eat*
> *in this way: "At first the new scavenger is filled with disgust and self-*
> *loathing" (p. 117).*

Boundary markers that indicate the shift back to the writer's ideas are often less clear. In fact, research has shown that the shift back to the writer's voice is not always understood to be in the same place by even experienced readers (Williams, 2010). Nevertheless, ending markers such as citations, paragraph breaks, and phrases that shift the discussion (*On the other hand, Kleinschmidt (2003) argued that…, From Juarez' work, we can see that…*) are used by academic writers.

The smooth incorporation of quotes in particular involves additional issues requiring a high level of language proficiency. First, quoting requires writers to clarify words in the quote that readers might not understand due to lack of context. Such words include names and deictic words (words whose meanings are dependent on context) such as pronouns and time adverbs (*then, tomorrow, today*). One way for teachers to help students think about words that need to be explained is to pose the question, what would you need to know if you had not read the source text? Writers deal with such words in a number of ways. Consider this sample sentence: "One advantage of bringing Lizbeth along as I make Dumpster rounds is that, for obvious reasons, she is very alert to ground-based fire ants" (Eighner, 1993, p. 123). In order to use this sentence as a quote, the writer needs to let the readers know that *Lizbeth* is a dog and that *I* refers to Lars Eighner. This can be made clear through the use of editor's brackets:

> *Eighner wrote: "One advantage of bringing Lizbeth [a dog] along as I*
> *[Eighner] make Dumpster rounds is that, for obvious reasons, she is very*
> *alert to ground-based fire ants" (Eighner, 1993, p. 123).*

Alternatively, it can be explained beforehand:

> *Eighner explained why he likes to bring his dog with him: "One advantage of bringing Lizbeth along as I make Dumpster rounds is that, for obvious reasons, she is very alert to ground-based fire ants" (Eighner, 1993, p. 123).*

Note that this second example clarifies the missing contextual information and introduces the quote with an independent clause at the same time, requiring the ability to contextualize the quote using a summary of part of the source text. A third possibility is that the writer could paraphrase the part of the sentence with the unclear words, and keep the rest:

> *Eighner (1993) explained that he likes to bring his dog with him when he dumpster dives because "she is very alert to ground-based fire ants" (p. 123).*

This type of incorporation requires the writer to know where the sentence can be cut to make a coherent quote. L2 writers sometimes cut a sentence in the middle of a clause in a way that makes the quote both ungrammatical and hard to follow.

A second issue that arises with quoting is the use of an author's turns of phrase quotes without attribution. It may be helpful to model the use of quotation marks around short, one- or two-word phrases as in *Eighner (1993) distinguishes between "scavengers" and "can scroungers" (p. 119).* Here, quotation marks are appropriate because these are terms that Eighner defines in a particular way to make a particular argument. Because research has shown that L2 student writers often use long, poorly integrated quotes (Borg, as cited in Petrić, 2012) and because papers with shorter quotes have been found to receive higher grades than papers with clause-length ones (Petrić, 2012), students should learn to use quotes for smaller pieces of text.

We have found that it is important to work with references not only at the sentence level but at the paragraph level as well. In order to be smoothly integrated into a paragraph, a paraphrase or quote should not be at the beginning of the paragraph with an explanation that follows, but rather in the middle, with contextualizing information beforehand and interpretation afterward. Contextualizing information often includes the topic, intended audience, and/ or purpose of the source text. When a writer-fronted citation is used, it should also include an explanation of who the author is and what expertise he or she has related to the topic. The interpretation should include an explanation and a connection to the line of argument. For quotations, the interpretation includes a paraphrase or discussion of the language of the quote that shows readers how the writer understood the source text. Thus, quoting in effect involves giving a paraphrase as well as a quote, and is not easier than paraphrasing, as some L2 writers imagine.

A paragraph with an ineffectively integrated quote might look like this:

> *"See the experiences or ideas in slow motion and in detail" (Joy, 2000, p. 6). That's what Joy asks us to do in order to learn about other cultures. She doesn't want us to misunderstand other cultures.*

This approach is typical of some of our L2 writers in that the quote comes first, followed by an explanation. It is problematic in that the reader gets to the quote before knowing how it connects to the argument that the writer is making. In addition, the author's name appears in the sentence but the readers have not been told who she is. The only contextualizing information is the explanation that *She doesn't want us to misunderstand other cultures*, which occurs after the quote and provides some insight into the purpose of the source text. However, without more contextualizing information, readers may feel like they are playing catch-up with the meaning of the text and there is little sense of authorial presence. As for interpretation, there is none. The word *that* refers back to the quote, but there is no discussion or paraphrase of the original words.

By contrast, here is the same quote, more effectively integrated into a paragraph:

> *People often have difficulty understanding unfamiliar cultures. In her discussion of cultural analysis, Joy (2000) gives us several strategies for analyzing cultures and avoiding cultural misunderstandings. She suggests, for example, that we "see the experiences or ideas in slow motion and in detail" (p. 6). By not rushing our analysis, we may also avoid judging the foreign culture by our own cultural values and come to understand it better.*

This paragraph begins with a topic sentence meant to connect to the argument of the paper; it is in the writer's words and thus gives a sense of authorial presence. Then the writer provides background information on the original context of the quote, including the topic (*cultural analysis*) and the fact that Joy was providing *strategies* for doing good cultural analysis. The writer also makes it clear that the quote refers to one sample strategy. After giving the quote, the writer paraphrases it (*by not rushing our analysis*) and connects it to her own argument by returning to the point of the paragraph (*come to understand a foreign culture better*).

In this paragraph, the writer also adds a new idea (*we may avoid judging the foreign culture by our own cultural values*). Arguably, she should have done a better job of making it clear whether this was her own idea or Joy's. However, it is common for paragraphs with quotes or paraphrases to include additional information. As discussed in Chapter 3, paraphrases frequently incorporate stance markers that indicate a writer's attitude or inference. Paraphrases have also been shown to contain comments on the source text information (Yamada, 2003), additional content knowledge (Shi, 2012), and information from another part of the text (Keck, 2010).

Thus, smooth incorporation of references involves choosing how much information about the source text to include; using citations appropriate to the surrounding sentences; introducing, interpreting, and adding to the ideas of references; and grammatically incorporating short quotes and boundary markers. These skills require a high level of linguistic proficiency.

## Connecting to the Classroom

We feel that it is important to acknowledge that unconventional source use, including patchwriting, attempted paraphrasing, and copying, help students to develop facility in academic discourse. The lessons we describe, however, are designed primarily to help students develop their skills in more conventional sentence-level source use, including separating their ideas from those of their source texts and representing source texts accurately. It seems clear from the discussions in this chapter that it is not enough for teachers to address paraphrasing, summary, and quoting in one lesson by quickly explaining the differences and moving on. Therefore, we suggest giving multiple lessons on these skills. Many of the lessons described here involve students in close readings of sentences that refer to source texts and of the source texts themselves. In addition, several of them connect with the lessons in Chapter 3 by asking students to consider rhetorical context. Lessons such as these are supported by research (e.g., Hsu, 2003; Wette, 2010) that has shown that explicit instruction can lead to more effective source use and reduced copying.

# Lesson 1:
# Patchwriting

**Focus:** Patchwriting

**Description:** Students do close readings of several samples of patchwriting and the corresponding source texts in order to identify copied words and similarities in sentence structure. They learn that effective paraphrasing involves making decisions about which words can be copied without attribution, about changing sentence structure, and about omitting specifics.

**Rationale:** Sometimes L2 writers do not realize that their ways of constructing texts lead to patchwriting, which is considered problematic source use by many teachers. This lesson, therefore, provides an opportunity for students to investigate patchwriting and develop their understandings of effective paraphrasing.

**Students:** High-Beginner to Advanced L2s

**Preparation:** Make a handout with some samples of patchwriting. Using samples from student papers from previous terms that are based on texts that the current class is reading allows the students to focus on the writing rather than the reading and helps them prepare for writing their own papers. Three examples of patchwriting along with excerpts from the source text, Eighner's (1993) memoir, *Travels with Lizbeth*, are provided.

## Patchwriting Sample A:

Eighner tried to discover the meaning of the word dumpster. Because of the lack of resources at that time, he wrote to Merriam Webster research service to find out the meaning of this word.

Source text: Long before I began Dumpster Diving I was impressed with Dumpsters, enough so that I wrote the Merriam Webster research service to discover what I could about the word *dumpster*. (p. 111)

## Patchwriting Sample B:

There are few courtesies among dumpster divers, "But it is common practice to set aside surplus items: pairs of shoes, clothing, canned goods, and such" (Eighner, 1993, p.120).

Source text: There are precious few courtesies among scavengers. But it is common practice to set aside surplus items: pairs of shoes, clothing, canned goods, and such. (p. 120)

## *Patchwriting Sample C:*

A great example is Eighner (1993), he wrote a narrative essay book that talks about his personal experiences and the values he had got and which was important and which was not. He mentioned being drunk in public, Eighner was not that type of person who accepts drinking at any time and did not like it, according to him after he drank a large jug of Pat O'Brien's Hurricane mix before realizing that rum was added, "Some divers would have considered this a boon, but being suddenly intoxicated in a public place in the early afternoon is not my idea of a good time." (Eighner, 1993, p. 116) Eighner's story shows us that homeless people have values and good attitudes and they respect rules and follow good principles.

<u>Source text:</u> One hot day I found a large jug of Pat O'Brien's Hurricane mix. The jug had been opened but was still ice cold. I drank three large glasses before it became apparent to me that someone had added the rum to the mix, and not a little rum. I never tasted the rum, and by the time I began to feel the effects I had already ingested a very large quantity of the beverage. Some divers would have considered this a boon, but being suddenly intoxicated in a public place in the early afternoon is not my idea of a good time. (p. 116)

**Procedure**:

1. Ask students to read Chapter 7 from Eighner's *Travels with Lizbeth.* This is the oft-anthologized essay, "On Dumpster Diving."

2. Explain the patchwriting metaphor; show a picture of a quilt and discuss what "patches" are. Then, ask students whether they write this way, deliberately piecing together sentences and/or paragraphs from other texts (either by copying or through memorization). Contrast this method with other methods for constructing texts, such as writing directly from one's head and translating.

3. Hand out the patchwriting samples. Ask students what they notice about how the student writers used the source text. You can use this opportunity to discuss incorporation issues before turning attention to patchwriting. For instance, in Sample A, there is helpful background information for readers living in the internet age who might wonder why Eighner wrote a letter (*Because of the lack of resources at that time*). On the other hand, there is no background information about what the "Merriam Webster research service" is, which would be helpful for readers who haven't read the source text.

4. Tell students that they will compare the patchwriting to the excerpts from the source text to see if any of the same words are used. Project the two texts on a screen so that all the students can see them at the same time, and ask a student to highlight the copied words in the patchwritten texts. Let the other students shout out when the student with the highlighter misses words so that the highlighting of copied words is thorough and the students are working together. Ask students to discuss what they see: Do the copied words occur in groups or are they sprinkled around? Do the student writers seem to have constructed their texts by sewing together patches? Is the overall number of copied words surprising?

5. Discuss each example as a class. Sample A provides a good opportunity to discuss the reuse of words without attribution. The patchwriting contains the copied words *discover, dumpster, wrote, Merriam Webster research service,* and *word.* For each copied word or phrase, ask students to consider whether the writer could have used quotes or a different word to make a more effective paraphrase. Arguably, the reuse of *dumpster* is necessary, as the word is essential to the meaning of the passage; it might have been quoted. The reuse of the words *wrote* and *word* is also necessary, as substituting synonyms for these words would sound odd, and quotes are not necessary for the reuse of such common words. However, *discover* could have been replaced by *learned,* and the phrase *Merriam Webster research service* could have been quoted if a paraphrase could not be generated. The uses of *discover* and *Merriam Webster research service* are closer to the source text than need be, and make the passage sound like patchwriting.

   Sample B provides a good opportunity to discuss the reuse of sentence structure as well as words. Ask students to compare the sentence structures and name the deletions and vocabulary substitutions in the patchwriting. The word *precious* is deleted and *dumpster divers* is substituted for *scavengers.* Capture this visually on the projected text:

   Source:        (There are)   precious   (few courtesies among)   scavengers.

                       ↕                           ↕                        ↕

   Patchwriting: (There are)                (few courtesies among)   dumpster divers,

   Explain that it is the copied words (*There are, few courtesies among*) in addition to the reused sentence structure that makes this sentence patchwriting.

Sample C provides a good opportunity to discuss the reuse of specifics. The patchwriting contains the copied words *a large jug of Pat O'Brien's Hurricane mix* and *rum,* specifics that make the text too close to the original. If the patchwriting had less specific words (*mixer* for *Pat O'Brien's Hurricane mix, alcohol* for *rum*), then it would be closer to an effective paraphrase.

6. Summarize the lessons of the class by going over the expectations for effective paraphrases (that they use copied words only when those words are common vocabulary that cannot be easily replaced, that they have a different sentence structure, that they are often more general that the source text). Explain that there is no absolute line between patchwriting and paraphrase. You may also want to discuss with students the contradiction between needing to learn English and academic discourse(s) through attempted paraphrases and the risk of plagiarism accusations.

**Adaptations:** Students can apply what they have learned to their own writing. Ask them to highlight paraphrases and patchwriting in a paper they have written and discuss their decisions to copy or substitute vocabulary, to change sentence structure, and to omit or use specifics.

# Lesson 2:
# Language Chunks:
# To Rephrase or Not?

**Focus:** Vocabulary—formulaic language

**Description:** Students discuss writerly moves and identify formulaic phrases in an academic paper that accomplish these moves. They make lists of the moves and formulaic language for future use.

**Rationale:** Academic language is full of formulaic phrases that do not lend themselves to rephrasing and do not require attribution, and knowledge of these phrases is essential to making one's writing sound scholarly and idiomatic. Because L2 writers often are not familiar with formulaic phrases, this lesson offers the opportunity to increase their knowledge of them.

**Students:** Intermediate to Advanced L2s

**Preparation:** Choose a text that is relevant to the course topic or to the students' areas of study and that contains a number of moves and formulaic phrases that you want to teach. Prepare a handout with a list of moves and corresponding formulaic phrases; you may want to match them to the part of the paper in which they occur:

## Moves in the Introduction

    a. Tell readers the main topic or argument of the article.

*This article explores....*

*In this article, I will discuss....*

*This paper reports....*

*In this article I examine....*

*I want to argue that....*

*The purpose of this paper is to....*

    b. Preview points in the paper.

*In the following, I will illustrate....*

    c. Establish common ground.

*Virtually no one would dispute that....*

*Few will disagree that....*

## Moves in the Body of the Paper

    d. Bring in a new supporting point.

*Now let us consider....*

    e. Give a contrasting viewpoint.

*Some evidence, however, questions the sufficiency of these explanations.*

*Although scholars generally agree that..., others have argued that...*

*It is true that.... However,...*

    f. Build on other work.

*Drawing on X's analysis of Y, we argue that....*

## Move at the End of a Paper

    g. Bring things to a close.

*Our focus has been on....*

*This paper has established that....*

*I have argued that....*

*The present study aimed at....*

**Procedure**:

1. Ask students to read the text and make sure that they understand it.

2. Hand out the list of moves and formulaic phrases. Explain that such phrases are often used and do not need to be cited. Explain that the phrases are formulaic but not set in stone. For example, *This article explores* could be changed to *This chapter explores* or to *This article investigates*, depending on the context. Students should generate some of their own adaptations to the given formulaic language.

2. Divide the students into small groups to skim the text looking for formulaic language like that on the handout. Assign one part of the article to each group. After locating some formulaic language, students should reread the relevant section of the text to determine the move that is being made and compare the formulaic language to the language on the handout to see if it is the same, different, or a variation.

3. Reconvene as a class to compare results. Students should add new formulaic phrases and moves that they have identified to the lists on their handouts so that they can keep them for later use.

**Adaptations:** For advanced students, you may want to focus on the formulaic language of research studies. Choose a study in a relevant field and provide a list of formulaic language for research studies:

a. State the goals of the study.

*The purpose of this study was to....*

*The aims of the project were:*

b. Create a space for the study (in a literature review).

*Few studies, however, have looked at....*

*Presently, there is no data to demonstrate a causal relationship between....*

*Not a great deal is known about....*

*This research raises questions about....*

*There has been little research that shows....*

*Other research supports the present hypothesis by....*

c. Describe the methods.

*Data were collected over the course of 9 months...*

*The participants were randomly assigned to either the experimental or the control group....*

*Ten male and ten female undergraduates were randomly assigned*

*Participants were recruited by....*

d. Report the conclusions.

*This study offers clear evidence that....*

e. Give the research implications.

*This paper calls for further research into....*

# Lesson 3:
# One-Sentence Summaries

**Focus:** Summary

**Description:** Students write and evaluate one-sentence summaries of several articles on the same topic; then they incorporate summary sentences into their own papers.

**Rationale:** Effective summarizing involves being able to distill the main idea and/or purpose of a text, produce a sentence capturing this distillation, and incorporate it into one's own writing. Student writers, however, may have difficulty with all three. Therefore, this lesson provides guidelines for producing short summaries and practice in incorporating them.

**Students:** Intermediate to Advanced L2s

**Preparation:** Choose three articles about a similar topic for the students to summarize and read. Use texts that students will later use as sources for a paper. Also, create two handouts. The first should provide a list of guidelines for summarizing:

a. The summary should be one or possibly two sentence(s) long.

b. The summary sentence should include the main point and/or purpose of the source text.

c. The summary sentence should not emphasize one part of the text but cover the whole text evenly.

d. The summary sentence should not include details, examples, quotes, metaphors, proverbs, or sayings from the source text.

e. The summary sentence should not include your ideas, comments, or critiques. You can add these in separate sentences after the summary sentence. The summary sentence should not have phrases like *I think*.

f. The summary sentence should be in your own words. You should not copy sentences or phrases from the source text.

g. The summary sentence should contain a citation with the author's last name and date of publication. It can be written following a number of sentence patterns:

- Author (date) explained/found/showed/demonstrated/concluded that....

- The main conclusion of author's (date) study/article was....

- It has been demonstrated/shown/argued that... (author, date).

The second handout is a list of possible functions for the summary:

- show that you are informed

- support a point that you are making by using the author's argument

- support a point that you are making by drawing on the author's reputation

- describe the context for the point you want to make

- introduce an idea that you will later apply to your own example

- explain a point that you go on to disagree with

- cast doubt on an earlier argument

**Procedure:**

1. Hand out the guidelines for summarizing and put students in small groups to discuss the three articles they have read and produce one-sentence summaries. Draw students' attention to the handout, and tell them to make sure that each of their summaries fulfills all the expectations for summary sentences. Tell them to pay careful attention to the different lines of argument in each article so that they can differentiate them in the summaries.

2. Ask each small group to join another small group to share their work. Groups should exchange summaries without telling the members of the other group which summary belongs to which article; the members of the other group should guess.

3. The combined groups should choose the more effective summary for each article. They should share these with the whole class by writing them on the blackboard or uploading them to a discussion board on a course website.

4.  Ask each student to choose one of the one-sentence summaries to use in their papers. Let them choose between the ones they wrote and the ones they collected from the shared summaries. Hand out the list of functions and remind the students that, when incorporating a summary sentence into their papers, they need to make it clear to their readers why they're using it. Tell them that, in addition to the author and date, they can include the title and/or genre of the article if they believe that this information is useful to their readers.

**Adaptations:** Ask the small groups to choose one article and write three summaries of different lengths: a 100-word summary, a 50-word summary, and a 25-word summary.

# Lesson 4:
# Paraphrasing Detectives

**Focus:** Paraphrasing—models of good paraphrases

**Description:** Students locate paraphrases in a sample student paper and identify the citation and boundary markers; they then compare the paraphrases to the source sentences, identify the differences in syntax and vocabulary, and decide whether the representation is accurate and whether any additions to the meaning were made.

**Rationale:** An effective paraphrase has several components, including a citation, the use of boundary markers, avoidance of the sentence structure and vocabulary of the source, accurate representation of the meaning of the source text, and possible addition of ideas. However, L2 writers may not be used to thinking about all of these things. This lesson, therefore, provides models of good paraphrases and has students analyze them for these considerations.

**Students:** High-Beginner to Advanced L2s

**Preparation:** Choose a piece of student writing with effective paraphrases of readily locatable source texts. Using writing from the previous semester works well. Also, prepare a handout with a list of common boundary markers:

## At the Beginning of a Paraphrase

*According to*

citation together with a reporting verb:
*Hawthorn (2008) argued that . . . .*

## *At the End of a Paraphrase*

phrases that shift whose ideas are being reported:
*On the other hand, Kleinschmidt (2003) argued that . . . .*

phrases that comment on the paraphrase:
*From Juarez's work, we can see that . . . .*

citation

paragraph break

**Procedure**:

1. Hand out the list of common boundary markers and discuss them with the students. Explain that it is important for writers to mark when they begin and end a paraphrase so that their readers know which ideas are theirs and which ideas come from source texts. Writers use boundary markers to do this; therefore, paraphrases are often identifiable by their boundary markers.

2. Hand out the student writing so students can locate paraphrases by scanning for citations and other boundary markers. Then students should highlight the paraphrases.

3. Ask students to work in pairs or small groups to track down the source texts of the paraphrases. To make the process efficient, ask different groups to track down different sources. The use of technology greatly facilitates this process—students can simply insert the quotes into a web browser to get links to source texts.

4. Ask students to read the source text and identify the sentences that were paraphrased. Then they should compare the source sentences to the paraphrases. Scaffold the process with a list of questions:

   ■ Were you able to locate a similar sentence in the source text? If not, why not?

   ■ What boundary marker, if any, did the writer use to indicate the beginning of the paraphrase or summary? What boundary marker, if any, did s/he use to indicate the end?

   ■ Does the paraphrase have the same grammatical structure as the similar sentence in the source text? Does it have any of the same words? Do you think that there are any issues of prototypical plagiarism with the paraphrase?

   ■ Did the writer accurately represent the meaning of the source text? Explain.

   ■ Did the writer add to the meaning of the source text by commenting on it, critiquing it, or adding information from elsewhere? Specify.

5. Reconvene as a class so students can share their findings. Some points to emphasize are: (1) that a good paraphrase should be accurate but can also add to the source text meaning and (2) that a good paraphrase needs to be different from the source text in terms of both vocabulary and syntax. You may also want to ask students to keep the list of boundary markers from this lesson to use in future assignments.

**Adaptations**: Provide the source texts rather than having the students find them. This saves time and focuses the lesson on paraphrasing.

# Lesson 5:
# You Be the Judge: How Close Is Too Close?

**Focus:** Paraphrasing—accuracy vs. copying

**Description:** Students choose the most effective paraphrase from among a group of paraphrases, some of which are closer to the wording of the source text than others.

**Rationale:** Students often produce paraphrases that are too close to the source text, either because their English proficiency level limits them or because they believe that a closer paraphrase preserves meaning better. This lesson provides an opportunity to discuss how close is too close in order to develop students' theories of acceptable paraphrase.

**Students:** Intermediate to Advanced L2s

**Preparation:** Make a handout with several paraphrases of an excerpt from Lee (2004):

> Source text: Non-violent games were predicted to have a higher rate of prosocial behavior and lower rate of antisocial behavior than those for violent games. However, during the period of preliminary and actual studies, antisocial behavior was not once observed. (Lee, 2004, p.14)

a. *Paraphrase by Fatima*: Non-violent games were estimated to have an increased rate of prosocial behavior and reduced rate of antisocial behavior than those for violent games. But, during the period of various studies, antisocial behavior was not noticed (Lee, 2004, p. 14).

b. *Paraphrase by Stephanie*: While antisocial behavior is frequently associated with violent video games, it has not been observed in actual research (Lee, 2004, p. 14).

c. *Paraphrase by Miguel*: Lee (2004) implies that violent video games do not lead to antisocial behavior but this is unlikely the case.

d. *Paraphrase by Ngoc*: According to Lee (2004), the common belief that violent video games lead to antisocial behavior has not yet been sufficiently corroborated by research.

e. *Paraphrase by Arnold*: Non-fierce pastimes were forecasted to have a bigger amount of pro communal conduct and lower degree of disruptive conduct than those for fierce competitions. Nevertheless, throughout the era of initial and real educations, disruptive conduct was not detected (Lee, 2004, p. 14).

**Procedure**:

1. Ask students to read Lee's (2004) "Effects of Video Game Violence on Prosocial and Antisocial Behaviors."

2. Hand out the paraphrases and tell students that they will be judges evaluating the paraphrases for a paraphrasing contest. Divide the students into small groups and ask each group to determine which paraphrase is the best one. Ask them to list three specific reasons why the chosen paraphrase is the best.

3. Groups should present their decision and supporting reasons to the rest of the class.

**Adaptations:** Choose an excerpt from a text that your students have already read and have each student generate a paraphrase of it. Ask students to tape their paraphrases to the wall and circulate to read everyone else's. Students should put a check on their three favorite paraphrases and tally the votes to declare a winner of the paraphrasing contest.

# Lesson 6:
# Introducing and Interpreting Quotes

**Focus:** Quoting—incorporating quotes

**Description:** Students write sentences to introduce a quote, attribute it, and interpret it. Then they put the sentences together into a partial paragraph.

**Rationale:** Students sometimes place their quotes at the beginning of the paragraph and follow them up with an explanation; other times they let the quotes speak for themselves. This lesson, therefore, teaches students how to introduce and interpret quotes.

**Students:** Intermediate L2s

**Preparation:** Choose a sentence from a reading text for your students to quote and make a handout that shows the sentence in its original context. Also include questions to scaffold the introduction of the quote. Adapt the scaffolding questions (*What are the topic, intended audience, and purpose of the source text?*) to the text you have chosen. Then do the same for the questions (*What are the key words? Are there any ambiguous words?*) designed to scaffold the interpretation of the quote.

Here is an excerpt from a first-year composition textbook that works; the sentence to be quoted is "Genuinely unique ideas and information are scarce commodities":

### The Qualities of Good Writing

Three qualities—fresh thinking; a sense of style including the use of correct grammar and punctuations; and effective organization—help to ensure that a piece of prose will meet your reader's expectations.

### Fresh Thinking

You don't have to astound your readers with something never before discussed in print. Genuinely unique ideas and information are scarce commodities. You can, however, freshen your writing by exploring personal insights and perceptions. Using your own special slant, you might show a connection between seemingly unrelated items, as does a writer who likens office "paper pushers" to different kinds of animals. Keep the expression of your ideas credible, however; farfetched notions spawn skepticism. (Reinking & von der Osten, 2005, p. 10)

## Questions for Introducing the Quote

<u>Topic</u>: What are Reinking and von der Osten writing about when they bring up "unique ideas and information"?

<u>Intended audience</u>: Who are the intended readers? What might the readers' beliefs about "unique ideas and information" be? Do they think they are common or uncommon? Hard or easy to achieve? Achievable or unachievable?

<u>Purpose</u>: Why are Reinking and von der Osten making this claim?

## Questions for Interpreting the Quote

What is the difference between "genuinely unique ideas and information" and "unique ideas and information"? In other words, how does the use of *genuinely* change the meaning of the sentence?

What does the word *commodities* mean, according to the dictionary? Why is the word used here? Is it just a turn of phrase or does it reflect the notion that ideas can be bought and sold?

**Procedure**:

1. Pass out the handout for students to read. Tell students that the excerpt is from a first-year college composition textbook, and ask them who the intended audience is (first-year college students taking a writing course), and what the purpose of the passage is (to describe the type of writing that college teachers expect; more specifically, to explain to student writers how to meet the teachers' expectations that it be "fresh").

2. Explain that the students will be working on building a partial paragraph around the underlined sentence, which they will quote. This involves three steps: introducing the quote, giving and attributing the quote, and interpreting the quote.

3. Scaffold the writing of sentences to introduce the quote in this way:

    Ask students to reread the quote and ask them: if you wanted to understand this sentence, what would you need to know if you had not read the source text? Explain that, when we read the sentence *Genuinely unique ideas and information are scarce commodities* all by itself, the context is lost. Therefore, in order to use this quote, writers need to supply some of the original context. The original context comprises a topic, an intended audience, and a purpose.

    Put students in small groups to analyze the context, using the scaffolding questions on the handout. Small groups should report back to the class. Ideas that are helpful for introducing the quote to their readers include that Reinking and von der Osten are discussing "unique ideas" in the context of writing, that their intended audience is first-year college students who may believe that all college writing should contain unique ideas, and that their purpose is to reassure students who are worried about not being able to come up with unique ideas that they do not have to.

    Ask the students to work individually to write a sentence that incorporates the contextualizing information. Explain that this is the sentence they will use to introduce the quote. The sentence might look something like this:

    *Reinking and von der Osten (2005) reassure first-year college writers that they do not have to worry about making their writing original.*

4. Ask the students to write a second sentence containing the quote, using quotation marks and a citation. You may need to provide some sentence starters, such as *According to Reinking and von der Osten* or *For example, they write that....*

5. Scaffold the writing of sentences interpreting the quote in this way:

    Tell the students that writers explain what they think a quote means after they give it. They interpret it and relate it to their own argument. Writers pay particular attention to words that are key to the point that they are making and/or words that are open to interpretation. Since, in this lesson, students do not have a larger argument to connect the quote to, direct them to focus on words that are open to interpretation, specifically, *genuinely* and *commodities*. Students should work in small groups to respond to the scaffolding questions on the handout.

Reconvene as a class to go over their responses. One point about the use of *genuinely* might be that it implies that there are ideas that we see as unique but that are not truly unique. One point about the use of *commodities* might be that Reinking and von der Osten are showing that they take a capitalist view of ideas as intellectual property.

Ask each student to write a sentence that interprets one of the words:

> *Reinking and von der Osten seem to be saying that it is okay for college students not to produce completely original ideas even though such ideas exist; instead, it is okay to use fresh or new ideas.*

6. Students should assemble their introductory sentence, sentence containing the quote, and interpretive sentence into a partial paragraph. Ask them to read the sentences together and decide what changes need to be made so that the passage flows. This may include changing names to pronouns or adding transition words. The goal is to write something like this:

> *Reinking and von der Osten (2005) reassure first-year college writers that they do not have to worry about making their writing original, stating that "Genuinely unique ideas and information are scarce commodities" (p. 10). They seem to be saying that it is okay for college students not to produce completely new ideas even though such ideas exist; instead, we can focus on fresh or new ideas.*

7. Reconvene as a class and use a document projector or the blackboard to display the passages so that students can examine one another's work.

**Adaptations:** Choose an embedded quote for students to introduce and interpret. Use scaffolding questions such as: Who is speaking here? What do you need to tell your readers about the person who is speaking? Students will learn why embedded citations are necessary as they complete this adaptation of the lesson.

# Take-Away Points

- Student writers may not be used to distinguishing different voices in their texts, so this skill needs to be taught explicitly.

- Patchwriting, including near and exact copying, helps students develop proficiency in academic discourse.

- Because what looks like copying to a teacher may be a paraphrase to a student, teachers should treat it as an imperfect paraphrase, not as deceitful plagiarism.

- Language learning and writing both involve reusing language, so calling some reuse inappropriate may strike some L2 writers as arbitrary.

- How difficult it is to paraphrase or summarize a source text depends on both the writer's language proficiency and the linguistic complexity of the source text; it also depends on a writer's ability to recontextualize the reference in their own writing.

- Teachers should encourage students to learn formulaic language so that they can recognize reusable phrases and make a variety of the moves of source-based writing.

- Paraphrasing effectively involves many skills, including being able to avoid the sentence structure and vocabulary of the source text, accurately represent its meaning, use boundary markers, introduce the paraphrase, communicate one's own stance, add commentary or other information, and cite.

- Summarizing effectively involves being able to distill the main idea and/or purpose of a text, produce a sentence capturing this distillation, incorporate it in one's own writing, and cite.

- Quoting effectively involves a number of linguistically demanding skills, including the ability to introduce and interpret quotes, integrate them into the grammar of one's sentence, select short quotes, and cite.

# 5

# The Process Dimension:
Helping Writers Develop Effective Strategies
for Reading, Thinking, and Writing

---

"I was watching my students work on their papers in class and was struck by the differences in how they approached the task at hand. Some of my students appeared to take detailed notes on their printed readings, while others only read from the screen. This made me realize how different we all are as readers and writers and made me wonder what strategies and processes I need to focus on to best support my students."

–Connor, a writing instructor in the U.K.

---

STUDENTS ARE TYPICALLY PLACED INTO WRITING CLASSES based on a general English proficiency or writing-specific placement test score, neither of which assesses all the skills required for source-based writing. Skills that are not tested may include planning, reading, and the integration of ideas from sources. Perhaps for this reason, we find that some of our students engage in the process of reading and writing from sources more effectively than others. We believe that thinking is the most important skill for effective source-based writing, as it is through thinking that writers develop their own ideas and integrate ones from sources into their arguments. This chapter provides an overview of the cognitive processes involved in writing and the various factors that affect these processes and then presents three subprocesses of the reading-thinking-writing process—namely planning, digesting sources, and integrating ideas into one's own writing—to highlight strategies that benefit student writers. We suggest ways that writing instructors can develop student writers' strategies in these areas.

### CONSIDER

Effective writing is often described as *clear thinking made visible*. When you envision the clear thinking that you'd like to see in your students' papers, how do you think about scaffolding to get them there?

# What We Know from Research and Theory

## The Role of Thinking in the Reading-Writing Process

Writing involves a number of cognitive processes, including identifying questions, planning inquiry, analyzing information and arguments, making credibility judgments, inferring meanings, categorizing information, formulating hypotheses, developing alternative views, solving problems, recognizing biases, drawing conclusions, providing reasons, assessing implications, and communicating the thinking process to others (Ennis, 1991; Paul & Elder, 2009). Although these ways of thinking are central to the development of one's own line of argument and to the effective use of sources, neither teachers nor students tend to give them the full attention they deserve. On the one hand, instructors may not give students credit for the amount of time and effort spent on tasks that are not directly evident in the student writing, tasks such as reading source texts and rejecting them for bias or irrelevance. On the other hand, students may be reluctant to search for additional source texts when their research raises new questions, or to disassemble their writing to try a new organizing structure once they have produced a coherent draft. We believe that it is important, therefore, for writing instructors to value all the thinking work of these processes and to support student writers as they develop their processes.

As teachers prepare source-based writing assignments, they should keep in mind that different tasks present different levels of difficulty. Certain source-based genres (e.g., summary papers or information-based synthesis papers) are cognitively easier than others (e.g., analytic essays, response tasks, or argument-based synthesis papers) (Asención, 2004; Durst, 1987; Li & Casanave, 2012). Moreover, other task-specific factors, such as time pressure and instructor expectations, affect the difficulty of the task as well. Personal factors, such as interest in the topic and fatigue, also affect students' levels of engagement, making a particular task more challenging for some students than for others. Finally, identity factors, specifically, the positioning of a student relative to a given topic, also affect engagement and difficulty. For instance, topics such as homosexuality as a medical diagnosis or craniometry may position some student writers as inferior, making the task harder for those writers.

Thus, a student may do a better job writing a summary paper of great personal relevance, especially if it is written in a high-stakes context (e.g., in a capstone course for an instructor with high expectations) than a more cognitively challenging analysis paper that is based on a reading text that does not interest him or her, written in a low-stakes context, or assigned under time pressure.

In this latter situation, the student may simply take a perfunctory approach to source use, referencing only to satisfy the requirement. What this means is that there are many more factors involved with effective source use than language proficiency. Writing from sources is a highly dynamic process involving the interaction of linguistic and cognitive resources, task demands, and individual and contextual factors. Next, we discuss three sets of strategies that writing instructors can use to scaffold this process.

## Effective Reading-Thinking-Writing Processes

### 1. Planning: Strategies for Countering Procrastination and Selecting Sources

Many L2 student writers become overwhelmed by the prospect of writing a paper from sources, but they react to the assignment in different ways. Some may procrastinate until the last minute, while others dive in, spending hours and hours reading texts they do not understand and, if they are L2 writers, perhaps translating every word that they do not know. Both behaviors may lead to issues with writing from sources that can be addressed by providing students with better strategies.

Anticipating students' tendency to procrastinate is necessary because procrastination has been associated with prototypical plagiarism among L1 students (Roig & Detommaso, 1995). Procrastination has also been shown in research with L2 students (Kim, Alhaddab, Aquino, & Negi, 2016; Lowinger, He, Lin, & Chang, 2014), albeit in lower numbers. One way to forestall procrastination is to promote students' engagement with the topic. No matter whether the topic is assigned or the students choose it themselves, students will need to narrow it down to fit the scope of their paper. Teachers should guide students through this process to ensure that students choose a topic that is engaging to them. For instance, instructors can ask students to read about topics in the popular press or on Wikipedia and then freewrite about their own knowledge and experience with the topic. Teachers can also take time in class to read an article on the general topic aloud to model how a single intriguing claim or statistic can lead to questions and then explain how these questions can lead to a literature search and eventually to a narrowed research topic.

Another way to help students avoid procrastination and thus facilitate their writing from sources is to encourage self-regulatory practices, such as adhering to deadlines (Ariely & Wertenbroch, 2002). Writing instructors can break

assignments into manageable subtasks—such as taking notes on reading, producing an outline or visual organizer of ideas from source texts, or drafting
a short section of the paper—and set deadlines for students to submit them
(Ackerman & Gross, 2005). Requiring and responding to intermediary products reinforce the message that teachers value all the tasks associated with the
reading-thinking-writing process. In addition, writing instructors can introduce
the strategy of goal-setting (e.g., Boice, 1989) to help students stay on track with
source-based writing assignments. Research has shown that even experienced
writers benefit from setting goals and, specifically, from checking their source
use against task guidelines (Plakans, 2009).

Once students are engaged with a topic and have an overview of the subtasks involved in writing their paper, they need to select source texts (unless
they are provided). Although some academic institutions offer library instruction and support in this area, student writers often find the process of navigating
their library's resources difficult to manage. They may find it hard to choose
appropriate keywords or, when working with online sources, they make use of
links that quickly move them from one source to the next without their realizing
it. We have found it helpful, therefore, to require students to select source texts
in class so that we can guide them in the choice of keywords and in the use of
search engines.

It is also important to teach students the criteria that academic writers use
to select source texts. Both L1 and L2 student writers have shown a preference
for sources that are available and easy to find (Bidix, Chung, & Park, 2011;
Burton & Chadwick, 2000; Stapleton, 2005). Choosing easily locatable texts
often results in the use of non-credible sources. It is possible that the reason L2
writers focus on selecting easily locatable texts is because of limited language
proficiency. For this reason, "L2 writers are therefore more prone to rely on
academically questionable Internet sources such as personal web pages and
commercial sites, and to source Internet information in an unsystematic manner (Slaouti 2002; Stapleton 2005; Radia & Stapleton 2008)" (Pecorari & Petrić,
2014, p. 283) because identifying appropriate sources is based on language proficiency. In contrast to students' preferences, writing instructors value credibility
as a very important criterion for choosing sources (Stapleton, 2005). Simply put,
this is because teachers do not want to spread misinformation, but approached
more deeply, it is because teachers tend to believe that written texts do not present the truth, but rather, a writer's truth claims, which is why it is important to
evaluate the credibility of those claims.

Teachers can have students evaluate the credibility of source texts using the following criteria:

1. Citation—If there is no citation, this detracts from the credibility of the text. The logic is that, if the author and/or publisher are not identified, their credibility cannot be evaluated. (Wikipedia does not follow this logic. Wikis are based on the premise that credible claims emerge when many writers pool their knowledge; however, this logic has not gained sway among all academic readers.)

2. Credentials—The author's education, experience, and seniority contribute to credibility.

3. Knowledge base—The more knowledgeable the author seems to be about the topic, the more credible.

4. Genre—In general, a text written for an academic audience is more credible than one written for a general audience. When considering blogs and websites, one sponsored by an established, respected institution is more credible that one written by an individual. Among academic texts, a review article may be considered more persuasive than an empirical study since it combines the results of multiple studies, and an empirical study may be considered more persuasive than a theoretical piece because it contains data.

5. Type of Support—Texts whose claims are supported with empirical data and citations tend to be more credible than those whose claims are supported with emotional appeals, repetition, exaggeration, and anecdotal evidence. Although personal narratives can be very compelling, many academic readers consider them to be anecdotal and require corroboration before they find them persuasive. Arguments that begin with acceptable premises and proceed logically without any gaps in the reasoning are more credible than those with unacceptable premises or missing steps.

6. Bias—Texts that contain biased words or omit perspectives tend to be less credible than those that appear fair-minded and balanced. Also, texts whose author or publisher has a vested interest in a particular perspective on the topic tend to be less credible.

For students who are inefficient in their reading, it is also useful to teach the strategy of evaluating sources for language accessibility. If the source text cannot be understood by the students, they may end up spending an inordinate amount of time reading it, or, alternatively, patchwriting from it (Abasi

& Akbari, 2008). In a survey of 543 L1 college writers, Burton and Chadwick (2000) found that accessibility was considered an even more important criterion than availability or credibility when choosing sources for papers. It seems reasonable to assume that L2 writing students also consider accessibility to be important.

Clearly, lack of language accessibility can have a negative impact on the effectiveness of L2 writers' writing. Li and Casanave's (2012) study of two first-year L2 college students in Hong Kong, for example, provided evidence of how selecting a source that is difficult to comprehend can lead to ineffective source use. Responding to an assignment requiring students to locate three sources relevant to their chosen topic and write a 500-word essay, one of the students, Iris, approached the literature search by typing the keywords from the assignment title into a search engine and selecting two articles that were among the first to appear. She then copied two passages from one and the abstract from another into a Word document, and these became the basis for her paper, together with the teacher's lecture slides. Iris' paper reproduced the ideas in her sources without her full understanding of them (Li & Casanave, 2012). To help students such as Iris, we believe it is important to guide students to choose accessible source texts. We are not suggesting that teachers promote the use of "dumbed-down" readings; rather, we believe that it is possible to find source texts that are academic and challenging but accessible.

In addition to credibility and language accessibility, relevance is an important criterion for writers to employ when selecting sources. While both experienced and novice writers read sources on their general research topics, at some point experienced writers decide not to include sources that do not have a particular relevance to their argument, while novice writers often include all the sources they initially selected. A study by Tomaš (2011) described one such novice writer. After spending only a little time selecting sources revolving around the same general topic, the writer, Aiko, wrote a fragmented paper, a list of summaries organized around seemingly random subheadings. Because the source texts were from four different geographical areas and disciplinary fields and focused on very different aspects of the topic (which was homosexuality), it was difficult for her to make connections among them. Relevance, like procrastination, can be addressed by helping students to find a topic that they are genuinely interested in. Like all writers, students need to identify what they are curious about. Once they have identified something that they really want to know, they are more likely to conduct a successful search for relevant sources. This is a first step in helping students fully integrate source ideas and avoid writing lists of summaries, or what Segev-Miller (2004) has called a "shopping-list approach."

## 2. Digesting: Strategies for Reading and Keeping Track of Sources

Once students have selected credible, accessible, and relevant sources, they need help reading them because reading comprehension has been linked to effective source use. Roig (1999), for example, found that ineffective paraphrasing was tied to difficulties in understanding source texts, and Howard (1995) argued that copying, or what she called "monologic patchwriting," is also evidence of incomplete reading comprehension (p. 141). To help students read more efficiently, comprehend more, and use sources more effectively, therefore, it makes sense to scaffold the reading of source texts and reinforce the reading-writing connections inherent in writing from sources (Hirvela, 2016).

One way to do this is by teaching active reading strategies. While teaching such strategies will not change the difficulty level of the reading, it can develop students' confidence in reading, which in turn can improve their engagement and writing performance (Spack, 1997). Effective note-taking is one active reading strategy that can facilitate students' comprehension of sources. Many students work directly from source texts, cutting and pasting ideas directly into their own texts, with multiple windows open on their computers at a time. This process bypasses the digestion necessary to developing a new line of argument. In previous decades, students were taught to write from sources using notecards; they were taught to use one card for each piece of information taken from a source. This approach meant that student writers could reorder the cards, mixing ideas from several source texts and interspersing their own ideas as well. We suggest teaching students to follow the idea behind this method using updated technology given that many students now prefer to read and write in the cyberspace (Hirvela, 2016).

Teaching students to work with the intermediary step of note-taking not only helps them integrate source ideas with their own, but it also helps them keep track of their citations. Students who cut-and-paste directly from sources into their own documents, as well as those who memorize texts in order to learn the information in them, often cannot identify their sources later. This may not only make it hard to attribute, but it may also lead to problems with source use, for difficulty in distinguishing where source text ideas end and one's own ideas begin has been found to contribute to ineffective paraphrasing (Pecorari, 2013). Therefore, we recommend that students be encouraged to develop a system for their note-taking that (1) provides for ways to record full referencing information and key it to each idea they record, (2) differentiates quotes from paraphrases (by means of quotation marks), and (3) clearly indicates which are their own ideas and which come from another source (perhaps by means of square brackets or different colored pens). When students have a process to help them keep ideas separate in their minds and their notes, it will, in turn, help them produce effective paraphrases with good boundary markers. Since, in our experience, many students also need help identifying the information required for a full reference for both print and online source texts, a good note-taking process is useful here as well. Developing the abilities to identify this information and keep track of it is an essential writing skill that students can take with them to writing tasks in other courses and contexts.

Another important aspect of note-taking is selection of ideas. When experienced writers take notes, they do not select random ideas to write down; neither do they select only those ideas that support their view. Instead, they take notes that capture the argument being made. This involves summarizing the main claims and noting how they are related to each other. When students are just beginning to learn to do this, it may be helpful to use reading texts with topic sentences in many of the paragraphs and direct the students to pay particular attention to these sentences. Students can be guided to continually reconsider the relation between the points in the topic sentences, the main point of the text, and the purpose in writing. Instructors can also ask students to underline repeated key vocabulary. Another approach is to ask students to write one-sentence summaries for each paragraph and then read the sentences to discover the shape of the argument. These summaries are useful later when integrating source ideas into the new line of argument; however, at this point the focus should be on understanding how ideas fit together rather than on constructing good summary sentences. (Guidelines for writing summaries are in Chapter 4, Lesson 3.)

Experienced writers are also known to ask questions about source texts, draw connections both to other texts and their own experiences (Bean, 2011; Plakans, 2009), and interrogate or challenge the claims of the author. Because L2 writers are often unaware of these active reading strategies and sometimes feel that "speaking back" to source texts is inappropriate, reading guides that provide questions scaffolding active responding are useful (Grabe & Zhang, 2013).

Active responding can also be modeled in class. In our experience, when students see each other in action, it encourages them to respond actively and to connect with their own experiences. A list of response strategies with responses from some L2 students to a text on volunteering is shown:

- Questioning a point: "That's interesting that young American people volunteer so much. I wonder if it's true for English language learners who grew up in the U.S., given that their parents may have come from cultures where ensuring the welfare of others is the responsibility of the state and not of individuals and community organizations?"

- Disagreeing with a point: "I find it very surprising that this researcher found that volunteering does not lead to improved employment opportunities. I just can't believe that that would be the case. It makes me wonder if the study was done correctly."

- Connecting a point to one's own life: "I really didn't like this article because it said that international students do not volunteer as much as American students. And it is true that it did mention the reasons for this, but I don't think the author really understands how overwhelming it is to function in a new culture. I just think he didn't address the issue in sufficient depth and instead made us [international students] seem lazy or not caring."

- Responding to a powerful quote: "I just love this quote because it feels like it's been written about me!"

- Evaluating a claim: "I am surprised that this author said this so confidently because the other two studies found the opposite of what he found. I don't know if it's really true like this author says. I think maybe we need more information, more research?"

Guiding students to choose the reading strategies that are most appropriate to the writing task is also beneficial. If, for example, the task is to synthesize a number of texts, then it is strategic to read the texts multiple times—the first time for general comprehension and the subsequent time(s) more deeply to mine ideas for later reuse (Plakans, 2009). If, on the other hand, the task is to write a reflection on an experience in one's own life using a reading text as a springboard, then it may be strategic to read more quickly, focusing on those parts that relate to one's own experience. In addition, it is sometimes useful to have students focus their attention on one part of the text because it is particularly relevant to the writing task. In an advanced class, for example, focusing on the methodology and limitations sections of a research report may help writers produce a critical analysis of the study. Thus, teaching students about text organization helps them make strategic decisions about what parts of the source text to focus on.

Finally, in order to most effectively help students write from sources, writing instructors should assess their students' reading processes. Doing so provides insight into the students' approaches to reading as well as their comprehension of and responses to the source texts at hand. One way to assess students' reading processes is to assign what Salvatori (1996) calls a *difficulty paper*, in which students discuss the specific reading issues they are encountering and reflect on their reading strategies. Other ways include observing the students as they work in class and conducting individual conferences in which you ask, for example, whether the students read online or paper texts, how they take notes, and whether they tend to memorize parts of the source text for later use. These approaches not only provide formative assessments and create opportunities for dialogue about the students' reading processes, but they also give instructors an opportunity to explain cultural references that may impede L2 writers' comprehension of source texts.

## 3. Integrating: Strategies for Reusing and Transforming Ideas

Using effective reading strategies sets writers up for being better able to integrate source ideas into their own writing. Effective integration includes both reusing ideas (with attribution) and transforming them.

L2 writers have been shown to struggle with source integration, as shown in the example of Aiko (Tomaš, 2011). When they struggle, L2 writers may end up using textual construction strategies that result in prototypical plagiarism. For example, the graduate-level L2 writer in Zhu's (2005) qualitative research study reused the line of argument of a source text, meaning that the student followed the logic and progression of ideas of another author. Even when L2 writers avoid prototypical plagiarism, they may not have command of an array of organizational techniques and so may not be effective in their source use. In looking at the genre of argumentation, for example, Qin and Karaback (2010) found that L2 writers tended to rely on basic argumentation strategies, such as backing up claims with evidence, over the more advanced strategies of making counter-arguments and rebutting claims.

According to Spivey (1990), three subprocesses characterize source integration: content selection, organization, and connection: (1) *Selection* entails choosing the source content most relevant to one's line of argument; (2) *organization* entails relating ideas from sources in meaningful, logical ways; and (3) *connection* involves bringing in one's own knowledge, experience, or thinking to the text at hand. While it is useful to separate these subprocesses in order to think in detail about how to scaffold the integration process, we recognize that writers do not go through the subprocesses sequentially but all at once and/or in a recursive manner and that these subprocesses are intertwined with those of planning and digesting previously discussed.

Spivey's subprocess of *selection* involves selecting ideas within texts, taking into account the importance of the idea and its alignment with one's own thinking. To help students select ideas, writing instructors might ask students to return to their source texts for a second reading. Teachers can model this reading/selection process in class by doing a think-aloud protocol and marking a text that the students are familiar with. As the instructor reads the text aloud, she can highlight parts that she may want to paraphrase or quote in a hypothetical paper and say what comes to mind as an experienced reader/writer—for example, "This example is similar to my experience . . . . So what I could do is paraphrase the claim that the example illustrates and then use my own example instead. That would bring more of my voice to the paper." This strategy is, of course, very similar to good note-taking strategies, but here the emphasis shifts from reading for ideas to reading to select ideas for reuse.

When it comes to *organization*, it is important to discuss organizing structures and moves with students. Nussbaum (2008) and Nussbaum and Schraw (2007) show three ways to organize an argument, including *weighting* (where a writer examines different sides of an issue and then focuses on the arguments with the most weight), *synthesis* (where a writer formulates a thesis that combines or reconciles aspects of different positions), and *refutation* (where a writer rebuts one or more arguments on the basis of merit, relevance, or evidence). Examining contrasting organizing structures of two papers fulfilling the same assignment may also help build students' repertoire of organizing structures. It is also useful to let students explore idea organizers, including graphic organizers, outlines, and charts. (See samples in Appendix 4.) Idea organizers can be used when planning and digesting, as well as when integrating to reinforce key ideas from source texts, to activate personal connections to them, and to test alternate schemes for relating ideas to one another. Because different writers find different types of organizers useful, asking students to evaluate sample organizers using the Five Cs is a good idea. (See Lesson 5.)

Finally, *connection* is the subprocess perhaps most intimately connected to transforming ideas, constructing authority, and being original. Of course, in an effective reading-thinking-writing process, students will have been connecting with their own ideas from the beginning, but as they sit down to write, writing instructors can scaffold their development of language to make these connections and build authorial voice. As students draft, they should work with their reading notes to match the questions they began with to the answers that they found in their research. They should also identify and reconcile differences in the positions of different authors. They can also reread sentences that they responded strongly to and freewrite on them to see if the strong response can be developed into a coherent position of their own. Throughout the connection process, instructors can help students work through their ideas and find language to make connections, build authorial presence, and smoothly incorporate references.

# Connecting to the Classroom

This chapter focused on the process of producing source-based assignments, foregrounding the fundamental role of thinking in each of its subprocesses—planning for source use, digesting source content and keeping track of sources, and integrating ideas into one's own writing. Our goal was to bring to light aspects of the reading-thinking-writing process that often go unexplored in writing classrooms, such as source selection and reading, so that instructors can scaffold them. An additional goal was to help instructors instill in students an appreciation for how much time and how many steps are actually involved in producing an effective piece of source-based writing. One way instructors can show students this is to shift the responsibility for planning to them by asking students to prepare their own timelines with specific goals and deadlines based on a careful reading of the assignment sheet and grading rubric. A second engaging way we use is to talk about our own writing experiences with specifics such as how many hours a revision took to complete. Next, several lessons that provide further ideas for teaching students about the complex process of writing from sources are presented.

# Lesson 1:
# Can I Trust This Text?
# Evaluating the Credibility of Sources

**Focus:** Evaluating sources—credibility

**Description:** Students apply criteria for evaluating credibility to a number of source texts and make arguments for which sources they would be comfortable using in a paper and which they would not.

**Rationale:** Teachers often hold up credibility as their primary criterion for source text selection, yet students have difficulty assessing the credibility of sources. This lesson, therefore, provides students with credibility criteria and practice in evaluating the credibility of source texts.

**Students:** High-Beginner to High-Intermediate L2s; L1s

**Preparation:** Choose several texts on the same topic that differ in credibility. For example, in a course with the theme of volunteering, you could use research articles, national news articles, non-profit organization newsletters, websites outlining benefits of volunteering, for-profit travel company brochures advertising volunteering trips, and private blogs by Peace Corps volunteers describing their experiences. Also, prepare a handout with a list of criteria for evaluating credibility and some questions to scaffold the students' work:

a. **Citation:** Does the text identify its author and publisher?

b. **Credentials:** What are the credentials of the authors? their education? their jobs? How long have they been doing these jobs?

c. **Knowledge base:** How knowledgeable do the authors seem to be about the topic? Have they taught about it? researched it? lived it? spoken to people who have lived it? written about it before? Do they refer to other people's work on this topic, showing that they have read about it?

d. **Genre:** Is this a scholarly text? Is the text written for the general public (like a news report), for a group of people (like a newsletter), or for an academic discourse community (like an article in a professional journal)? If the text is a blog, is it a blog of an individual writing on his/her own or a blog associated with a news organization?

e. **Type of support:** Are the claims of the text supported through logical argument, beginning with an acceptable premise, and moving to a conclusion without skipping any steps? Are the claims supported by empirical data? Or are the claims supported by emotional appeals, anecdotes, repetition, or exaggeration?

f. **Bias:** Does there seem to be bias evident in word choice or omissions of certain perspectives? Is there a sponsor for the text that has an interest in making a certain claim on the topic?

**Procedure**:

1. Hand out the list of criteria for evaluating the credibility of academic sources and go over them as a class. Take time to engage students in a discussion of what makes a source credible for academic readers. While it is obvious for some of the criteria what makes a text more credible, this is not the case for all of them.

2. Divide students into three groups. Assign the first three criteria to one group (citation/credentials/knowledge base); assign the next two criteria to the second group (genre/type of support); assign the last criterion to the third group (bias). Ask students to read the texts and work in their groups to evaluate them on their criteria. Point out that some of the questions, such as the author's credentials or the interests of the sponsoring organization, may require a bit of research; if the students have laptops in the classroom and internet access, they can use them to do this research.

3. Form new small groups, with at least one person from each of the old groups in the new ones. Ask the students to report on the work they did in the old group. The new group should pool all of the information about each source text. Then, ask students to determine, for each text, whether it would be a credible academic source or not. Tell them to be ready to justify their answers.

4. Reconvene as a class so groups can share their work.

**Adaptations:** Advanced students can compare examples of academic genres for their credibility. Choose an empirical study, a theoretical piece, and a review article. Or, choose one academic text and underline several different types of claims in it (a claim based on the results of an empirical study, a claim based in their theoretical approach) and ask students to evaluate how credible they find each claim.

# Lesson 2:
# Can I Handle This?
# Evaluating the Accessibility of Sources

**Focus:** Evaluating sources—language accessibility

**Description:** Using one of three electronic tools, students assess how difficult the vocabulary in several potential source texts is for them to understand. (An alternative technique developed for print sources is given in the Adaptations section for instructors who do not have access to the internet.)

**Rationale:** If students choose source texts that are beyond their comprehension, it raises the likelihood that their source use will be ineffective. This lesson, therefore, provides students with tools to evaluate the accessibility of sources based on the comprehensibility of vocabulary.

**Students:** Intermediate to Advanced L2s

**Preparation:** Choose two credible sources on the same topic that differ in language accessibility. A good way to locate a text that is largely inaccessible to students at the intermediate level is to select an article from a highly specialized disciplinary journal. A good way to locate a text that is more accessible is to look for a book or textbook chapter (perhaps even written by the same author as the journal article). You will also need computers for your students to use and a computer with a projector for the whole class to use.

Instructors should familiarize themselves with the websites used in this lesson:

- Word and Phrase (www.wordandphrase.info/analyzeText.asp)

- LexTutor Vocabulary Profiler (www.lextutor.ca/vp/eng/)

- Text Fixer (www.textfixer.com/tools/online-word-counter.php)

For these electronic concordancing tools, users copy and paste a piece of source text into an input box and receive an immediate linguistic analysis of it showing the most frequently used content words. Word and Phrase and Lextutor Vocabulary Profiler also show the percentage of words in the text that are considered frequently used based on their own lists of frequently used words. In addition, Lextutor shows words from the Academic Word List. Instructors can acquaint themselves with Word and Phrase and Lextutor Vocabulary Profiler by watching tutorials about them on YouTube. Text Fixer has instructions on its website; look for information on Word Counter.

**Procedure:**

1. Give students five minutes to begin reading the articles. When they stop reading, they should freewrite about their ability to comprehend them.

2. Ask students to compare their ideas in pairs.

3. Reconvene as a class to discuss what makes some texts more accessible than others. Some factors are linguistic density (a large number of content words), discipline-specific jargon, complex grammatical structures, and difficult content (e.g., complex statistical analyses). Tell the students that they will judge the linguistic accessibility of their sources based on the comprehensibility of the vocabulary in them.

4. Using a computer and a projector, model using the three electronic tools. Cut and paste one of the articles into the input box in Word and Phrase. Use the entire article. Go over the linguistic analysis together with the students. Then repeat the process with the same article for LexTutor Vocabulary Profiler and Text Fixer.

5. Ask the students to try using the websites themselves. They should cut and paste the second article into the input box of the tool that they liked the most. Let the students help one another and point them toward the online tutorials and instructions if they need them.

6. Ask students to compare the linguistic analyses of the two articles and then look at the top 10 to 20 content words and determine how many of them they know. Then ask them to consider the percentage of the words in the text that are on the frequently used word list and the Academic Word List. Tell them that, generally speaking, texts with fewer unknown content words, more words on the frequently used word lists, and fewer words on the Academic Word List are more accessible. Let them determine the accessibility of each text for themselves.

7. Debrief as a class about the three tools. Which ones did the students find easy to use, and why?

**Adaptations:** In contexts where internet access is not available, ask the students to read the print sources one at a time. As they read, they should guess the meaning of unknown words from context. When they are able to make a reasonable guess, they should continue reading, but when they come across a word that impedes their understanding of the text, they should stop and write it down. Once they have reached five words that impede their progress, they should stop reading and summarize what they have understood up to that point. After students do this for the second source, they should compare how far into each text they were able to get and how much of each they were able to restate. Based on these two criteria, students can decide whether the sources are accessible to them or not.

# Lesson 3:
# Do I Care? Choosing Interesting
# Topics and Relevant Sources

**Focus:** Evaluating sources—relevance and interest

**Description:** Students choose paper topics that they are interested in and source texts that are on topic and that suit the scope of the assignment.

**Rationale:** Students often struggle to select a topic and source texts interesting enough to keep them engaged and narrow enough for the scope of the writing task. This lesson, therefore, guides students through the process of narrowing the topic and selecting relevant sources.

**Students:** High-Beginner to Advanced L2s; L1s

**Preparation:** This lesson is designed for a course in which students choose research topics that are connected to a course theme. Prepare abstracts of credible sources related to the theme (e.g., volunteering) that have specific foci (e.g., benefits of volunteering for seniors, effects of volunteering on employability).

**Procedure:**

1. Pique the students' interest in choosing research topics by having them watch this short video: *How do you choose and refine a topic?* available at https://youtu.be/bEOxnWbbgvA (Tomaš, Marino, & Pantelides, 2015c). Briefly discuss the video.

2. Discuss the scope of the paper with the students and explain that the course theme is too broad a topic for their paper. Ask students to read the prepared abstracts to see how the theme can be divided into narrower paper topics.

3. Introduce interest as an important criterion for selecting a paper topic. Ask students to decide which abstract is the most interesting to them and explain their reasoning in a short piece of informal writing. If there are students who are not interested in any of the abstracts you selected, suggest that they choose a paper topic related to an outside interest or another course they are taking (e.g., a student studying Business may choose to write about volunteering in non-profit organizations).

4. Once the students have selected a tentative topic, ask them to find several additional abstracts that are directly relevant to their topics. If you have laptops and internet in the classroom, this can be done in class; if not, it can be done as homework.

5. Assign a writing task in which the students explain how each source text meets the criteria of interest and relevance. They should respond to these questions:

- What makes this source interesting to you?
- What ideas from this source do you think would be interesting to share with your readers?
- How is the source connected to your topic?
- How does this source add to the topic compared to the sources you already have?

**Adaptations:** If there are time constraints in covering source selection, combine Lessons 1, 2, and 3, and ask students to reflect on how their source texts meet all four criteria (credibility, accessibility, relevance, and interest) at once.

# Lesson 4:
# Note-Taking Strategies
# for Different Writing Tasks

**Focus:** Note-taking

**Description:** Students examine three note-taking strategies for the same text and consider which strategy would work best for writing a summary paper, a response paper, and an argument paper.

**Rationale:** Experienced writers use a number of different note-taking strategies depending on the writing task they need to accomplish. Since students often do not have a well-developed array of note-taking strategies, this lesson provides examples of three different strategies, matched to different writing tasks.

**Students:** High-Beginner to Advanced L2s; L1s

**Preparation:** A short, annotated text is needed for this lesson. Sample 5 in Appendix 3 can be used. If you would prefer to use a different text, you will need to prepare it: Make three copies of the text so that you can model three different note-taking strategies. On the first copy, take notes that would facilitate writing a summary paper. For example, highlight the topic sentences of each paragraph, write a one-sentence summary next to each paragraph, and underline repeated, key vocabulary. On the second copy, take notes helpful for writing a personal response. Highlight powerful quotes, take notes in the margins on connections to your own life or ask questions of the text. Finally, on the third copy, demonstrate effective notes for writing an argument. Your notes could reflect an evaluation of claims or evidence in the source text and present possible counter-arguments.

**Procedure**:

1. Ask students to read a copy of the text with no notes on it.

2. Divide students into small groups and hand out the three copies with the different types of notes. Ask the groups to describe the differences that they notice. Then, students should decide which copy lends itself best to writing a summary paper, a personal response, and an argument paper.

3. Reconvene as a class and ask the groups to explain their decisions and reasoning.

4. Draw the students' attention to the usefulness of paragraph summaries for writing summary papers and argument papers, and provide a list of guidelines for writing short summaries (see Chapter 4, Lesson 3). Also, discuss the usefulness of responding actively to source texts when writing response papers and argument papers.

**Adaptations:** Select a text that you want your students to write an argument paper about. In class, model active responding to the text and elicit responses from the students as well.

# Lesson 5:
# Idea Organizers: Tools for Digesting Content, Organizing Information, and Finding Connections

**Focus:** Source use—integration

**Description:** Students evaluate three types of idea organizers (graphic organizers, outlines, and charts) according to The Five Cs guidelines and develop their own organizers for a set of source texts; then they analyze the structure of the source texts and compare them to the argument structures that they developed.

**Rationale:** Organizing is essential for the effective synthesis of source ideas and one's own ideas into a line of argument, and idea organizers facilitate this planning. This lesson provides an opportunity for students to analyze the organizing structures of three texts, experiment with three types of idea organizer, and compare their own lines of argument to those of the source texts.

**Students:** Advanced L2s; L1s

**Preparation:** Prepare a sample graphic organizer, outline, and chart. The content of all three idea organizers should be the same; only the format varies. Samples of the organizers appear in Appendix 4. Prepare a handout that includes the 5 Cs Guidelines: Also, choose three texts on the same topic, preferably ones that the students have already read.

- ❏ **Clarity:** The organizer represents the key ideas from source texts clearly.
- ❏ **Completeness:** The organizer includes enough notes to develop a line of argument. The ideas do not come from a limited number of pages in a given source (e.g., only from an abstract or an introduction).
- ❏ **Conciseness:** The organizer does not include too much information to develop a clear line of argument.
- ❏ **Connections:** The organizer shows the logical connections between ideas from the texts and the writer's knowledge and experience.
- ❏ **Credit:** The organizer keeps track of citations for paraphrases and/or quotes.

**Procedure**:

1. Begin a discussion of source-based writing by asking students how they keep track of information from multiple sources, whether they take notes, and whether they organize ideas visually. You might also want to mention how you do these things, that there are multiple ways of doing them, and that visual organizers can be helpful.

2. Divide students into small groups and hand out the sample organizers. Each group should analyze the samples using the handout with the Five Cs Guidelines.

3. Reconvene as a class so small groups can present their findings. Point out that all three organizers integrate the writer's ideas with ideas from the sources. Also, the graphic organizer facilitates narrowing the topic and keeping track of key concepts from many different sources, the outline orders the ideas for writing the paper, and the chart allows for a quick comparison of ideas across sources.

4. Ask students to choose the organizer they would prefer to use and list their reasons. Then, put students in new groups with classmates who want to work on the same type of organizer.

5. Provide the groups with the three texts you have chosen and ask them to develop their own organizers.

6. Students will then post their organizers on the wall in the classroom so their classmates can walk around and examine their
peers' work.

7. Students should take a closer look at the organizing structures of
the three texts. Ask the small groups to compare the structures,
looking for similarities and differences in content, progression of
ideas, and balance between the authors' voices and referenced
ideas. Questions such as these can guide them:

   ■ What are the similarities in the content of the three texts?
   Name the specific ideas used in more than one text.

   ■ Looking at the ideas used in more than one text, decide
   whether they are foregrounded or backgrounded in each.
   Are the ideas used for the same purpose in each argument?

   ■ Are there any differences in content between the three texts?
   What are they?

   ■ In what ways do the organizational structures of the texts
   differ?

   ■ Which of the three examples do you consider the most effective in terms of its organization and argument development?
   What makes it effective for you?

   ■ Is the organization of any of the texts similar to the organization of ideas in your own organizer? If so, look for ways to
   reorganize the ideas in your organizer. Also, look for ideas
   that you could add or delete to make your line of argument
   more different from the one in the text.

8. Reconvene as a class to discuss any similarities between the
organizing structure and those of the texts.

**Adaptations:** Students compare two versions of the same graphic organizer, one
from the beginning of the reading-thinking-writing process that comprises the writer's own brainstorms and another later version with ideas from sources and merged
categories added. A sample of the early version of the graphic organizer used in
this adaptation also appears in Appendix 4. How did the shape of the argument
change as the writer learned more? Is the student surprised by the level of detail
in the early organizer? What advantages are there to creating an early organizer?

Also, tech-savvy students may want to make use of a website such as https://
bubbl.us/ where they can create visual displays.

# Lesson 6:
# Revising to Integrate Source Ideas and Bring Out Your Own

**Focus:** Source use—integration

**Description:** Students contrast two drafts of a piece of writing and analyze differences in the number of references, consider how the textual revisions connect to the writer's concerns, and trace the use of the writer's and source ideas in the line of argument in the revised draft.

**Rationale:** Sometimes student writers do not realize the extent to which the development of a line of argument and the smooth integration of source ideas with one's own ideas relies on revision. This lesson, therefore, models the revision process of (an) experienced writer(s) that demonstrates these two things.

**Students:** High-Intermediate to Advanced L2s; L1s

**Preparation:** For this lesson, you will need two drafts of a piece of academic writing for which you have some insight into the thinking of the author. Two such drafts appear in Sample 6 in Appendix 3.

**Procedure**:

1.  Introduce the topic (student procrastination when writing papers from sources) and the purpose of the text (to show teachers ways to help students avoid procrastinating).

2.  Hand out the two versions of the text so students can see the versions side by side. Note the differences. In our sample, the revised version is quite a bit longer and is comprised of three paragraphs as opposed to just one.

3.  Ask students to compare the number of references in the early and later drafts. The students should highlight the sentences containing references, using different colors for each cited text. They then count the number of sentences with and without references. In our sample, the earlier version has eight sentences, four of which contain references (50 percent reused ideas), while the final version has fifteen sentences, six of which contain references (40 percent reused ideas). The six source texts cited in the early draft are all cited in the final version, and there is an additional citation in the final version as well. Thus, the final draft has more sentences with the writers' own ideas relative to reused ideas than the earlier one, despite the fact that the final version has an additional reference. This reflects the fact that the writers made revisions with an eye toward amplifying their own ideas.

4. Read the earlier version aloud with the students and answer any questions they may have about the meaning.

5. Tell students that, after writing the first version, the writers were concerned that L2 student writers were stereotyped as procrastinators. The writers wanted to avoid this overgeneralization because it is both negative and inaccurate.

6. Divide students into small groups and ask them to read the revised version and identify the changes that they notice related to the writers' concerns about stereotyping. The changes in our sample include:

   ■ Reframing the discussion by adding the idea that, in addition to students who procrastinate, there are others who spend a lot of time on assignments; this entailed deleting the first two sentences and writing three new ones, which became the introductory paragraph.

   ■ Reframing the discussion to begin with *many student writers*, a phrase that encompasses both L1 and L2 writers.

   ■ Focusing on the behavior of procrastination as opposed to student writers as procrastinators; this entailed deleting the precise statistics and the mention of specific ethnic groups in the sentence citing Lowinger et al. and Kim et al.

7. Put students in small groups to identify other textual changes through comparison of the two versions.

8. Reconvene as a class so each group can name a textual difference between the two versions. Working together as a class, lead them through a discussion of the writers' concerns that prompted the textual changes:

   ■ The writers wanted to argue that connecting the writing topic to one's own life can help students overcome procrastination, so they added five sentences, beginning, *One way to forestall procrastination is by promoting students' engagement with the topic....*

   ■ The writers felt that the point about deadlines had gotten lost, so they separated the discussion of goal-setting that cites Boice from the discussion of deadlines that cites Ariely & Wertenbroch.

   ■ The writers wanted to make goal-setting more important than deadlines, so they reversed the order of the two discussions, feeling that goal-setting stood out more when it came second.

   ■ The writers wanted to firmly establish their knowledge of the field, so they added the sentence with the Plakans citation.

■ The writers wanted to reconnect with the main line of argument beyond this excerpt, namely, that the entire reading-thinking-writing process affects source use and therefore needs to be taught, so they added the sentence *Requiring and responding to intermediary products reinforce the message that teachers value all the tasks of the reading-thinking-writing process.*

9. Ask students to work in small groups again to trace the line of argument in the revised version. As they read the underlined sentences, they should decide which sentences form the backbone of the argument and name the move made in each one:

   a. Defining the problems. (*Many student writers become overwhelmed....*)

   b. Offering an overarching solution. (*Issues...can be addressed by providing students with better strategies.*)

   c. Establishing the relevance of the first problem to the larger topic of source use. (*Anticipating students' tendency to procrastinate is necessary because ....*)

   d. Offering a suggestion to solve the first problem. (*One way to forestall procrastination is....*)

   e. Offering a second suggestion to solve the first problem. (*Another way to help students ....*)

   f. Offering a third suggestion to solve the first problem. (*In addition, writing instructors can... to help students stay on track with source-based writing assignments.*)

10. Ask students to determine which of the underlined sentences contain the writers' ideas and which contain ideas from sources. The first two contain the writers' own ideas, the third contains information from a source, the fourth is the writers' idea, and the fifth and sixth contain ideas from sources (or the writers' ideas which they chose to support with citations).

11. Reconvene as a class. Discuss how the line of argument is constructed by combining the writers' ideas with ideas taken from the source texts. Point out that the phrases *anticipating students' tendency to procrastinate, forestall procrastination, avoid procrastination,* and *help students stay on track* function as synonyms and help create the coherence of the line of argument.

**Adaptations:** Ask students to prepare short presentations on their own revising processes in which they share an earlier excerpt from their paper and compare it with the final version, articulating their reasons for making changes. These kinds of presentations not only push students toward rigorous revising, but also build their confidence as developing academic writers by allowing them to showcase their own progress.

# Take-Away Points

- Teachers should consider the entire reading-writing-thinking process when teaching and assessing source-based writing.

- The reading-thinking-writing process can be divided into three parts: planning, digesting ideas, and integrating ideas into one's writing; these processes are not undertaken sequentially, but are intertwined.

- Effective source-based writing involves many factors, including linguistic and cognitive abilities, task demands, and individual and contextual factors.

- Taking an interest in students' ideas and argument-building sends the message that clear thinking is the most important aspect of written communication.

- It is important to address procrastination, scaffold reading comprehension, and teach idea integration, as issues with all are known to lead to prototypical plagiarism.

- Showing students how to select source texts that are credible, accessible, and relevant to their paper topics results in better writing from sources.

- Teachers should help students develop their own systems of note-taking because they help students digest source texts, keep track of citations, and develop their own ideas in response to source texts.

- Idea organizers such as visual organizers, outlines, and charts are useful tools for student writers.

- Students need to learn to select the reading strategies that are most appropriate to the writing task.

- Integrating sources into one's writing includes reusing ideas and transforming them and can be divided into the intertwined subprocesses of selection, organization, and connection, all of which require complex skills that teachers need to scaffold.

- Modeling is a good way to bring the various parts of the reading-thinking-writing process into the classroom.

- Observing students as they read and write in class and then interviewing them about their writing processes are two good ways to assess students' use of strategies.

# 6

# The Response Dimension:
## Developing Discussions around Source Use Decisions

"I just spent a whole class on citing, and then when I read their drafts, half of them didn't even have any cites! It's driving me crazy -- Were they not listening, did they not get it, or do they just not care?!"

–Hyungsook, instructor in a first-year ESL
integrated reading-writing course at a U.S. university

"My teacher wrote, 'Your reason for using this cite is not clear' on my paper. I used it for support! What doesn't she get? I don't know what she wants me to do!"

–Jean, student in a first-year seminar course in a U.S. university

MANY TEACHERS HAVE FOUND THEMSELVES IN HYUNGSOOK'S SHOES, frustrated by student papers that do not seem to reflect their teaching. When teachers read papers like this, it may be a very short step from assessing the paper as lacking citations to drawing the conclusion that the student writer is inattentive, lazy, or did not follow the lesson. However, teachers must remember that learning to reference conventionally is a long process that requires a tremendous amount of feedback and practice as well as exposure to concepts and rules. This chapter discusses several types of feedback—teacher response to student writing, peer review, and self-assessment. This chapter is not concerned with correction of error, but rather, with discussing and applying decisions about source use that influence the clarity, persuasiveness, authority, originality, and effectiveness of a piece of writing. The chapter opens with an argument for a pedagogical approach to response that is positive in tone, integrated into the work of the class, and supported. Then, response as dialogue is discussed, as is the importance of understanding students' reasons for their referencing decisions. The chapter closes with an examination of peer review and self-assessment and a discussion of ways that students can respond to referencing issues in both their peers' writing and their own.

---

**CONSIDER**

Read these teachers' views (as quoted in Ferris, Liu, & Rabie, 2011):

"Responding to student writing IS the job of teaching writing. If they don't write and we don't respond, then how else are they going to learn to write? I can't learn to ride a bicycle by talking about it or watching PowerPoint presentations about it or even thinking about it." (p. 40)

"…whether they [students] choose to use it [feedback] is entirely up to them…." (p. 48)

- In what ways is learning to write like learning to ride a bicycle?
- In what sense is the use of feedback the student's decision? In what ways is it not?
- Should students should be held accountable for how they incorporate feedback into their papers? Why or why not?

---

# What We Know from Research and Theory

## Formative Response: A Pedagogical Approach

Chapter 1 argued for a non-punitive, pedagogical approach to students' unconventional but non-deceitful source use, an approach bolstered by research that has shown that punitive responses do not adequately deal with the problem (Chandrasoma, Thompson, & Pennycook, 2004; Howard, 1999; Pecorari, 2003, 2013) and may in fact exacerbate it, causing students to lose motivation and self-confidence (Gu & Brooks, 2008). This non-punitive approach to source use fits well with general theories of writing response that claim that positive response (including both praise and constructive criticism) builds confidence, which in turn helps students take more control of their writing. Furthermore, it fits with Knoblauch and Brannon's (2006) argument that the positive tenor of response is probably more important to the effectiveness of response than the form (e.g., margin comments, conferences, audio recording) in which it is delivered. Response needs to be given in ways that show teachers value the work of student writers, even when their papers contain problematic source use. One way to do this is to make feedback selective rather than exhaustive; seeing too many comments can make some students feel as overwhelmed or attacked as seeing negative ones. Commenting only on those aspects of source use that have most recently been taught (and grading only those that have been taught) are good suggestions.

In addition to being positive in tone, response should be integrated into the work of the class. This means that students should receive feedback on early pieces of writing so they can use it when writing later assignments. Building opportunities to provide feedback into the syllabus helps avoid crises at the end of the semester when a student hands in a paper with too much copying, and it is too late to fix. Teachers can communicate the importance of dealing with feedback by establishing grading criteria for it on their syllabi. Holding students accountable for their understanding and application of feedback encourages them to take it seriously.

Teachers also need to find ways to support students' understanding and application of response (Ferris, 2003, 2014; Knoblauch & Brannon, 2006). They can support students by, for instance, defining the terms they use when giving feedback; modeling revision; having students revise in class so that the teacher is available for consultations; putting students in pairs or small groups or with tutors to apply teacher feedback; and apprising students of resources (such as writing centers, library staff, and the Purdue OWL) that they can turn to for assistance outside of class. Several studies of L2 student writers have shown the validity of supporting students in understanding and applying feedback. For example, Goldstein (2006) reported on the case of Hisako, a graduate L2 writer who received electronic comments in the margin from her writing instructor. Goldstein found that Hisako failed to revise her problematic source use in each of the subsequent drafts, which the instructor attributed to laziness and oversight; Hisako's lack of revision, however, was due to her inability to understand the teacher's comments. Other cases include Diana, a student in Currie's (1998) study, and Yang, a student in Leki's (2003) study, who struggled with paraphrasing source information effectively. When they received constructive feedback from their instructors, both students used more copying, which ironically resulted in their receiving better grades. In Yang's words, "If you change, you are wrong . . . . If I copy correctly, there is no error" (Leki, 2003, p. 91).

Another study that provides evidence that teachers should support students in the way to respond to feedback was conducted by Fiona Hyland (2001), who found that feedback that was not direct enough was not understood by some L2 writers. In her study, teachers were hesitant to directly address students' inappropriate source use in margin comments because they felt that doing so would be accusatory. Instead, they addressed the issue indirectly by, for instance, asking open-ended questions about one student's source use without explicitly indicating that it was unacceptable. As a result, this student and others felt uncertain about how to improve their writing (Hyland, 2001). While the way the feedback was presented could be seen as the problem here, we would suggest that feedback that is not direct is not bad, if it is supported. Open-ended questions can be quite useful for engaging students in dialogue about their referencing decisions since students know that textual reuse is a fraught topic. But the dialogue must then continue so that the student writers can learn specifically what types of reuse are conventionally acceptable and effective.

## Understanding Source Use Decisions: Feedback as Dialogue

We believe that dialogue is one of the best ways that students can critically examine and understand their referencing decisions. Dialogue allows students to ask questions and teachers to respond in an individualized manner. It also allows teachers to learn important information about the students' referencing decisions and to provide a clear understanding of their expectations regarding source use. Dialogues are also more authentic in that they more closely represent the ways that scholars and other professional writers receive feedback from one another, both informally and during the publication process, about how to improve a piece of writing.

Several types of response lend themselves well to dialogue. Some teachers ask students to write letters or memos about the papers they are working on and to highlight areas they would like to receive feedback on, explain how they have addressed their teacher's feedback (Ferris, 2007), or describe how they applied a particular lesson on source use. Similar exchanges can be accomplished directly on an electronic copy of the student paper using the text boxes that are available in Google docs or in Track Changes in Word, in which case the students do not have to worry about organizing their ideas into extended prose. These exchanges can also occur in face-to-face conferences, but since some students may not be used to meeting alone with a teacher, it makes sense for teachers to scaffold the process so that students know what their role is. Ferris's (2014) recommendations for conferencing are that teachers should:

> (a) discuss goals and format of conferences with students ahead of time
>
> (b) suggest that the student take notes or record the conference for later review
>
> (c) consider holding conferences with students in pairs or small groups to minimize discomfort any students might feel with one-to-one meetings with the instructor and to maximize instructor time (particularly with small groups of students struggling with similar writing issues). (p. 8)

It is also helpful for teachers to understand why students make the decisions they do. Chapter 4 discussed how to smoothly incorporate quotes and paraphrases, but how do writers choose whether to quote or paraphrase? Studies have shown that L2 writers make decisions for several reasons. Some quote because they feel tired or daunted due to the high cognitive load involving both language and content issues of the academic L2 writing process (Petrić, 2012) and they believe that quoting is faster or easier than paraphrasing and less likely to result in plagiarism (Hirvela & Du, 2013). They also choose to quote in an effort to meet their instructors' demands for "more accessible, less awkward text that contain[s] the appropriate disciplinary terminology" (Currie, 1998, p. 9). Some students apply idiosyncratic theories in their decisions to quote or paraphrase; according to Shi (2010), one student believed that paraphrasing was the preferred skill at the university level, in contrast to quoting, which had been taught in high school, while another student said she "decided to paraphrase because she believed that quoting was not appropriate at the beginning of the paper" (p. 20).

Knowing students' reasons for choosing when to quote and when to paraphrase helps teachers decide how to respond. If students are quoting because they think it is easier than paraphrasing, then perhaps they do not understand the readings and the instructor should incorporate more scaffolding of the reading process. Or perhaps students need more vocabulary to paraphrase well on the topic. It is also likely that the easily produced quote is not well incorporated and the student needs more practice interpreting quotes. Teachers can also share with students reasons academic writers choose to quote, which include: "to indicate a higher degree of objectivity by attributing the quoted words to a credible source, to distance themselves from the quoted material in order to convey some attitude or reduce their own responsibility or to create a lively and dramatic way of reporting" (Petrić, 2012, p. 103).

## Centering the Student: Peer Review and Self-Assessment

Student-centered response, including both peer review and self-assessment, offers students an opportunity to develop the metalanguage of referencing. As students explain their reasons for reusing an idea, choosing to quote rather than paraphrase, or patchwrite, they develop the terminology they need to talk about referencing. Fluency with this language allows students to better negotiate their referencing decisions and may also result in better transfer of referencing skills from writing class to other contexts. Peer review also increases writers' independence and confidence.

While some L2 writing instructors may have mixed feelings about peer review, a fair amount of literature has indicated that it can be beneficial for L2 writers (Berg, 1999; Ferris, 2003; Liu & Hansen, 2002; Lundstrom & Baker, 2009; Rollinson, 2005). Peer review not only provides an opportunity for students to learn from the responses of different readers to their writing (Ferris, 2014), but it also provides an opportunity to practice reading and evaluating a draft in the way that experienced writers do. It works well when teachers provide the time and training necessary for students to learn to trust one another's feedback (Rollinson, 2005), carefully design response tasks and the composition of peer groups (Ferris, 2014), and model the process by first providing feedback on students' papers themselves (Liu & Hansen, 2002). Peer reviewers, like teachers giving feedback (Ferris, 2014; Stern & Solomon, 2006), should be selective. Teachers should structure peer review tasks around particular issues related to what has previously been taught, the goals of the class, and/or misunderstandings identified in dialogues, and monitor reviewers so that they do not get caught up in other concerns, such as correcting grammar.

The rhetorical functions of references and how they fit into the line of argument is a key element of feedback. Peer responders can be taught to make comments that help the writers learn to anticipate what a reader will understand (Knoblauch & Brannon, 2006); for example, "I find this hard to believe without supporting statistics." Peer responders can also be taught to reflect what they are reading in rhetorical terms (e.g., "What I see you doing here with this reference is illustrating the concept"). Students can also be shown how to give feedback on originality by commenting on those aspects of a paper that strikes them as unique to that writer, such as discussions of their own experiences.

Because of their familiarity with the same writing task, peers can give excellent feedback on how the paper fulfills the assignment. If the task is based on a set of source texts used by all of the students, peers are well positioned to say whether the student text is an accurate representation of the source, whether patchwriting is evident, and whether ideas from the sources are attributed. The type of response known as error correction may be usefully applied by peers to the formatting of in-text citations or misleading reporting verbs. It is probably best to have students respond to such concerns only on later drafts of a paper because research has shown that this is when error correction is most appropriate (Ferris, Liu & Rabie, 2011). Since research has shown that pointing out errors has more lasting effects than actually correcting them (Ferris, 2014; Li, 2010) and teachers may also be concerned about the students' ability to provide good corrections, we recommend asking peers to only point out possible errors.

In our experience, it is useful to use a buddy system to lay the groundwork for peer review. By pairing students early in the semester, each student is encouraged to invest not only in their own work but that of their partner. The buddies take a few minutes at the beginning of each class to check in with each other, sharing challenges and providing each other with ideas for tackling the current writing assignment (e.g., How is the new article you found fitting in with your argument?). These sessions can be guided by a set of questions, but they do not have to be, and the teacher can monitor the sessions and address issues that multiple pairs of students are grappling with. Once the buddies have established trust in this way, they become better peer reviewers on more structured tasks.

Self-assessment is another process that can help students develop the metalanguage of source use and independence in their writing. Self-assessment is particularly useful for revealing the "occluded features" of source use (Pecorari, 2006, 2013). Source use is "occluded" when it is hard to recognize that an idea or quote has been reused due to lack of conventional attribution. In self-assessment, students identify reused ideas so that they can be discussed. One method for doing this requires students to submit their sources with their drafts, with the reused parts highlighted, and to describe why they chose to quote or paraphrase a particular passage.

Matched text detection programs that look for matches in two or more electronic texts are popular today with teachers and students. Turnitin is the most popular of these programs, currently used in more than 10,000 institutions in more than 140 countries (Turnitin, n.d.). While these programs have been criticized for violating students' intellectual property (Foster, 2002; Marsh, 2004; Pecorari, 2013; Purdy, 2005; Vanacker, 2011) and creating distrust between instructors and students (Howard, 2007), they can be beneficial. Only a few studies have examined the use of matched text detection software for self-assessment of source use. One study of 141 L2 undergraduate writers at a U.S. university found that nearly 75 percent of students used technological tools (i.e., search engines and matched text detection software) to help them analyze the accuracy of their paraphrases, revise their citations, understand the concept of plagiarism, and reassure themselves that they were referring to sources conventionally (Bikowski, 2012). If students are already using such technological tools, it may make sense for teachers to scaffold their use. Another study presented the case of an undergraduate L2 writing course at a U.S. university that provided opportunities for student writers to analyze their source use and locate the original sources they had cited using Turnitin (Kostka & Eisenstein Ebsworth, 2014). The study found that the color-coding feature of the software reinforced the notion that an academic text should include a balance of the writer's words and reused material and made students aware of text matches that they might need to address, either through attribution or paraphrase.

## Connecting to the Classroom

This chapter discussed the usefulness of teaching students how to apply and respond to teacher feedback and how to become good reviewers for their peers and themselves. To achieve these goals, students need to take an active role in feedback processes. Students who assume that applying feedback is a simple matter of substituting in a correction, for instance, need to be shown that giving and applying good feedback entails making complex decisions. Six lessons to help students become more engaged in response are presented. Because giving and applying feedback is a routine part of teaching (cf. Lunsford & Straub, 2006), teachers may want to use them repeatedly throughout the term.

# Lesson 1:
# Making Sense of Teacher Feedback

**Focus:** Feedback—how to apply it

**Description:** Students read sample paragraphs with instructor feedback on source use and work together in small groups to figure out how to revise the paragraphs or to explain why they do not want to.

**Rationale:** There are several hurdles to making teacher feedback effective, such as having students read it, making sure they understand it, and making sure that they can apply it or can express why they do not want to. This lesson supports students in overcoming these hurdles by having them work on them together in class.

**Students:** All levels of L1 and L2

**Preparation:** Prepare several sample paragraphs with feedback for the students to read. These paragraphs could come from student work or examples you made up, but it is important that you write the feedback since the goal is to teach students how to communicate with you. Make the feedback selective and align it with a recent class lesson. You could address complex referencing issues such as using references for a clear rhetorical function, paraphrasing effectively, incorporating quotes, finding ways to include one's own ideas, or developing a line of argument.

**Procedure:**

1. Post the paragraphs with your comments in different stations around the room, divide students into small groups, and assign a paragraph to each group. Ask students in each group to work together to figure out how to respond to the feedback on their paragraph. They may choose either to revise or to give the reason that they choose not to revise, and they should write their response on the posted paragraph.

2. After 10–20 minutes, ask the groups to move to another paragraph and consider it along with both the teacher feedback and their peers' revision or response. If they like the revision or response, they should explain why in writing. If they do not, they should write a response and, if they see fit, a more effective revision.

3. Continue in this manner until all the groups have read all the paragraphs.

4. Reconvene as a class and have the groups discuss their decisions.

**Adaptations:** If you want to review a number of source use issues, prepare the sample paragraphs such that each one focuses on a different issue. Let one group work on each paragraph and present the issues and their solutions to the class.

# Lesson 2:
# Training for Peer Review

**Focus**: Feedback—how to give it

**Description**: Together, the instructor and the students read a sample student paper and write comments focused on a specific aspect of source use.

**Rationale**: Giving feedback requires the ability to recognize source use issues in a text. Since students need to be able to do this to revise their own writing and participate in peer review, this lesson models how to give feedback.

**Students**: Intermediate to advanced L2s; L1s

**Preparation**: Prepare a paper written by a student writing at about the same level as the students in the class and perhaps responding to the same assignment prompt. Choose a paper that illustrates the particular aspects of referencing you want to discuss. Sample 4 in Appendix 3 can be used; it was written by an L2 writer. Version A is an unmarked copy with no teacher comments; Version B illustrates feedback on the line of argument and integration of source texts; Version C illustrates feedback on incorporation of quotes.

**Procedure**:

1. Explain to the students that, when giving feedback, they should focus on a particular aspect of writing or source use and not respond to everything they see. Explain that they should not correct errors but describe and ask questions about the text; they should point out strengths as well as weaknesses.

2. Ask students to read the sample paper and make sure that they understand it.

3. Project a copy of the paper for the class so that you can highlight parts of it as you discuss them. If you are modeling response to a complex aspect of source use such as how to give feedback on line of argument and integration of sources, engage students in a careful second reading of the text. Focus the students on the basic structure of the paper, highlighting the structuring devices on the projected paper as you go.

4. Bring students' attention to the references. If using our sample, show students that the writer drew on three source texts (Zebroski, Romano, Renalds) to make the argument. Point out that each key element is discussed in its own paragraph and each paragraph draws on only one source. In other words, the writer did not synthesize information from several sources to discuss each element. Discuss how, for the first key element, the writer drew on the source to support what seems to be his idea that

"strong determination" is important to the success of intercultural marriages. Contrast that with elements two, three and four, which seem to be less the writer's own ideas as they all come from the same source. Finally, point out that the reference in the fifth key element ("self-disclosure") is used to specify Asian spouses, though no particular ethnicity is mentioned prior to this, and it is unclear why the writer has done so.

5. Work together with the students to decide what particular comments to make and where to make them in the text. Model the language to use, writing directly on the projected text. Some sample comments are provided on Version B of Sample 4 in Appendix 3.

6. Immediately after modeling how to comment on line of argument and source integration, allow students to comment on these things during peer review.

**Adaptations**: Use this lesson to model the smooth incorporation of quotes. Identify, together with the students, all the sentences in a sample paper that contain quotes. Then, go through them one by one, using Chapter 4, Lesson 6, to decide whether they are properly introduced and interpreted. Model the writing of comments for a few quotes, and ask the students to break into small groups to write comments for the remaining ones. Examples of comments on quotes are provided in Version C of Sample 4 in Appendix 3.

# Lesson 3:
# Peer Review:
# Working with Common Sources

**Focus**: Source use—peer review

**Description**: Students read their writing partners' papers, give feedback on a specific aspect of source use, and either apply or respond to their partners' feedback on their own papers.

**Rationale**: Peer review helps students develop independence in their source use decisions. Furthermore, when students in a class write papers based on the same reading texts, their knowledge of the readings places them in a good position to respond to one another's source use. This lesson, therefore, has students draw on that knowledge to provide focused feedback and respond to it.

**Students**: Intermediate to Advanced L2s; L1s

**Preparation**: Students should make their drafts available to a writing partner; they could exchange papers by email, upload them to a course website, or give their partners an extra print copy. Also, choose the aspect of source use that you want the students to focus on and prepare guidelines for them to use when writing feedback. You could, for example, choose one of the following three types of focus and sets of guiding questions:

## a. Accuracy

- Does the paper reflect the meaning of the source as you understood it?
- If there is a summary, does it capture the overall meaning or does it seem to overemphasize a detail?
- If there is a quotation, is it exact?
- For quotes and paraphrases: Does the text give enough of the original context that the source text is not misrepresented?

## b. Attribution

- Based on your own knowledge of the source texts, are there any instances of unattributed source use?
- For summaries and paraphrases, can you tell when the reused idea begins and ends?
- If the source text contained ideas or quotes from someone who was not the author, is it clear in the student paper whose ideas or words they are?
- Is there a citation for every quotation? For every paraphrase?
- Does every quotation have quotation marks?
- Do the citations all contain the last name of the author and the year of publication?
- Do the citations contain page numbers (if necessary)?
- Does each citation have a corresponding entry in the reference list?

## c. Rhetorical Functions

- What is the main argument of the paper?
- How does the reused information relate to the main argument? Does the reference:
  - provide an example or illustration?
  - support a claim or build authority by citing an expert?
  - support a claim by providing data or evidence?

- support a claim by showing that the idea has already been published?
- support a claim by providing a supporting argument?
- show a gap that the writer intends to fill?
- describe the context for the argument?
- cast doubt on someone else's argument?
- direct readers to more information?

**Procedure**:

1. Ask students to read one another's papers and discuss them to make sure that they understand them; this is best done face-to-face.

2. Then, using their intimate knowledge of the source texts, students will write comments about source use. It is important that they give written feedback because sometimes oral peer review sessions turn into chatting sessions and also so that teachers can collect the written feedback and assess it. Students can write their comments outside of class.

3. Give the partners time in class to discuss the feedback and apply or respond to it.

**Adaptations**: Follow the peer review session with a self-assessment memo. Focusing on the rhetorical functions of references, the students write a memo discussing similarities and differences between their partner's and their own source use.

# Lesson 4:
# Bringing Source Use Decisions to Light

**Focus**: Source use—self-assessment

**Description**: Working with a paper they are writing, students choose three sentences with reused ideas, describe their source use decisions for each, and discuss the sentences and decisions with their writing partners.

**Rationale**: Students are often not sure about how their teachers expect them to use sources, and some aspects of their source use may not be visible in their papers. This lesson, therefore, provides an opportunity for students to initiate discussions of aspects of source use that they are unclear about. It also allows teachers to view students' referencing decisions not to cite.

**Students**: Intermediate to Advanced L2s; L1s

**Preparation**: Prepare a handout with these guiding questions:

a. Is there a sentence in which you reused a part of a source, but you weren't sure whether it was better to quote or paraphrase? If so, which did you choose? How did you make the choice? How might the other choice have changed the effect of your writing?

b. Is there a sentence in which you wrote a paraphrase, but you were not confident about it? If so, what worried you? accuracy? grammar?

c. Is there a sentence that you wrote containing an idea that you are not sure is your idea or not? What made you unsure?

d. Is there a sentence that you wrote for which you weren't sure if you needed a citation? What made you unsure? Did you use a citation?

e. Is there a sentence that you wrote using an idea from a source that you weren't sure if you should use? What was the source? What made you unsure about it?

f. Is there a sentence that you wrote in which you used words from a source because you thought the writing style was good? Or because you didn't have the vocabulary to say the idea in another way? Or because you liked the sentence structure of the original? If so, did you use quotation marks? Why or why not? Did you use a citation? Why or why not?

g. Is there a sentence that you wrote with information or words that you memorized a long time ago? If so, can you remember the source? Did you cite it?

h. Is there a sentence with an idea that you got from a classmate, teacher, friend, tutor, roommate, or the internet? If so, did you cite it? Why or why not?

i. Is there a sentence with an idea of your own that you are worried might be mistaken for prototypical plagiarism? Why do you think it might be mistaken?

Also, remind students to bring copies of their papers to class.

**Procedure**:

1. Ask students to highlight the sentences in their papers that are based on ideas or words drawn from sources, including sentences that contain in-text citations as well as those that do not.

2. Students should select three sentences from among the highlighted ones and respond to one of the sets of the guiding questions for each. Then they should write their responses so that you can collect them.

3. Ask students to compare notes with their writing partners.

**Adaptations**: After this lesson, students can write a memo in which they compare their source use to other approaches, as expressed in the quotes from students in Chapter 2, Lessons 2 and 4.

# Lesson 5:
# Turning Turnitin into Opportunities for Self-Assessment

**Focus**: Attribution and patchwriting—self-assessment

**Description**: Students use Turnitin to identify instances of matched text in a paper they are writing; then they explain if they intended each instance to be a quote, paraphrase, or their own words and make revisions.

**Rationale**: Teachers may not recognize problematic textual reuse in student papers if there is no citation, and students may not recognize it because they have idiosyncratic understandings of attribution. This lesson, therefore, identifies instances of textual reuse, providing an opportunity for students to improve both their understandings of attribution and their abilities to produce conventional references.

**Students**: All levels of L2s; L1s

**Preparation**: Arrange for classroom access to computers, either students' laptops or a computer lab. Make sure that you have institutional access to Turnitin. (If you do not, suggestions for using other websites or for working on paper are given in the Adaptations section.) If you are not familiar with the Turnitin website, watch the instructor video at https://guides.turnitin.com/01_Manuals_and_Guides/Instructor/01_Instructor_QuickStart_Guide. Prepare a handout with guidelines for making citing decisions:

- ❑ Reused idioms (*go hand in hand, shift gears, bottom line, big picture*), collocations (*stimulate circulation, successive generations, limited resource, bridge the gap*), and formulaic phrases (*For this reason, The purpose of this study is to…*) do not require attribution.

- ❑ Terminology of a field (multiword vocabulary) (*carboxylic acids, bilabial fricative, subject position*) does not require attribution, unless the writer is comparing or contrasting different terms to make a point or the writer does not demonstrate mastery of the topic.

- ❑ Turns of phrase unique to an author require attribution, even when they are not whole sentences.

- ❑ Attribution rules are the same for internet sources as they are for print sources.

- ❑ Paraphrases should change both the vocabulary and the sentence structure of the sentence in the source text.

- ❑ Sometimes you need to use quotes around just a word or a phrase, rather than around the whole sentence.

**Procedure**:

1. Orient students to what Turnitin does (matches text) because if the students have heard about the site and think it checks for prototypical plagiarism, they may feel anxious about using it. Introduce the students to Turnitin by showing an originality report from a previous semester and pointing out that the text is highlighted, with each color matched to a particular source, and that the percentage listed on the top right refers to the percentage of the student's overall text that is matched to other sources. The student training video on the Turnitin website (www.turnitin.com/en_us/training/student-training) may also be helpful.

2. Assign students to submit a draft of a source-based paper that they are writing to Turnitin to generate an originality report. (Since this takes time, you may want to continue with Step 3 on another day.)

3. Hand out the guidelines for making citing decisions, and ask students to examine the matches listed in the report one at a time. For each, they should explain whether they intended the sentence to be a quote, paraphrase, or their own words. If they intended it to be a quote, they should make sure that they used a citation and quotation marks. If they intended it to be a paraphrase, they should make sure that they used a citation and work on revising to make it more effective through substitution of vocabulary, sentence restructuring, and/or by some quoting words or phrases. If they intended it to be their own words, they should make sure that the matched text is reusable language such as common vocabulary, an idiom, collocation, or formulaic phrase. As the students work in class, they should consult with you or with one another as questions arise.

4. Examine the text matches that the students do not believe require attribution to see if you agree. You may want to review attribution expectations that the students are not familiar with.

5. Ask students to incorporate the revisions into their paper drafts.

6. Collect anonymous feedback from students about the lesson and discuss any misgivings they may have about using Turnitin.

**Adaptations**: If you do not have access to Turnitin, use a major search engine (e.g., Google or Bing) to locate text matches and/or use a free "plagiarism checker" website (e.g., http://plagiarisma.net/; http://www.plagiarismchecker.com/). You can also require students to check their attribution decisions on paper. Ask students to find a part of their paper that has some source use and number ten consecutive sentences. Then, on a separate piece of paper, the students should list their reasons for citing or not citing each sentence. By using ten consecutive sentences, it is likely that there will be sentences with and without citations. In this way, the idea that a citation may not be needed if the attribution remains clear from the previous sentence is also addressed.

# Lesson 6:
# Promoting Independence
# with the Purdue OWL

**Focus**: Source use—self-assessment

**Description**: Students explore the Purdue OWL website (https://owl.english.purdue.edu/) and complete a task that requires them to use information on source use from the website.

**Rationale**: Student writers need to gain independence in making good source use decisions. This lesson, therefore, familiarizes them with the Purdue OWL, a widely used website that provides information on many aspects of source use.

**Students**: Intermediate to Advanced L2s; L1s

**Preparation**: Before doing this lesson, explain to the students that different referencing style guides, such as APA, MLA, and Chicago, are used in different disciplines, by different publications, or by different teachers. Suggest that the students find out which style most of the teachers in their major courses use so that they can focus on learning that style. As homework, students should spend some time familiarizing themselves with the Purdue OWL website and should describe, in writing, the major sections of it.

**Procedure**:

1. Ask students to work in pairs to complete a scavenger hunt, searching for the answers on the Purdue OWL. Sample questions relevant to source use might include:
   - How many different style guides are provided on the website? List their names.
   - Where would you go if you had a question about formatting an in-text citation in APA format? Give the title of the page and the URL.

- Where would you go if you needed to create a reference page entry for an edited book in MLA format? Give the title of the page and the URL.

- Where could you find paraphrasing exercises? Why do you think these exercises were placed in the section they were in?

- In the research section, what different elements are listed for evaluating a source? (Hint: there are more than 10 bullets!)

- How are the differences between quoting, paraphrasing, and summarizing explained?

- What are some of the "intellectual challenges" of U.S. academic writing that the site discusses?

2. Ask students to complete a task using the website.

- Read the section about paraphrasing, quoting, and summarizing, and then practice summarizing the sample essay provided on the website.

- Look up how to format a reference page and apply the formatting to sources they are using in a paper.

- Write a full reference for a book, journal article, article in a book, and/or website that you are using in class in a particular style.

3. To check that students are indeed learning to navigate the website, require them to cite the URL they used to complete the task.

**Adaptations**: If you do not have internet access, help students gain independence in making source use decisions by familiarizing them with a print style guide.

## Take-Away Points

- Learning to use sources is a process that requires practice and feedback, as well as exposure to concepts and rules.

- The best way to practice effective referencing is in the context of one's own writing.

- Feedback on source use should be non-punitive and positive in tone, whether among peers or between the student and instructor.

- Formative feedback should be ongoing and integrated into the work of the class.

- Students should be taught how to respond, how to negotiate referencing issues, and how to apply feedback when making revisions.

- Teachers should seek to understand the reasoning behind the source use decisions that students make; having a dialogue is a good way to achieve this.

- Student-centered response, including peer review and self-assessment, helps students develop the metalanguage of source use and makes them more independent as writers.

- Self-assessment can reveal the occluded referencing features in students' texts.

# 7

# Bringing It All Together:
## Teaching the Dimensions of Source Use

FIVE DIMENSIONS OF SOURCE USE HAVE BEEN PRESENTED because we believe that, if we want students to use sources effectively, then teachers must focus on much more than just how to avoid prototypical plagiarism. Teachers need to lay the basis for source use through a discussion of the concepts that underlie Western approaches to it. They should address the use of sources from a rhetorical perspective, with respect for the intricacies of language at the sentence level and an understanding of the reading-thinking-writing processes that allow writers to repurpose source ideas and integrate them into an argument. They should also promote dialogue around contextualized practice.

Writing instructors can help students with all of these dimensions, but students need more time to master them than any teacher has in one term. In her longitudinal study of the literacy development of one undergraduate named Yuko, Spack (1997) found that it was not until her third year in college that Yuko developed the understandings fundamental to effective source use, that "acquisition [of academic discourse] involves being engaged in a process of constructing knowledge" (p. 44) and "that referring to published authorities was tied to critical thinking; for in selecting key points...she could analyze an author's stance toward a subject" (p. 46). This was true despite the fact that Yuko had entered as a first-year student with a quite high English proficiency score (640 on the paper-based TOEFL®). Because the development of these understandings takes so much time, we need to set realistic goals for the progress that can be made in one term and celebrate even the small successes we see our students achieve.

This final chapter describes how each of the authors has selected and used some source use lessons in the writing courses we teach. Although effective source use is just one aspect of writing, the descriptions presented emphasize the source use aspects of our courses. The courses are similar in that they were all for L2 writers and at four-year U.S. universities, but they differ in significant ways. The first course described is a first-year college composition course, the

138

second is an upper-level (primarily third- or fourth-year) L2 writing course with a required research paper, and the third is a graduate writing course.

What these descriptions reveal is that, although each of us uses lessons from all five dimensions, we focus on certain ones that are appropriate to the courses we teach:

- In her first-year college composition course, Jennifer aims to introduce students to the basics of college-level writing, so she begins with an assignment that encourages students to develop their own ideas and connect them with ideas from sources. Then, because she wants to give students the knowledge and skills they will need to avoid prototypical plagiarism accusations, she goes on to focus primarily on the concept and sentence dimensions.

- In her L2 writing course that focuses on the research paper, Zuzana leads with discourse lessons that focus on academic writing as a conversation in order to help students visualize the endproduct of the assignment that they will work on all term. She also draws heavily on process dimension lessons to carefully scaffold the reading-thinking-writing processes essential for producing a good research paper.

- In her graduate writing course, Ilka has yet another approach: because her students are on their way to becoming scholars, she begins with a discussion of prototypical plagiarism and then promptly takes up the peer review lessons from the response dimension that will allow her students to build independence and learn to respond to referencing issues in both their peers' writing and their own. Ilka also finds it necessary to teach lessons on citing, paraphrasing, and prototypical plagiarism, despite the fact that such topics are considered by some teachers to be basic.

The descriptions of the three courses also reveal commonalities, such as the fact that we all use assignments that serve multiple purposes because we so often feel strapped for time: Jennifer's second major writing assignment has students learn about different attitudes toward "plagiarism" while at the same time practicing synthesizing ideas from multiple texts; Zuzana's first lesson, What Does Our Class Believe? not only shows the students that referencing is a way of capturing the conversation of a discourse community, but it also serves as an icebreaker to help the students get to know one another; Ilka's lesson on peer review aims to prepare students to be excellent reviewers while providing models of source-based papers for analysis.

We hope that the ways we have found to efficiently integrate lessons from the dimensions into our courses will offer teachers ideas for designing their own courses and that teachers can develop lessons in the book to complement the material in textbooks or simply use these lessons in the absence of a good textbook on source-based writing.

## Teaching the Basics: Jennifer's Approach

### "I haven't done any writing since fourth grade—and then it was just paragraphs."

For the past several years, I have been systematically surveying my first-year college students about their past experiences writing in school. My purposes were to improve my teaching by better meeting the students' needs, to explore cultural differences in approaches to teaching writing, and to gather data that I could use to suggest to administrators that students really do need to be taught about prototypical plagiarism. I was prepared to learn that my students differed widely in their past experiences—to learn, for instance, that some students had written a variety of essay genres and could converse in a sophisticated way about form and style while others had cut-and-pasted entire research papers that were accepted by their teachers, and many had written only as a form of knowledge display and never to develop their own thinking. I was also prepared to learn that none of my students had ever used Western-style attribution (in-text citations paired with a reference page) and that many had never used any type of attribution at all. I was not prepared to discover that so many students had never written anything longer than a paragraph.

How could I design an L2 college composition course that fulfilled the requirements of the English departmental syllabus to teach expository writing to students so diverse in terms of their writing background? How could I balance learning to develop one's ideas in writing with learning to write from sources?

As I forged ahead, what I saw over the semesters in terms of source use was two things: (1) students working hard to develop their own ideas in writing with a lot of attribution errors and patchwriting and (2) students who became so overwhelmed by course demands that they resorted to full-scale copying or cheating. I found myself wanting to protect the former group from the institutional plagiarism policy and to punish the latter group. I know that the difference in these behaviors does not stem from differences in the students' ethical convictions. I know that both behaviors are heavily influenced by things beyond individual students' immediate control, such as the assumptions about source use that influence university policy (including the erroneous belief that students know what "plagiarism" is and know how to avoid it), differences in the role that writing plays in schooling in different countries (that leave many students unfamiliar with U.S. source use expectations), and, perhaps most important, the globalizing knowledge economy (that values going to college in an English-speaking country). Despite knowing these things, in more than 25 years of teaching, I have not resolved the difficulties of teaching source-based writing and have, in fact, come to see new ones, which have motivated me to write this book.

## Context

My college composition course is housed in the English department, which offers mainstream and ESL sections of the course (as well as stretch, hybrid, and online sections). Students find their way into my course in a number of ways. Most are newly accepted first-year students coming directly from countries abroad; they have met the university admission requirement of a score of 61 on the internet-based TOEFL® or a 5.5 on the IELTS. As incoming students, their schedules are made up for them so most take composition right away. Because they are L2 international students, the admissions office directs them to the ESL sections. Other students have just finished at the university intensive English program and are placed into the course by the faculty there, after scoring a 500 on an in-house paper TOEFL® test. Unfortunately, L2 immigrant students are not identified by admissions, so they are not told about the ESL sections of first-year English and do not tend to find their way there. Once in my course, we have 75 minutes together twice a week for 15 weeks.

## Course Goals

The goals of the course are shaped by the university, the department, and my own commitments. Since the course is one of two first-year core requirements for graduation, the other being a first-year seminar that "covers" the research paper, I am supposed to focus more on writing and less on research skills. In addition, the departmental syllabus that assures that all sections of first-year composition (150 or so per year) have something in common requires that I teach (or, actually, assess) mechanics and how to develop a line of argument and support it using sources. My own commitments involve goals that can be divided into four categories:

1. **process writing goals**—helping L2 writers learn to develop their own writing processes and become more fluent in writing

2. **rhetoric/genre goals**—teaching the language of writing for students to take with them to upper-level courses and teaching the rhetorical relationships among topic, purpose, writer, reader, and form

3. **source use goals**—teaching students how to evaluate reading texts for credibility so that they begin to think of writing less as mastery of facts gleaned through reading and more as weighing claims of one author against claims of others, and giving students the tools they need to defend themselves against charges of "plagiarism"

4. **thinking goals**—challenging students to think more deeply, more analytically, more critically, and with less bias.

With these myriad goals, the course touches on all of the dimensions of effective source use. However, I find that at this level I am most focused on teaching the concepts behind Western understandings of effective source use.

## Teaching the Dimensions

The syllabus I describe is structured around three units, each based on a major writing assignment. Each unit has its own topic because I have found that my students prefer not to stay with one theme the entire semester. In the first unit, students focus on developing their own lines of argument and they write a reference page. In the second unit, they work on in-text citations, one-sentence summaries, how to qualify claims, and the concepts of originality and "plagiarism." They also revise their source use in response to my feedback and discuss the difference between patchwriting and effective paraphrase. In the third unit, students learn to evaluate the credibility of sources, read for the rhetorical functions of sources, and use *I* to establish authority. They also learn how to introduce source texts and incorporate quotes and paraphrases, and they use peer review or self-assessment to improve their own source use.

In each unit, I assess intermediary tasks, response tasks, and source use tasks in addition to the major paper. I grade the papers holistically. For Papers 1 and

3, the primary things I look for are students' development of their own analyses and a clear line of argument; for Paper 2, which is a dialogue, I primarily look for synthesis of ideas. For all three papers, I also pay attention to whether the students support their claims with explanations and examples, accurately represent the source texts, write in an organized and coherent way, follow directions, apply class lessons, and make progress between drafts.

## Unit 1

Because I have students who have never developed an argument and because I want to establish that the purpose of writing in my course is not knowledge display, I always begin with an informal writing task to engage students by asking them to write about their own lives. Then, I connect this to the first major writing task, which is an application assignment that has the students do their own thinking and connect it to their own experiences. The topic for the first unit changes each semester in response to student interests and what's going on in the world.

In addition, because there is so much to cover when it comes to attributing sources, I introduce the reference page. I start with this because most students know about reference pages even if they cannot produce them. I find that the students need quite a bit of background information: they need vocabulary (*volume, issue number, initials, hanging indents, alphabetical, entry*), and they need to understand the various genres of the source texts they will cite (journal articles online, websites, articles in books, whole books). After reviewing this information and the basic formats of reference page entries, students work in class to gather the information they need to write references for their sources. This class is workshoppy and productive, with students conferring with one another and with me. In the first unit, I also encourage students to use in-text citations if they can, but I don't grade them on doing so because it hasn't been taught yet.

## Unit 2

Recently, I made the concepts of originality and "plagiarism" the topic of the second major writing assignment so we could explore them in depth. (For other approaches to making textual reuse a course topic, see Bloch, 2012; Robillard, 2008.) I find Chapter 2, Lesson 2: That's What I Do! Relating to Other Writers' Source Use (pages 22–23) invaluable for establishing a non-judgmental framework for our discussions of source use. Then, the students read several texts about originality in writing and textual reuse, including the academic integrity policy of our institution. They learn things that surprise them in this policy, such as the fact that, if one student copies the paper of another, both are considered to have cheated, that copying from a paper that you wrote before is considered cheating, and that making mistakes in attribution or patchwriting is considered to stem from a lack of integrity. We also discuss why some people get really upset about prototypical plagiarism and how patchwriting and unconventional attribution may be usefully distinguished from cheating. Sometimes we also use Chapter 4, Lesson 1: Patchwriting (pages 78–81) to look at patchwriting in more detail.

I help students structure their reading processes by asking them to take notes in a chart that distinguishes quotes from paraphrases and their own ideas. We also discuss the readings in class so that I can help students digest them and choose ideas to use in their papers. For every source text, we do a version of Chapter 4, Lesson 3: One-Sentence Summaries (pages 84–86) to make sure that the students understand the main points of the texts and are not just cherry-picking sentences from them for reuse in their writing. In this unit I also begin the discussion of when to cite, using Chapter 2, Lesson 4: Discussing Reasons to Cite: Attribution and Common Knowledge (pages 25–27), and when I grade the major paper, I look for in-text citations in addition to a reference page. Usually after students have written their first drafts, I use Chapter 3, Lesson 5: How Much Will Readers Accept? Avoiding Overgeneralizations and Unfair Claims (pages 55–59) and ask students to apply this lesson in their revisions.

The major writing assignment of the unit is from Chapter 2, Lesson 5: Differing Attitudes toward Textual Reuse (pages 28–30), which presents the students with a number of quotes about source use and then asks them to develop characters around the quotes and go on to write a dialogue between the characters. In this course, students work individually to compose the dialogue. They may write themselves into the dialogue if they wish, and they may pretend that their characters have read the same source texts about the constructs of originality and "plagiarism" so that they have something specific to discuss. This assignment not only develops the students' understandings of these constructs but provides an opportunity to synthesize ideas from a number of source texts.

An especially good excerpt from one of these dialogues is shown in Sample 1, Appendix 3. This writing, by JuiChun Chou, shows her ability to summarize one of our reading texts (Gladwell, 2004), to draw on her own experience to name some reasons that student writers reuse text, and to relate one to the other in support of her own argument, which is that student writers' textual reuse should not be considered "plagiarism." This excerpt from JuiChun's paper demonstrates a strong ability to establish authority and synthesize ideas:

*Jean:*      "Sometimes I see students use a significant amount of words or sentences from another source, almost made me believe this was plagiarism. However, when I saw the result or the idea coming out of it, which was totally different from the original, it was totally acceptable. They maybe used the same vocabulary because of the limitation of their knowledge of the language, or they think the way other people are saying it is valuable, instead of paraphrasing or alternating with other words, they decided to go with the original. Yet the conclusion or the idea came out of it was totally amazing and brand new. Do you call plagiarism? I don't think so."

*Zeke:*     "Can you explain further about this? I don't quite understand."

*Jean:*      "Sure. For example, there was a Broadway show called *Frozen*, which was supposedly written by Bryony Lavery. However, a journalist whose name is Gladwell found out the work of his, called *Damaged* was tremendously used in *Frozen* without his permission in advance. You would think he must be angry, but he wasn't. Surprisingly, he was appreciative and glad that Lavery took his work and reproduce it. Even though his idea and words were taken from his work, Lavery interpreted it in a totally different way and created a brand new story line to wow the audience. If it was shown in his original way, would it have the same effect? Probably not. Thus, when we are talking about plagiarism, you can look at it from a very different angle." (Gladwell, 2004)

## Unit 3

The topic of the final unit changes but is always a complex issue that requires deep analysis, such as homelessness, exile, an environmental issue, or the politics of English (see Mott-Smith, 2016). It is designed around a writing task that brings together the basic skills for producing a good piece of source-based writing at this level. The students all read the same source texts and we evaluate them using a version of Chapter 5, Lesson 1: Can I Trust This Text? Evaluating the Credibility of Sources (pages 106–107). I also try to find a source text with good references that I can use to begin a discussion of the rhetorical functions of references. Then the students are given a choice about how to approach the writing task; they can write a persuasive, analytical, or personal essay, as long as it draws on the source texts. As they draft, I teach them how to use one-sentence summaries to introduce their sources, and using Chapter 4, Lesson 6: Introducing and Interpreting Quotes (pages 89–92) how to recontextualize their quotes. For some students, knowing how to develop an entire paragraph around one quote helps them understand how they can make their paper long enough and have enough to say without reading multiple additional sources. I look for both one-sentence summary introductions of source texts and well-incorporated quotes when I grade their papers.

I also use Chapter 3, Lesson 6: Exploring Academic Uses of *I* (pages 60–63) because I have found that most of my students prefer to avoid *I* and that this avoidance inhibits their ability to write smooth prose for this assignment. Because the students are all using the same source texts, we are able to make use of Chapter 6, Lesson 3: Peer Review: Working with Common Sources (pages 129–131). These classes become workshops in which students' understandings of conventional and effective referencing are applied.

## Connecting Experience with Theme-Based Source Content: Zuzana's Approach

**"Your paper is very good. Maybe a bit too good.**
**Did you write it yourself?"**

This seemingly simple question posed to me by my American literature professor at a university pre-service teacher training program in an EFL setting some two decades ago shaped my view of teaching writing from sources ever since. The question implied that I "plagiarized" or received outside help without which I would not be able to produce the paper. In the few seconds that it took the professor to articulate her accusation, the weeks I had spent reading, thinking, and writing were minimized and the final product I had felt so proud of devalued. I remember feeling hurt and angry. I remember my heart thumping as I searched for an appropriate response.

Truth be told, it is possible that my paper included copied or nearly copied chunks of source texts, which some may view as prototypical plagiarism. I did not keep the paper, so I cannot know for sure. What I do know, however, is that I did not copy and paste (in fact, I do not think I even knew how to do that at the time!). I also know that I read more sources than was required and that I spent countless hours thinking carefully about how I could synthesize the different sources while still saying something interesting about my topic. If I did do something inappropriate, it was because I did not know any better—the course focused solely on analyzing literary works and did not include examples of student papers or expected genres, opportunities for practice using sources, or peer and instructor feedback on early drafts. Somewhere between the feelings of hurt and injustice, I promised that as a future English teacher, I would find a better way to teach writing. It was not until just recently—when I developed and taught an undergraduate theme-based academic writing course while I was collaborating on this book—that I finally felt like I had.

## Context

The writing course that I find to be particularly successful is an upper-level undergraduate course housed in the ESL program, prior to which, most students complete a credit-bearing intermediate ESL writing course (though some are placed directly into the upper-level course). In the intermediate course, students use a limited number of sources in short academic essays with the key rhetorical function being to provide evidence for one's claims. The main assignment in my course, in contrast, is a six-page research paper with the minimum requirement of four scholarly sources.

The course typically meets for two 75-minute sessions a week. I devote a 45-minute portion of one of the sessions to working on the research paper. During the sessions when we are not working on the research paper, I highlight one or two issues that seem problematic for several students, model effective strategies and practices, and engage students in lessons from the five dimensions, further analysis of the readings, and peer review of each other's developing drafts. I find this format very effective because it allows me to organically tailor instruction to my students' needs as they emerge, rather than being tied to a writing textbook that dictates the progression of activities.

I typically base the course on a theme; the most popular theme so far has been volunteering. I like this particular theme for several reasons. First, as an advocate of service-learning pedagogy, I am aware of the linguistic, cultural, civic, and personal benefits that volunteering provides to international students, and I hope to implicitly encourage my students to volunteer and thus take advantage of such benefits. (During the term students can choose to attend one or more of three volunteering events.) Second, the theme lends itself to meaningful cross-cultural discussions, such as examination of cultural values, the role of government in providing welfare services for less privileged populations, and the view of poverty or disability across cultures, among others. At the same time, the theme is amenable to different "spins" that make it relevant to students from a variety of disciplines. I have also found that good scholarly texts on volunteering are easily accessible. Finally, my personal interest in the theme helps sustain my enthusiasm while teaching this course.

## Course Goals

The goals of the course come from an established syllabus in our ESL program and fall into four categories:

- **academic writing goals**—recognizing the characteristics of academic writing genres, improving fluency and accuracy in writing, and expanding key vocabulary and formulaic language common in academic writing
- **research writing goals**—developing effective strategies and processes employed during the reading-writing-thinking process; learning to identify, evaluate, and use academic sources; learning to summarize, synthesize, and critically analyze source materials; and following established citing conventions
- **revision goals**—ability to revise, edit, and proofread their and their peers' work
- **critical-thinking goals**—developing a greater awareness of one's own attitudes and thinking critically about the world.

The ability to develop an original line of argument and authorial voice is assumed rather than explicitly articulated in the syllabus, but my personal pedagogical goal is to foreground these concepts and make them integral to the course. I feel strongly that a deep engagement with the theme that includes a personal experience enhances students' authority and argument development.

## Teaching the Dimensions

The course typically begins with a writing sample that allows students to reflect on past experience with volunteering (or the reasons for lack thereof). Thus, from the start of the term, students are engaged in developing their own ideas about the theme. A follow-up discussion helps build background and interest in the course theme as does Chapter 3, Lesson 1: What Does Our Class Believe? Writing in a Mini-Discourse Community (pages 45–46), which is the first lesson from this book that I incorporate in my course. The lesson gives students an opportunity to interview classmates and collect sample quotes on volunteering (students often quote something they wrote in the writing sample) and repurpose them in a written paragraph that synthesizes information on a small scale. This efficient lesson is extremely well-received by the students. On a personal level they feel that they get to know their classmates, while on the academic level they are excited to put to use important academic phrases outlined in the lesson. I find that the lesson provides a perfect transition from writing in previous courses, where students generally drew upon few (if any) sources, to my advanced writing course, which centers on effective use of published sources.

Chapter 3, Lesson 2: Whose Idea Was This? (page 47) effectively builds on the first by framing academic writing as a conversation between scholars and introducing different functions of source use. For this lesson, I use a peer-reviewed article entitled "A Cross-Cultural Examination of Student Volunteering: Is It All About Résumé Building?" written by eleven authors from ten different countries (Handy et al., 2010) that reflects on the motivations of undergraduate student volunteers in their respective cultures. Beyond the practice in source use, the lesson and the text help build student background in the selected theme and provide one common source that we can refer back to as a community of writers.

Once students have a good grasp of the volunteering theme, we brainstorm possible topics or "angles" from which students could approach this theme in their own papers. I write the students' ideas on the board as they offer them, which models a basic way of organizing thoughts—something we examine in more depth later in the course. Then I ask that students pick two topics that seem interesting to them and do an exploratory source search for both topics, identifying at least one appropriate source per topic. The articles students bring to class are then used as a basis for source evaluation in a lesson that combines Chapter 5, Lessons 1, 2, and 3 (pages 106–107, 108–109, and 110–111). Students consider their identified sources in light of the four criteria outlined in these lessons—credibility, accessibility, relevance, and interest. This is helpful not only in reinforcing these criteria to the students, but also in helping them decide which of the two initially selected topics lends itself better to the course assignment. Students interested in the same topics are able to support each other throughout the semester by sharing sources and clarifying meaning. They become research buddies of sorts, invested in each other's work, often choosing to work together during group work and peer review tasks.

Given that the number of required sources is relatively small in this course, I insist on a careful digestion of sources and a clear articulation of authors' arguments. To make students accountable for such in-depth reading, I adapt Chapter 5, Lesson 4: Note-Taking Strategies for Different Writing Tasks (pages 111–112) by asking students to compare their notes on the first reading on volunteering that everyone in the class has read. I highlight effective reading strategies and prompt students whose notes seem lacking to interact with the text more by asking questions such as those highlighted in the lesson. I assess students' note-taking to reinforce the message that without an in-depth comprehension of source content, students cannot produce good research papers.

Once students complete their third reading, I introduce Chapter 5, Lesson 5: Idea Organizers: Tools for Digesting Content, Organizing Information, and Finding Connections (pages 112–114) using the idea organizers in Appendix 4 or an idea organizer for a paper I may be working on during the semester. As suggested in the follow-up to that lesson, students also prepare idea organizers based on their own texts and have opportunities to receive peer and instructor feedback.

I now encourage students to move forward with drafting as soon as they have read and digested the first three sources; in the past I used to suggest that students wait to start drafting their papers until after they had read all the sources and organized their ideas. The idea of drafting prior to fully completing the reading and organizing tasks may seem rushed or messy to some, but I have found that, in a course structured around the research paper, the advantages of doing so considerably outweigh the disadvantages. Students draft a paragraph or two during one class session and submit them to me as their instructor. I then select a manageable number of source-related issues and create materials and activities that target them; the students work on these in a subsequent class period. In the response-focused lessons, I utilize many ideas from Chapter 6, Lesson 3: Peer Review: Working with Common Sources (pages 129–131). The in-class peer review sessions are often followed by graded homework assignments focused on the specific source-related issue(s) addressed, practiced, and peer-reviewed in class.

Contrary to my own experience described at the beginning of this narrative where the instructor did not provide feedback until the final draft, breaking the assignment into manageable parts and observing and evaluating students' writing continuously provides students with ample support and formative assessment and helps avoid bad (or suspiciously good) surprises at the end of the semester. Additionally, when students produce writing regularly, it allows me to complement the Discourse and Process dimensions I focus on in the early part of the semester with the lessons from the Sentence, Concept, and Response chapters that are best aligned with the particular needs of my students.

It often becomes clear after the first round of drafting that most of my students need to think carefully about their source text language at the sentence level. Following our recommendations in Chapter 4, Lesson 1: Patchwriting (pages 78–81), I select samples (with students' prior permission) and ask groups of three to reflect on the source use in the examples utilizing the questions included in the lesson. I monitor the groups to make sure they are on the right track prior to leading a discussion on each example in front of the whole class. I highlight any positive aspects of students' writing that the groups may forget to mention because I find that it is useful to start with student examples that have strengths as well as areas that merit improvement. Doing so fosters a pedagogical rather than punitive atmosphere in the class. Time constraints often force me to adapt Chapter 2, Lesson 2: That's What I Do! (pages 22–23) only as a brief discussion of students' approaches to textual reuse and not a full-length lesson. Even a short discussion complements the patchwriting lesson very well, and I recommend that instructors consider doing these two lessons in tandem.

In the process of reviewing students' developing drafts, three more issues that I am able to address effectively with the lessons from this book frequently present themselves. Chapter 4, Lesson 6: Introducing and Interpreting Quotes (pages 89–92) is invaluable in helping students avoid unincorporated quotations and instead learn how they can weave quotes into their texts in ways that help further their argument. While the quote-building "formula" scaffolds students' paragraph development and presents them with concrete ways to incorporate ideas of other writers, many students continue to express frustration at not knowing how to be "more original." Therefore, I employ ideas from two lessons to address this concern. First, I adapt Chapter 2, Lesson 1: Developing Something to Say (pages 21–22) by modeling my own process of working with a source text for a paper on volunteering. The goal is to show students how I am precise in distinguishing my ideas from those of the source text. Using an overhead projector, I list the main points of the text as bullet points; then I add my own ideas in a different color font. Next, I choose a subset of points from the text and organize them in a different way, interspersed with my own, to match the focus I want to maintain in my paper.

The second lesson I use to show students how they can communicate their originality and thus distinguish their ideas from those of published authors is Chapter 3, Lesson 6: Exploring Academic Uses of *I* (pages 60–63). At this point in the semester, all of the students have either had a volunteering experience from their home cultures or have attended one of three suggested volunteering events announced in class. However, they often still struggle to make connections between these experiences and the sources on volunteering that they read. This is not so much because they do not see them, but because they have been warned against the use of *I* in past academic writing courses. The lesson is empowering to my students; the additions of *I* to their papers help establish their authority and, beyond that, appear to help students re-invest themselves in writing as the semester draws to a close and energy starts running low. The example given illustrates how one student established her authority as an opinion-holder by using the personal pronoun in her academic paper:

> And while volunteering cannot be an adequate enough solution, it can be one of ideas for conquering International students' spouses circumstantial difficulties in their sojourn. Fundamentally, I suggest it is required to revise the anachronistic and obsolete immigration law for ameliorating the conditions of ISS [International Student Spouses] under 'Zombie Visa.' By doing this, their volunteering could shine as the completely spontaneous and voluntary best plan, not the best alternative plan.

By the end of the semester, I have typically used about 13 lessons from this book, building most lessons around students' own attempts at using sources. My students appreciate the flexibility that the lessons provide and often comment on how helpful it is to work through the problems in their own work in class with the support of the handouts and PowerPoint presentations based on the lessons. Most of my students are able to produce high-quality papers that they often choose to present at the university's undergraduate research and/or ESL symposium. Every time I teach this course as described, I rejoice in my students' interest in volunteering both as an area that they can research and an activity they can meaningfully incorporate into their lives.

# Developing Independent Learners: Ilka's Approach

**"Chinese students copy and paste everything.
You have to keep an eye on them."**

The reason I became interested in researching source-based academic writing many years ago as a doctoral student was because of comments like these that I heard too often from other writing teachers. These kinds of stereotypical statements always made me cringe because I felt they were unfair and untrue, and I knew that there had to be more to the story. The more I have researched "plagiarism," taught academic writing, given workshops to other teachers, reflected on my own experiences writing graduate-level papers in a second language (German), and thought about the nature of source-based writing, the more I have come to appreciate the complexity involved. Academic writing is a multi-layered and complex skill, and it is one that all writers have to learn, practice, and continue to work on. No one is born an excellent academic writer!

Approaching source-based writing with a pedagogical mindset has completely changed the way I think about and teach source use. I hardly worry about prototypical plagiarism because I try as hard as I can to build in as much support, guidance, and feedback at every stage of the writing process. Over the years, as I have worked on these activities and honed my teaching, I have found that I seldom, if ever, encounter prototypical plagiarism. Along the way, I have also found myself advocating for L2 writers more than I ever did before. There are many misconceptions about international students similar to the ones I mentioned, which fuel a punitive mindset in teachers. I strongly believe that intimidating or warning them about "plagiarism" and "getting caught" is both ineffective and detrimental to learning. My focus is and will continue to be helping L2 writers become skilled and confident academic writers who are prepared to tackle any assignment they need to complete their academic studies.

## Context

My graduate course is situated in one of two pathways programs at the university that offer conditional admission to international students who need additional English language instruction before matriculation. Our programs separate undergraduate and graduate students but are taught by the same faculty and run by the same administration team. Students are required to take both

English language courses (integrated reading-writing and integrated listening-speaking) and content courses (e.g., philosophy, calculus, and history, among others), and they enroll in our programs for either one, two, or three semesters, depending on their English language proficiency placement test scores. Students must achieve a sufficient GPA and a particular score on a language proficiency test (as determined by their destination degree program) in order to leave the pathway program and matriculate to the university.

## Course Goals

The primary objective of the graduate L2 writing course I describe is to prepare first-semester master's students for the academic writing tasks they will encounter in their graduate studies, many of which are source-based assignments. The reading skills we work on in the course include finding and evaluating academic texts for credibility and relevance to the topic they will write about in their four main assignments; identifying rhetorical strategies (e.g., ethos, pathos, and logos); distinguishing fact and opinion; and determining a text's purpose, audience, and tone. The writing skills we focus on include embracing writing as an iterative process (i.e., writing and receiving feedback on multiple drafts and revising accordingly); organizing ideas logically and coherently; supporting claims by summarizing, paraphrasing, and/or quoting credible sources and qualitative data the students have collected; formatting papers according to MLA style standards; and editing for grammar, style, vocabulary, and mechanics.

## Teaching the Dimensions

Students write four sequenced assignments in the course, all of which center on the same topic that students choose and are connected in some way to students' intended major of study. We start the semester by talking about "plagiarism," and I use Chapter 2, Lesson 5: Differing Attitudes toward Textual Reuse (pages 28–30) to help students explore their understandings of source use. This activity is particularly useful for students in this course, as they have just arrived in the U.S. and have not yet taken any writing courses here. Although students in our programs hear about prototypical plagiarism and academic integrity policies at the beginning-of-semester program orientation, we know that students need much more conceptual background in order to avoid it. This lesson is an engaging way for students to get to know each other and delve more deeply into the notion of prototypical plagiarism by using the role-playing and adaptation.

Students write three drafts for every assignment and receive feedback from their peers and me on the first two drafts; the third draft is what students submit for a grade. Individual student-instructor conferences are also built into the course, which meets for six hours per week, and I meet with each student individually after they have written the first and second draft. During individual conferences, students work on peer review activities, exercises, quizzes, and/or reflective journals when not in a meeting with me. When we meet to discuss the second draft, I ask students to bring their first draft so I can see how they have incorporated the feedback they have received. Then, before students submit the final draft, I collect the first two drafts so I can see how they have incorporated the feedback from me and their peers. Once I have graded students' final drafts, I set up an online journal in our course management software and ask students to reflect on my feedback and on their progress.

One of the first activities I do with students at the beginning of the semester is prepare them for peer review, using Chapter 6, Lesson 2: Training for Peer Review (pages 128–129). I like to do this early in the semester since students engage in peer review for each of their assignments. I have learned that there is increased student buy-in for peer review when students can provide specific and useful comments on each other's drafts and when I read through the comments their peers have left to address any lingering questions and issues. Students also come to value the practice of peer review for both helping their peers and developing their own critical-reading skills. I began checking students' peer review worksheets because I have often heard from students that "peers aren't as good as the teacher"; nonetheless, I rarely have to "correct" what a peer has written on a student's paper. Students of all levels, when trained and prepared, can do an excellent job of providing feedback. Finally, I try to cultivate a sense of community among my students, and to do so, I often share my own working manuscripts so they can see that peer review is very much a common academic practice. This also helps students realize that peer review is a real activity and not one that writing teachers have come up with as busy work.

I also introduce students to Turnitin early on in the semester (sometimes even in the first week of class), as they submit every draft of each assignment to Turnitin. Teachers in our program are not required to use Turnitin; however, the majority of them do. I often find that most students in both my undergraduate and graduate courses have never heard of the program, yet they are usually curious and willing to learn more about it. The lesson we describe in Chapter 6, Lesson 5: Turning Turnitin into Opportunities for Self-Assessment (pages 133–135) is useful for ensuring that students learn to use the program to work *for* them, not against them. I pull up students' originality reports in the two individual conferences I have with them, and we go through each match to determine whether a revision has to be made (e.g., when a source is directly quoted but an in-text citation is missing). I also want students to feel comfortable using the program because many instructors in our program and at the university use Turnitin.

Because I want my graduate students to become independent learners, I like to familiarize them with the Purdue OWL early on in the semester using Chapter 6, Lesson 6: Promoting Independence with the Purdue OWL (pages 135–136). I have noticed in many classes that students do not have a consistent go-to resource (besides a course textbook) that they use while writing. I have also found that when I simply show students the Purdue OWL and include the link to the website in our course page, they do not use the website much and tend to forget about it. However, since asking them to peruse the website, explore each of its sections, and bookmark the page, I have found that they use the website far more often during the course of the semester. I have been pleasantly surprised on many occasions to hear students tell each other, "I'm not sure. Check the OWL." I have learned that if I want students to develop a habit of using a formatting guide, I need to show them how to do so and hold them accountable to it.

During the second week of the term, we begin preparing for the first assignment, in which students write an annotated bibliography paper of two credible sources that they choose. The assignment mirrors the skills that students will need to write a literature review, including finding and evaluating credible and relevant sources, summarizing, contextualizing information from sources within the broader topic, and creating a Works Cited page. This assignment is often the first time that students work with sources, so we spend quite a bit of time discussing why ideas have to be cited at all (Chapter 2, Lesson 4: Discussing Reasons to Cite: Attribution and Common Knowledge) (pages 25–27). I have found that students come to our program with a wide range of experiences and understandings of source use, so this lesson helps ensure that everyone begins the term on the same page.

As the second assignment, students write a survey report for which they design survey questions, create an electronic survey, distribute it, and describe their findings. The assignment's primary objective is to acquaint students with the skills of summarizing and analyzing data that they may need when conducting a quantitative or mixed-methods research study in graduate school. Chapter 4, Lesson 2: Language Chunks: To Rephrase or Not? (pages 81–84) aligns well with this assignment, particularly when using the adaptation focused on language chunks that refer to research (e.g., *The remainder of this paper will highlight…; From my findings, it is evident that…* ). I give students excerpts from different research articles to read, and they highlight and compile all of the academic language chunks into a Google doc and provide a brief explanation of how the language chunk was used in context. The students can then refer to their lists throughout the semester, as all information is stored in one place and accessible to everyone in the class.

The third assignment is an interview report, for which students interview a person with either expertise or extensive experience in their topic. Similar to the survey report, students create interview questions, arrange the interview, and describe their results in the paper. Because students include direct quotations from their participant, Chapter 3, Lesson 4: Reporting Verbs: Does the Writer Agree? (pages 52–54) is a useful activity for reinforcing the idea that writers need to be cautious about which verbs they use to refer to authors' ideas. Students are often surprised that they cannot use reporting verbs interchangeably. Interviewing a person face to face, rather than reading an author's words, helps students understand the nuances in the interviewee's attitudes and encourages them to use a variety of reporting verbs. For instance, if the interviewee made a clear and passionate assertion about his or her stance, the student could not write that the interviewee simply "mentioned" the topic; thus, the interview assignment is a good place to review the writer's stance activity that focuses on reporting verbs. I ask students to audiorecord the interviews so I can provide feedback both on their writing and on their interviewing skills. I also use Chapter 4, Lesson 4: Paraphrasing Detectives (pages 86–88) to work on paraphrasing, a skill that students need in this paper to report what their participant has said. My sense is that students feel less daunted by the idea of paraphrasing someone else's words after this lesson because they come to see paraphrasing as a real-life skill.

In the final assignment, students write an argumentative essay, choosing a controversial issue related to the topic they have researched all semester and writing a paper that takes a stance on that issue. Students are encouraged to use any of the data they collected during the semester (i.e., academic sources described in the annotated bibliography or additional ones, survey data, or interview data) to support their argument. Our lesson on hedging (Chapter 3, Lesson 5: How Much Will Readers Accept?) (pages 55–59) has helped students realize that they should not make overly general claims about their issue because this can undermine their credibility and misrepresent the author's claims. After doing this activity and generating the kinds of hedges they need, students are able to identify these kinds of statements in their papers and make revisions accordingly.

# Teaching Values

Despite the differences in teaching contexts and approaches, the courses we designed and teach demonstrate many of the same teaching values. For example, we all prefer authentic writing assignments: This is seen in Jennifer's decision to stop assigning the paper on "plagiarism" as an expository or analytical essay and to redesign it first as a letter to a friend thinking about coming to the U.S. to study and then as a dialogue between people with different positions. Zuzana's commitment to authenticity is clear in her use of the volunteering theme, which contextualizes the students' writing in their own volunteering experiences and allows them to choose subtopics that they feel passionate about. Ilka's final assignment, an argument essay, was designed specifically to give students experience with the authentic research writing processes that graduate students use, including conducting library and empirical research, synthesizing data, and taking positions.

In addition, we all draw on our own experiences as language learners. Jennifer's strongest second language is Japanese, and she has had experience writing in Japanese about teaching English for an audience of Japanese teachers; Zuzana's first language is Slovak, so she comes at the teaching of English from a nonnative English-speaking teacher perspective; and Ilka's first language is English, but she has both taught and pursued graduate studies in German, her second language. From these experiences, we gain empathy and our belief in teaching rather than punishing. These values translate into the classroom as commitments to scaffolding learning in as many ways as we can think of, including breaking large writing assignments into smaller, more manageable ones; modeling processes in class; holding conferences; continuing to create new lessons and materials; encouraging students to make use of the resources available to them, including writing tutors and online information; and, of course, sharing our own writing experiences as both L2 academic writers and language learners.

Most important, we value students—their cultures, their experiences, their ideas, and their ways of writing. We would never want students' non-deliberate act of breaking the rules to lead to expulsion, and we are committed to advocating for L2 writers by discussing these issues with teachers of disciplinary courses; developing resources, such as writing centers, that can support them throughout their college careers; and serving on academic "honesty" committees to ensure that they have advocates at the institutional level. Nor would we would ever want adherence to referencing conventions to eclipse students' development of ideas. We believe that its is possible for everyone to express their ideas in academic discourse, but we know that it can be harder for some than for others. To encourage the development of students' ideas, we seek to open dialogues in which we discuss various ways to construct texts rather than imposing Western conventions. It is when students become aware of the assumptions behind the Western conventions that they feel empowered to search for their own balance between adhering to them and pushing the envelope to advance both their own rhetorical purposes and their professional careers.

## Final Thoughts

As we did the research for this book, we were struck by how many of the common, hegemonic understandings of concepts related to source use are erroneous. The most obvious of these is that "plagiarism" is always deceitful, but there are many others, including that "plagiarism" is one, identifiable behavior; that people can agree on individual instances of it; that common knowledge is the same in all contexts; that it's easy to tell whether an idea is your own or someone else's; and that good writers never copy. It was brought home to us that if we want to become good teachers of effective source use, we need to root out assumptions like these in our teaching materials and in our own minds.

In researching the book, we were also struck again and again by how little is actually known about effective source use. We found that further research is needed to understand how writers do many things, including how they decide whether to cite or not, choose to quote or paraphrase, and transform ideas. Research is also needed to ascertain how teachers define "plagiarism" and how referencing expectations vary from person to person, genre to genre, and discipline to discipline. And we found that research is needed on teaching source-based writing, including how best to teach students who feel that the requirement to cite squelches their voices and what role patchwriting might play as a strategy for teaching and learning academic discourse. We realized that, as research goes forward, we will need to continue to think about effective source use and redesign our lessons.

Countless times as we wrote this book, we found ourselves asking, shall we use a citation here or claim this as our own? And many times, as we read over notes, we realized that we had a citation that we had not included. The process brought home to us the very complex process of balancing ideas that one claims as one's own with references to source texts. In the Chapter 3, we argued *both* that using references establishes a writer's authority by showing that she or he is informed *and* that using the first person establishes authority by showing that a writer is the originator of ideas. If both moves establish authority, then how do writers choose which one to make? Reflections such as these on our own writing processes continue to inform how we teach, just as reflection on our teaching led to the writing of this book.

# Appendix 1: Lessons Chart

| Lesson | Focus | Description | Pages |
|--------|-------|-------------|-------|
| **Concept Lesson 1:** Developing Something to Say | Authority and originality | Students develop a line of argument on a controversial topic, drawing from their own experiences and two source texts. | 21–22 |
| **Concept Lesson 2:** That's What I Do! Relating to Other Writers' Source Use | Source use—different approaches | Students read L2 student writer remarks about their source use and discuss the remarks in a non-judgmental context. | 22–23 |
| **Concept Lesson 3:** When Is Attribution a Must? | Attribution—genre differences | Students read texts looking for ideas that may have come from other texts and note whether or not they are attributed; they then develop explanations for why the information is or is not attributed and draw conclusions about whether the source is credible for academic writing. | 24–25 |
| **Concept Lesson 4:** Discussing Reasons to Cite: Attribution & Common Knowledge | Attribution—common knowledge | Students read sentences from student papers that contain unattributed ideas and the explanations the students gave for not citing and consider whether they agree with the stated explanations or not. | 25–27 |
| **Concept Lesson 5:** Differing Attitudes toward Textual Reuse | "Plagiarism" — what is it? | Students read statements about "plagiarism" made by people with differing attitudes toward it; then they use their imaginations to develop characters around these statements and write dialogues between the characters. | 28–30 |

| Lesson | Focus | Description | Pages |
|---|---|---|---|
| **Concept Lesson 6:** Facing Charges of "Plagiarism" | "Plagiarism"— facing accusations | Students learn the definition of "plagiarism" and the process for adjudicating it as laid out in their institution's policy. Then, they analyze a case of textual similarity and apply the policy to the case by writing either a letter of appeal defending the student or a paper stating the case against him or her. | 31–35 |
| **Discourse Lesson 1:** What Does Our Class Believe? Writing in a Mini-Discourse Community | Referencing— introduction | Students write paragraphs summarizing data from a survey taken by their classmates. They use provided language to smoothly capture generalizations, contrasts, and similarities. They also include their own ideas and quote and cite their classmates. | 45–46 |
| **Discourse Lesson 2:** Whose Idea Was This? | Referencing— conversation in academic writing | Students highlight the ideas from different authors in different colors in a piece of academic writing in order to visualize academic writing as a conversation; they then evaluate the source use. | 47 |
| **Discourse Lesson 3:** What's the Point of Referencing Anyway? | Referencing— rhetorical functions | Students read several excerpted texts that refer to the same source and identify the rhetorical functions used in each. | 48–51 |
| **Discourse Lesson 4:** Reporting Verbs: Does the Writer Agree? | Vocabulary— reporting verbs | Students read sample sentences and determine the writer's stance toward the cited idea based on the choice of reporting verb and contextual cues; then they develop three lists of reporting verbs: verbs that indicate agreement, those that indicate doubt, and those that vary according to context. They use the lists to revise reporting verbs in their own writing. | 52–54 |

| Lesson | Focus | Description | Pages |
|---|---|---|---|
| **Discourse Lesson 5:** How Much Will Readers Accept? Avoiding Overgeneralizations and Unfair Claims | Hedging | Students read a text and compare it with claims based on it. They determine whether the claims are fair or not and whether they are overgeneralizations or not. They are introduced to hedges as a way of fixing unfair and overgeneralized claims. | 55–59 |
| **Discourse Lesson 6:** Exploring Academic Uses of *I* | Authority— first-person pronouns | Students locate the first person pronouns in a published text, categorize the uses, and learn that *I* can be used to establish authority and ownership of ideas. | 60–63 |
| **Discourse Lesson 7:** What Am I Supposed to Do? Differences in Referencing Expectations across Disciplines | Referencing— disciplinary differences | Students read samples of academic writing from different disciplines and contrast the referencing by examining citation type, reporting verbs, and use of quotes. | 63–64 |
| **Sentence Lesson 1:** Patchwriting | Patchwriting | Students do close readings of several samples of patchwriting and the corresponding source texts in order to identify copied words and similarities in sentence structure. They learn that effective paraphrasing involves making decisions about which words can be copied without attribution, about changing sentence structure, and about omitting specifics. | 78–81 |
| **Sentence Lesson 2:** Language Chunks: To Rephrase or Not? | Vocabulary— formulaic language | Students discuss writerly moves and identify formulaic phrases that accomplish these moves. They make lists of the moves and formulaic language for future use. | 81–84 |

| Lesson | Focus | Description | Pages |
|---|---|---|---|
| **Sentence Lesson 3:** One-Sentence Summaries | Summary | Students write and evaluate one-sentence summaries of several articles on the same topic; then they incorporate summary sentences in their own papers. | 84–86 |
| **Sentence Lesson 4:** Paraphrasing Detectives | Paraphrasing— models of good paraphrases | Students locate paraphrases in a sample student paper and identify citations and boundary markers; they then compare the paraphrases to the source sentences, identify the differences in syntax and vocabulary, and decide whether the representation is accurate and whether any additions to the meaning were made. | 86–88 |
| **Sentence Lesson 5:** You Be the Judge: How Close Is Too Close? | Paraphrasing— accuracy vs. copying | Students choose the most effective paraphrase from among a group of paraphrases, some of which are closer to the wording of the source text than others. | 88–89 |
| **Sentence Lesson 6:** Introducing and Interpreting Quotes | Quoting— incorporating quotes | Students write sentences to introduce a quote, attribute it, and interpret it. Then they put the sentences together into a partial paragraph. | 89–92 |
| **Process Lesson 1:** Can I Trust This Text? Evaluating the Credibility of Sources | Evaluating sources— credibility | Students apply criteria for evaluating credibility to a number of source texts and make arguments for which sources they would be comfortable using in a paper and which they would not. | 106–107 |
| **Process Lesson 2:** Can I Handle This? Evaluating the Accessibility of Sources | Evaluating sources— language accessibility | Using one of three electronic tools, students assess how difficult the vocabulary in several potential source texts is for them to understand. (An alternative technique developed for print sources is also given.) | 108–109 |

| Lesson | Focus | Description | Pages |
|---|---|---|---|
| **Process Lesson 3:** Do I Care? Choosing Interesting Topics and Relevant Sources | Evaluating sources—relevance and interest | Students choose paper topics that they are interested in and source texts that are on topic and that suit the scope of the assignment. | 110–111 |
| **Process Lesson 4:** Note-Taking Strategies for Different Writing Tasks | Note-taking | Students examine three note-taking strategies for the same text and consider which strategy would work best for writing a summary paper, a response paper, and an argument paper. | 111–112 |
| **Process Lesson 5:** Idea Organizers: Tools for Digesting Content, Organizing Information, and Finding Connections | Source use—integration | Students evaluate three types of idea organizers (graphic organizers, outlines, and charts) according to The Five Cs guidelines and develop their own organizers for a set of source texts; then they analyze the structure of the source texts and compare them to the argument structures that they developed. | 112–114 |
| **Process Lesson 6:** Revising to Integrate Source Ideas & Bring Out Your Own | Source use—integration | Students contrast two drafts of a piece of writing and analyze differences in the number of references, consider how the textual revisions connect to the writer's concerns, and trace the use of the writer's and source ideas in the line of argument in the revised draft. | 115–117 |
| **Response Lesson 1:** Making Sense of Teacher Feedback | Feedback—how to apply it | Students read sample paragraphs with instructor feedback on source use and work together in small groups to figure out how to revise the paragraphs or to explain why they do not want to. | 127 |

| Lesson | Focus | Description | Pages |
|---|---|---|---|
| **Response Lesson 2:** Training for Peer Review | Feedback— how to give it | Together, the instructor and the students read a sample student paper and write comments focused on a specific aspect of source use. | 128–129 |
| **Response Lesson 3:** Peer Review: Working with Common Sources | Source use— peer review | Students read their writing partners' papers, give feedback on a specific aspect of source use, and either apply or respond to their partners' feedback on their own papers. | 129–131 |
| **Response Lesson 4:** Bringing Source Use Decisions to Light | Source use— self-assessment | Working with a paper they are writing, students choose three sentences with reused ideas, describe their source use decisions for each, and discuss the sentences and decisions with their writing partners. | 131–132 |
| **Response Lesson 5:** Turning Turnitin into Opportunities for Self-Assessment | Attribution and patchwriting— self-assessment | Students use Turnitin to identify instances of matched text in a paper they are writing; then they explain if they intended each instance to be a quote, paraphrase, or their own words and make revisions. | 133–135 |
| **Response Lesson 6:** Promoting Independence with the Purdue OWL | Source use— self-assessment | Students explore the Purdue OWL website and complete a task that requires them to use information on source use from the website. | 135–136 |

# Appendix 2: Teaching Materials

## Print

Flaherty, C. (2014, May 13). New book, new allegations. *Inside Higher Ed*. Retrieved from www.insidehighered.com/news/2014/05/13/arizona-state-professor-accused-plagiarism-second-time

This medium-length article (2852 words) reports on a case of a history professor being accused of plagiarism. It contains side-by-side text comparisons that students could do close readings of. It could also be used to show how seriously academics take plagiarism. It has a short discussion of the American Historical Association's plagiarism standards, with a link to its Statement on Standards of Professional Conduct, which could be used to discuss standards of one academic discourse community.

Gladwell, M. (2004, Nov. 22). Something borrowed: Should a charge of plagiarism ruin your life? *The New Yorker*. Retrieved from www.newyorker.com/magazine/2004/11/22/something-borrowed

This long article (6537 words) relates the author's experience having his words reused and shows how his attitudes changed over time. It is useful for examining how transformation (repurposing ideas and text) makes textual reuse different from prototypical plagiarism, the fallout of plagiarism accusations, and the emotions associated with plagiarism from both the point of view of the person who reused text and the person whose text was reused. It can be excerpted.

Holtzman, A. (2009). Original misunderstanding. *Knowledge Quest, 37*(3), 62–64.

This short article (3 pp.) gives a high school student's perspective on his attempts to be original when writing a history paper. It shows how he moved away from the belief that he had to say something no one had ever said before to the belief that originality lies in how he constructs and supports his argument. It is useful because it approaches originality from a student perspective and argues that the Romantic notion of originality is not relevant to student work.

Howard, R.M. (1995). Plagiarisms, authorships, and the academic death penalty. *College English, 57*(7), 788–806. Excerpt: "A PROPOSED POLICY ON PLAGIARISM" (pp. 798–802).

Howard's "proposed policy on plagiarism" makes several moves that are not commonly found in institutional plagiarism policies, including suggesting that it is not possible to write completely new work; distinguishing cheating, non-attribution, and patchwriting as three types of plagiarism; suggesting that some forms of plagiarism are not deceitful; offering advice to students for avoiding plagiarism; and proposing pedagogical responses to non-deceitful plagiarism. This is one of the sample texts we discussed in Concept Lesson 1: Developing Something to Say.

Kirkpatrick, D.D. (2002, Jan. 5). 2 Accuse Stephen Ambrose, Popular Historian, of Plagiarism. *The New York Times*. Retrieved from www.nytimes.com/2002/01/05/national/05AMBR.html

This short news article (839 words) reports on plagiarism accusations made against a historian. It includes examples of similarities in wording that could be compared in the classroom and used to spur discussion.

Leopold, T. (2014, Aug. 8). 'True Detective' writer accused of plagiarism. Retrieved from www.cnn.com/2014/08/08/showbiz/tv/true-detective-pizzolatto-plagiarism/

This short news article (567 words) reports that a writer for the TV show *True Detective* was accused of plagiarism. It could be used to initiate a discussion of common knowledge, as the writer claims that the philosophical ideas that he put in the mouth of one of his characters do not belong to any one writer.

Moore, V. (2002, Aug. 15). Playing dirty in the war on plagiarism. *The Chronicle of Higher Education*. Retrieved from http://chronicle.com/article/Playing-Dirty-in-the-War-on/46035/

This short, satirical article (1476 words) looks at the type of "plagiarism" that we consider to be cheating (e.g., buying or downloading a whole paper) and suggests that teachers upload terrible papers to the internet so that when students submit them in a course, they will receive a failing grade. The article demonstrates how the ethical discourse surrounding discussions of textual reuse turn teachers and students against each other.

Mullin, B. (2014, September 16). Is it original? An editor's guide to identifying plagiarism. Retrieved from www.poynter.org/news/is-it-original-an-editors-guide-to-identifying-plagiarism/

This short article (920 words) presents a series of steps that could be used to judge whether an article is prototypically plagiarized or not. It also contains a flowchart of the process. It could be used to discuss plagiarism standards in the journalism community. Students could also create their own flowcharts for judging plagiarism charges in the schooling context and compare them to this one.

Popova, M. (2012, June 12). Combinatorial creativity and the myth of originality: The power of the synthesizing mind and the building blocks of combinatorial creativity. *The Smithsonian*. Retrieved from www.smithsonianmag.com/innovation/combinatorial-creativity-and-the-myth-of-originality-114843098/?no-ist

This short article (540 words) challenges the notion that original creations come from nowhere and endorses the notion that new ideas are formed by recombining old ones.

Shi, L. (2011). Common knowledge, learning, and citation practices in university writing. *Research in the Teaching of English, 45*(3), 308–334.

> This full-length research article (26 pp.) presents an interview study conducted at a U.S. university that explored instructors' (n=27) and students' (n=48) understandings of textual reuse. It concluded that there was little consensus on how to make attributing decisions among teachers or students, or among people from the same language or cultural backgrounds. This is the article from which we took the student quotes for Concept Lesson 4: Discussing Reasons to Cite: Attribution and Common Knowledge. The article could also be used in its entirety in a graduate course to explore attribution in more depth, and the literature review section could be used as a model.

Toor, R. (2011, June 20). Unconscious plagiarism. *The Chronicle of Higher Education*. Retrieved from http://chronicle.com/article/Unconscious-Plagiarism/127928/

> This short article (1388 words) gives a creative writing teacher's perspective on textual reuse. She discusses her commitment to letting students learn through imitation, her negative feelings at having her own work reused, and the fact that sometime we reuse ideas and text without realizing it. She suggests that textual reuse is not discussed enough in academia.

Walling, D.R. (2009). The creativity continuum. *TechTrends, 53*(4), 26–27.

> This short article (946 words) encourages teachers to show students how to use their creativity to create more original media while at the same time respecting copyright rules. It is useful for introducing students to the idea that plagiarism and originality exist on a continuum.

## Multimedia

Garrett, M. (2008). *College cheating story*. Retrieved from www.youtube.com/watch?v=gpPnjWP59MU

> This short video (2 min., 42 sec.) presents plagiarism as a form of academic dishonesty, placing it beside copying someone's work and bringing notes into an exam. It can be used as a quick way to get a discussion of prototypical plagiarism started with your students.

Murdoch University of Dubai. (2011). *Plagiarism*. Retrieved from www.youtube.com/watch?v=7lmp3-0UIFM

> This video (11 min., 13 sec.) presents four cases of prototypical plagiarism resulting in the expulsion of all students involved: a student who cut and pasted from the internet; one who bought a paper; one who reused a paper written by a student who had taken the course before; and two study partners, one of whom copied

the other's work. We suggest analyzing this representation critically with your students, both in terms of the definition of "plagiarism" and in terms of the social identities (cultural, racial, linguistic) of the teachers and students.

Primo. (2016). Peer-Reviewed Instructional Materials Online Database. Retrieved from http://primodb.org

This is a database that allows users to enter keywords such as "plagiarism" or "paraphrasing" to locate online tutorials on effective source use. Teachers should be aware that some tutorials vary in terms of how much cultural knowledge and vocabulary are required to follow them, the use of decontextualized versus contextualized examples, and the speed of narration. While we do not recommend that online tutorials be used to teach about effective writing from sources instead of classroom instruction, they can be helpful in reinforcing concepts discussed in class, or utilized in a flipped classroom manner—with students watching the tutorial at home to build background knowledge which is then clarified, discussed, and practiced during class.

Purdue University. (2016). OWL Purdue Online Writing Lab. Retrieved from https://owl.english.purdue.edu/owl/

The Purdue Online Writing Lab (OWL) is a widely used free resource for writing teachers and students. The website provides a *Research and Citation* section, which includes information about citing sources (i.e., quoting, paraphrasing, and summarizing), definitions of plagiarism, paraphrasing exercises, descriptions of fair use, guidelines for writing an abstract, and guidelines for finding and evaluating sources. The Purdue OWL also includes videos ("Vidcasts") about a wide range of topics, including second language writing, grammar, and MLA and APA formatting of in-text citations and reference lists.

Ryssdal, K., & Hill, A. (2015, Aug. 24). Joke stealing is no laughing matter. Retrieved from www.marketplace.org/2015/08/24/life/joke-stealing-no-laughing-matter

This very short article (246 words) and accompanying audiocast (4 min., 32 sec.) discusses whether reusing jokes is a copyright infraction and raises the issue of the applicability of copyright law to social media.

Tomaš, Z., & Marino, B. (Developers). (2014). *Departing from punishing plagiarism: Toward addressing ineffective source use pedagogically.* Retrieved from www.youtube.com/watch?v=t EskWSfrwzo&feature=youtu.be

This video (18 min., 32 sec.) contains two scenarios. The first, "A punitively oriented consultation," is short (about 4 min.) and models a teacher-student conference in which the teacher dismisses the work a student did on his paper because of the problematic source use. The second, "A pedagogically oriented consultation," is longer (about 13 min.) and models a teacher-student conference in which the teacher situates response to source use in the context of response to the student's entire draft, offering useful suggestions to address the problematic issues. The video also contains slides of talking points to help viewers isolate the difference in the approaches. Instructors could use this video to spur discussion about how teachers react to prototypical source use.

Tomaš, Z., Marino, B., and Pantelides, K. (Developers). (2015a–j). "Straight from the Students: Sharing Strategies of Effective Writing from Sources" series.

These short videos can be used as conversation starters on a variety of topic related to writing from sources:

- *Describe an assignment in which you had to use and cite outside sources.* Retrieved from https://youtu.be/_mwaHicYZmY. (2 min., 33 sec.). This video presents clips of L1 and L2 college students describing source-based writing tasks that they completed in a variety of courses.

- *Describe your process for completing research-based assignments.* Retrieved from https://youtu.be/BjsTWCAm0_k. (2 min., 48 sec.). This video presents clips of L1 and L2 college students describing their processes of writing a research paper.

- *How do you choose and refine a topic?* Retrieved from https://youtu.be/bEOxnWbbgvA. (1 min., 20 sec.). This video presents clips of L1 and L2 college students explaining how they choose a paper topic, touching on using Wikipedia, making connections between courses, asking for the professor's advice, and choosing something that resonates with you.

- *How do you find and evaluate sources?* Retrieved from https://youtu.be/vGKRhBtq_GA. (3 min., 7 sec.). This video presents clips of L1 and L2 college students explaining how they find source texts, including using Wikipedia, Googlescholar, and the university library, asking people, mining reference lists from other sources, and scanning abstracts for relevance.

- *How do you manage your time when you are challenged with an extensive assignment?* Retrieved from https://youtu.be/Fi9BgRH0aVg. (2 min., 11 sec.). This video presents clips of L1 and L2 college students talking about breaking up an assignment into smaller tasks, setting deadlines and using a calendar, and leaving time for revision.

- *How do you track information from different sources?* Retrieved from https://youtu.be/_0rF0jWRTJ8. (1 min., 37 sec.). This video presents clips of L1 and L2 college students briefly discussing their system for keeping track of ideas in sources, including print and electronic approaches.

- *What are your strengths and challenges as a writer?* Retrieved from https://youtu.be/brNr_pzLrc4. (2 min., 6 sec.). This video presents clips of L1 and L2 college students naming their strengths and challenges as writers.

- *What resources do you use when writing a paper?* Retrieved from https://youtu.be/iFo2okhyCp8. (3 min., 12 sec.). This video presents clips of L1 and L2 college students talking about the writing resources they use, including university resources such as the library and advisors and online resources such as YouTube, PurdueOWL, Kightcite, EasyBib, Facebook, and GoogleScholar.

- *What strategies do you find useful when completing research?* Retrieved from https://youtu.be/mmgHArN8TiY. (1 min., 53 sec.). This video presents clips of L1 and L2 college students naming some of their research strategies, including freewriting in response to source texts, highlighting parts of source texts, downloading more source texts than will ultimately be used, and reading source texts in their first language.

- *What writing advice would you give a less experienced university student?* Retrieved from https://youtu.be/5rI5FYW10KY. (2 min., 6 sec.). This video presents clips of L1 and L2 college students naming their strengths and challenges as writers.

# Appendix 3: Writing Samples

## SAMPLE 1

### "Behind Plagiarism" by JuiChun Chou

(Dialogue written for a first-year composition course at a four-year university in the U.S. Citations and full references are formatted as the student writer formatted them. The Mott-Smith 2016 citation refers to a handout with the quote shown on pages 28–30. The characters are fictional.)

■ Concept Lesson 5: Differing Attitudes toward Textual Reuse

Character #1: Zeke Franco, a blogger for the *Chronicle of Higher Education*, who earned his Ph. D in Academic Environmental Research. He is in his late 30's and likes to be in a slim fit suit with his stylish glasses frames. He lives alone in a New York City apartment, even though he had many relationships in the past, but none of them went well. You would think he must be someone who has prejudice against people and owns a high self esteem, the truth is, he is very considerate and has a personality that every girl can be easily persuaded. For someone who is intelligent like him and makes good money, it is hard to find a perfect match. With his background in Academic Environmental Research, he has published many articles in education and delivered many speeches for academic purposes.

Character #2: Jean Linthicum, a professor who studies in Social Work, believes the most important thing to educate people is patience. She has learned many life stories after working with people with disabilities and the elderly for many years. Not only she is passionate with her job, but also she likes to do researches and learns how to improve the condition for her clients. Therefore, she decided to travel around the world and visit those kids in the third world country. She is now in her late 50's, and she has been to many countries such as Ethiopia, Congo, Madagascar and etc. In 2010, she had won the Swedish human rights award for NSA. She gladly accepted it and thanked everyone who was in her life. Last year, she retired from Harvard University where she has been teaching for more than twenty years, and is now touring and giving speeches voluntarily, wish to share her experience and spread her thoughts to the world.

(Professor Linthicum and Zeke Franco were both invited to attend a conference for Academic Environmental Research in Sweden. They met in the lunch after the conference…)

**Zeke**: "Hello Professor, it's been a while since Harvard. How have you been?"

**Jean**: "Hi Zeke, It's good to see you here. I have been busy, just came back from South Africa two days ago, how about you?"

**Zeke**: "I did the same. Just landed this morning, I came straight from England for a conference I went to. Still dealing with some jet lag."

**Jean**: "Oh I know your pain, flying around does mess up your body clock, doesn't it?"

**Zeke**: "You know it does. How did you like the conference this morning by the way?"

**Jean**: "I think it was right to the point, especially when they were talking about plagiarism while doing academic research. It really is an issue that existing in every country and in different research fields."

**Zeke**: "I agree. It is one of the major issues that we should confront as far as doing academic research."

**Jean**: "Do you remember while you were in my class, I asked all of you to read the article *"Chinese researchers debate rash of plagiarism cases"*, which was written by two Chinese researchers named Li and Xiong?" (Li & Xiong, 1996)

**Zeke**: "Yes, definitely, that article helped me to see how different cultures look at the problem of plagiarism, and how they could make mistakes by not knowing the other language enough. From what I remember, they tried to conduct an experiment in the field of Genetic Science; however, even knowing the results came out differently, but because of the replicate words were being used in the research paper, they were accused of plagiarism. One of the most important factor that caused this situation was because of language barrier. If those Chinese researchers could have known the language better, they could express thoughts in their own words, which would avoid the problem completely. What do you think professor, does that happen to you while you doing human rights research for Social Work?"

**Jean**: "Exactly, while I was doing research on human rights, I noticed that there was one article published in Indonesia that was nearly alike from the one I wrote for a non-profit organization which was published in a journal back in 1995. The words were similar, but the concepts delivered behind the article were not the same."

**Zeke**: "Did you think that was plagiarizing your work?"

**Jean**: "Well, you know, it really is critical to say if people are copying your words, especially in doing the research on human rights. We use evidences from past incidents and establish our theory thus to explain it. You can't really say it's plagiarism when delivering facts such as the speech given out by Martin Luther King. But when you are borrowing material from others, citation is important. Always indicating your source is not only to avoid the possibility of being accused of plagiarizing, but also to show your respect to the author."

**Zeke**: "That makes sense. I agree on the importance of citation. But from what I have noticed nowadays, the issue of plagiarism is getting more serious among students because technology has become so convenient. In order to get good grades or to save some time, they can easily go online and search for the reference with putting in the keywords or quotes. Furthermore, they conveniently 'forget' to cite the source. They don't want their professors to think they were copying and pasting the word from other people so they can get good grades by doing this." (Mott-Smith, 2016) The academic purpose is to help students build fundamental structure of knowledge, therefore, students can use the knowledge they have earned to expand their views and creativity. Professors are looking for students' creativity they have developed and how much they have comprehended, not the copying of words or the ideas from others."

**Jean**: "You were in the same position; do you think it's acceptable for students to 'reuse' other people's work? How do you look at this situation?"

**Zeke**: "To be honest, I understand for those students who can't write well or write in languages they are not comfortable with, the possibility to copy from the internet or any other source is higher. They choose to go the other way around and use different methods to accomplish their work. Some of my classmates borrowed other friends' works and alternated the words a little to use it as their own project, some of them even paid other people to do it and ended up getting good grades. I do not agree with those behaviors; I know it was not legitimate and unfair to other students. But I don't blame them, when I was a student, I had the same stress, and I know how terrifying that was."

**Jean**: "But to think about it in a different way, if those students can put more effort in practicing and enhance their writing skills, instead of taking other people's work, they could come up with their way to accomplish the work with their own strength. This is the purpose of education, students learn from mistakes, and improve from establishing the fundamental skills. "

**Zeke**: "True, that is why we go to school, to be educated. But like what you said, 'students learn from mistakes'. What if a student copied an article but forgot to credit the author unintentionally, would you think it is an unacceptable mistake?"

**Jean**: "As for me, I wouldn't go deep with looking for student's possible copying word for word, I am more focused on seeing if they can understand the concept behind a theory and use it on the application in a useful way. Therefore, I would rather ask students to work on applications such as creating their own products or designing campaigns than ask them to write research papers, by doing that, I can see if students are really understanding the concept and be able to apply them correctly.

**Zeke**: "That is very good insight."

**Jean**: "Sometimes I see students use a significant amount of words or sentences from another source, almost made me believe this was plagiarism. However, when I saw the result or the idea coming out of it, which was totally different from the original, it was totally acceptable. They maybe used the same vocabulary because of the limitation of their knowledge of the language, or they think the way other people are saying it is valuable, instead of paraphrasing or alternating with other words, they decided to go with the original. Yet the conclusion or the idea came out of it was totally amazing and brand new. Do you call plagiarism? I don't think so."

**Zeke**: "Can you explain further about this? I don't quite understand."

**Jean**: "Sure. For example, there was a Broadway show called "*Frozen*", which was supposedly written by Bryony Lavery. However, a journalist whose name is Gladwell found out the work of his, called "*Damaged*" was tremendously used in "*Frozen*" without his permission in advance. You would think he must be angry, but he wasn't. Surprisingly, he was appreciative and glad that Lavery took his work and reproduce it. Even though his idea and words were taken from his work, Lavery interpreted it in a totally different way and created a brand new story line to wow the audience. If it was shown in his original way, would it have the same effect? Probably not. Thus, when we are talking about plagiarism, you can look at it from a very different angle." (Gladwell, 2004)

**Zeke**: "Now you remind me of when I was writing for the *Chronicle of Higher Education*, I had seen many scholars doing similar research for the same topic. However, when I was reading their articles, I don't have the feeling of plagiarism. When they conduct the experiments, there might be numerous same situations occurring during the process, but once they came out with different results and established their points of view, it doesn't seem to be the same anymore."

**Jean**: "That is the point of reproduction. And there has always been a critical issue between original and reproduction. "

**Zeke**: "So that is where education come into play. People have more knowledge and better writing skills, they can adapt from the previous and inject their own thoughts to the overall discussion. "

**Jean**: "Correct. Instead of spending time and energy catching if a student is stealing other people's work or copying from his/her classmates, I rather to put more effort into teaching and inspire them to come up with their own idea and incorporate it with references. (Mott-Smith, 2016)

**Zeke**: "That also requires having trust in the students. Do you think having the trust in students will help them grow?"

**Jean**: "Definitely, no one wants to be treated as a prisoner that is monitored 24/7, they need some rooms to develop their interest. The more space you allow them; the more creativity will be developed. If you ruled them strictly and asked them to follow the path you set, they will always be restrained in the box, thus never grow. Everybody has their own personality and intelligence. There is no certain rule has to be followed, you will be surprised to find how much creativity can come out of a kid when there is no prejudge or restriction involved. Donovan Walling once said '*Children are innately creative, and the youngest often are the most original because they have yet to be influenced by the creativity of others*'" (Walling, 2009)

**Zeke**: "And that's what we lack nowadays, creativity!" Professor, what do you think is creativity? Sometimes it is hard to distinguish between creativity and plagiarism.

**Jean**: "Creativity is a continuum, just like when a series of signals are being transmitted analogously, they do not stop, they go on and on. We use the original idea and if we make a slight change, there could be a million changes in between until it hits the mark where a different concept shows up. The process involves many people's ideas and numerous attempts, and finally it turns out to be something innovative and new. In the mean time, it is hard to determine precisely when the 'original' idea occurs."

**Zeke**: "That being said, creativity comes from the original, while we copying people's words we are also copying from the originals. If we can add some of our own ideas or to tweak the words somehow, we are on the process of developing creativity. In order to reach creativity, we need to give people room to think and discover. That is, we need to give people full trust and believe they can grow themselves. Mistakes such as plagiarism are also a learning process, they learn from where they fall. We rather teach them more writing skills than spending time on judging one's integrity. Therefore, education is the important element. Education is to creativity just like the fundamental support is to a spectacular skyscraper. A strong base is the support for the fancy high rise. And that's what we should all focus on and make the progress upon."

**Jean**: "You are still as smart as you were, I am so proud of you. And guess what, you are now in an important position to spread thoughts and help the academic environment move forward."

**Zeke**: "Certainly!"

## Works Cited

Gladwell, M. (2004, Nov. 22). Something borrowed: Should a charge of plagiarism ruin your life? Retrieved Nov. 24, 2014, from *The New Yorker*: http://www.newyorker.com/magazine/2004/11/22/somthing-borrowed

Li, X., & Xiong, L. (1996). Chinese researcher debates rash of plagiarism cases. *Science, 274*(5286), 337–338.

Mott-Smith, J. (2016). *Differing attitudes towards textual reuse*.

Walling, D. R. (2009). The creativity continuum. *TechTrends, 53*(4), 26–27.

# SAMPLE 2

## "Interpretations and Assumptions: A Re-Examination of 'Human Sacrifice' at the Royal Cemetery at Ur" by Abigail Murphy

(First paragraph excerpt, with corresponding references from the reference page. Citations and full references are formatted as the student writer formatted them.)
(Written for a 300-level undergraduate history course called Ancient Near Eastern and Anatolian Civilizations at a four-year university in the U.S.)

- Discourse Lesson 2: Whose Idea Was This?
- Discourse Lesson 6: Exploring Academic Uses of *I*
- Discourse Lesson 7: What Am I Supposed To Do? Differences in Referencing Expectations across Disciplines

Sir Leonard Woolley discovered the Royal Cemetery at Ur in the 1920s and 1930s, and there he found "thousands of human skeletons."[1] Woolley interpreted the rows and rows of bodies as evidence that the individuals buried there had taken poison willingly, "ready to continue their service to a king or queen in the netherworld," and many scholars have accepted his interpretation.[2] However, some scholars, like Baadsgaard et. al., Pollock, and Sürenhagen argue for different interpretations of the tombs. Baadsgaard et. al. argue for a less willing, more violent end to the court attendants' lives,[3] and Pollock examines how ideology and ritual could have made the attendants willingly end their lives.[4] Sürenhagen, however, offers an interpretation that foregoes the idea that human sacrifice occurred, instead arguing that the multitude of bodies in a single tomb was due to the fact that multiple burials occurred there.[5] Despite the overwhelming amount of scholars that argue that human sacrifice occurred at Ur, I will argue that it did not, as I believe that these interpretations rely too much upon assumptions made by Woolley about a practice that would have occurred rarely and over a short period of time, if at all.

[1]  Aubrey Baadsgaard, et. al, "Human Sacrifice and Intentional Preservation in the Royal Cemetery of Ur," *Antiquity* 85 (2011): 27.
[2]  Ibid., 29.
[3]  Ibid., 38.
[4]  Susan Pollock, "The Royal Cemetery of Ur: Ritual, Tradition, and the Creation of Subjects," in *Representations of Political Power: Case Histories from Times of Change and Dissolving Order in the Ancient Near East,* ed. M. Heinz and M. H. Feldman (Winona Lake, IN, 2007), 105.
[5]  Dietrich Sürenhagen, "Death in Mesopotamia: The Royal Tombs of Ur Revisited," in *Of Pots and Plans: Papers on the Archaeology and History of Mesopotamia and Syria …,* ed. by L. Werr et al. (London 2002), 330.

## Bibliography

Baadsgaard, Aubrey, Janet Monge, Samantha Cox, and Richard L. Zettler. "Human Sacrifice and Intentional Preservation in the Royal Cemetery of Ur." *Antiquity* 85 (2011): 27–42.

Pollock, Susan. "The Royal Cemetery of Ur: Ritual, Tradition, and the Creation of Subjects." In *Representations of Political Power: Case Histories from Times of Change and Dissolving Order in the Ancient Near East,* edited by M. Heinz and M. H. Feldman, 89–110. Winona Lake, IN, 2007.

Sürenhagen, Dietrich. "Death in Mesopotamia: The Royal Tombs of Ur Revisited." In *Of Pots and Plans: Papers on the Archaeology and History of Mesopotamia and Syria* ..., edited by L. Werr et al., 324–348. London, 2002.

# SAMPLE 3

## "Updated Review of the Biosynthetic Pathways of Polyunsaturated Fatty Acids in Lower Eukaryotes" by Caitlin McMahon

(First paragraph excerpt, with corresponding references from the reference page. Citations and full references are formatted as the student writer formatted them.)

(Written for a 400-level undergraduate biology course called Honors Internship in Molecular Biology at a four-year university in the U.S.)

- Discourse Lesson 2: Whose Idea Was This?
- Discourse Lesson 7: What Am I Supposed To Do? Differences in Referencing Expectations across Disciplines

Polyunsaturated fatty acids (PUFAs) are carboxylic acids with a long hydrocarbon chain that contains more than one double bond, giving the acid its nominal unsaturated characteristic. The position of the first double bond proximal to the methyl end of the hydrocarbon chain is important for classification: PUFAs can be $\omega$-3 or $\omega$-6 (Tanaka et al. 2009, 1). PUFAs are important biological molecules because they serve as important structural components of cell membranes and are intermediates of eicosanoids, which mediate fever, inflammation, blood pressure, and neurotransmission in humans (Uttaro 2006, 563). Linoleic acid (LA), is an $\omega$-6 18 carbon PUFA, often short-handed as C18:2n-6, that is essential for the normal growth of all eukaryotes as an integral component of cell membranes (Chodok et al. 2013, 901). Other $\omega$-6 PUFAs are $\gamma$-linoleic acid (GLA; C18:3n-6) and arachidonic acid (AA; C20:4n-6), which has a $\omega$-3 homologue called eicosapentaenoic acid (EPA; C20:5n-3), which in turn is a precursor of docosahexaenoic acid (DHA; C22:6n-3). All of these PUFAs are known for reducing the risk of rheumatoid arthritis and other inflammatory diseases, cardiovascular disease, neuropsychiatric disorders like dementia and depression, and depression in humans (Chodok et al. 2013, 901).

In addition, AA and DHA have gained popularity and brought attention to the human health benefits as a result of their discovery as important compounds for neonatal neural and retinal development (Uttaro 2006, 563). AA and DHA are present in human mother's milk and are now are deemed necessary for inclusion in commercial infant formulas (Uttaro 2006, 563-4). PUFAs are now known to be vital constituents of human metabolism, but humans have a limited capacity to synthesize these fatty acids de novo and can only obtain them through dietary intake (Venegas-Calerón et al. 2010, 109)....

## References

Chodok, P., Eiamsa-ard, P., Cove, D. J., Quatrano, R. S., & Kaewsuwan, S. (2013). Identification and Functional Characterization of two Δ12-fatty Acid Desaturases Associated with Essential Linoleic Acid Biosynthesis in *Physcomitrella patens*. *Journal of Industrial Microbiology and Biotechnology*. *40*, 901-913. doi: 10.1007/s10295-013-1285-3

Tanaka, T., Shen, J., Abecasis, G. R., Kisialiou, A., Ordovas, J. M., Guralnik, J. M., Singleton, A. et al. (2009). Genome-Wide Association Study of Plasma Polyunsaturated Fatty Acids in the InCHIANTI Study [Introduction]. *PLoS Genetics*. *5*(1), e 1000338. doi: 10.1371/journal.pgen.1000338

Uttaro, A. D. (2006). Biosynthesis of Polyunsaturated Fatty Acids in Lower Eukaryotes. *IUBMB LIFE, 58*(10), 563-571.

Venegas-Calerón, M., Sayanova, O., & Napier, J. A. (2010). An Alternative to Fish Oils: Metabolic Engineering of Oil-Seed Crops to Produce Omega-3 Long Chain Polyunsaturated Fatty Acids [Introduction]. *Progress in Lipid Research*. *49*, 109. doi: 10.1016/j.plipres.2009.10.001

# SAMPLE 4

## "Tips for Successful Intercultural Marriage" by Hiroki Tanabe

(Excerpt from the body of a research paper, with corresponding references from the reference page. Three versions are included.)

(Written for an upper-level undergraduate ESL writing course at a four-year university in the U.S.)

- Version A: Unmarked Copy for Discourse Lesson 2: Whose Idea Was This?

Among intercultural marriages, the couples have more possibilities of having conflicts than monocultural couples have. It seems to that couples have to have special elements to overcome the various difficulties. Arguably, it has been suggested that the key elements that intercultural married couples should know to avoid the conflicts or overcome the conflicts by many interviews to intercultural couples. The key elements are strong determination, flexibility, liking the other culture; sensitivity to each other's need and self-disclosure.

The first of all, to be a successful couple, people should know that intercultural marriage brings various kinds of problems which are mentioned in the beginning part of this paper. In addition, Zebroski (1999) stated Marriage across racial lines is often perceived negatively by family, friends and community. This means that for intercultural couples usually difficult to get supports from their relatives or acquaintances. As a result, intercultural couples should understand the situation that the couples are difficult to get support from others and build strong determination to overcome the problems or conflicts to keep relationship with a partner before they get marriage.

The second element is a being flexible. According to "Intercultural Marriage promises & pitfalls," flexibility is a necessary characteristics for intercultural couples. "Being flexible means being like a reed swaying in the wind, bending this way and that according to the circumstances" (Romano, 2008, p. 180) In other words, flexibility is essential to adapt to rapid changes and different environments. In intercultural marriage, the couples are likely to face the sudden changes because of cultural differences and different nationalities. Sometimes, you have to move to your partner's country that has different lifestyles. To become confortable in another cultural environment, flexibility is a necessary element.

The third element is "a liking for the other culture" (Romano, 2008, p. 178). In case of intercultural couples, a couple should respect the culture that partner belongs to. This is because person can know about their partner through learning partner's culture such as how the partner educated, how the spouse is brought up. In other words, by knowing partner's culture, the person is able to know and understand their partner more. In addition, in case of intercultural marriage, one dislike one's partner's culture can mean that partner disrespect and dislike the partner because culture usually becomes a part of identity. In addition, if person likes his or her partner's culture, the person is highly motivated to learn partner's culture more. Future more, being familiar with partner culture, the person can adopt himself or herself easily when people move to their mate's native country. A liking partner's culture brings to intercultural couples a lot of benefits to their marriage life.

The forth element is "sensitivity to each other's need." (Romano, 2008, p. 177) Sensitivity is one of the essential skills for successful marriage lives especially for intercultural marriages. Incidentally, What is a being sensitivity? According to Romano (2008), "Being sensitive means being able to feel or perceive and respond to out side stimuli" (Romano, 2008, p. 177). In other words, partner should perceive or feel what their partner wants to do or hopes for and take an appropriate response to their desire. In addition, the book also stated "it also means learning to understand and tolerate (if not share) the other's values, beliefs and needs, and comprehending how the other interprets life" (Romano, 2008, p. 177) Being sensitive can be good opportunities to know more about partner's characteristics, desire and their culture.

The fifth element is self-disclosure. If one of the partners hide his or her feeling, it is very hard for his or her spouse to know what to do for their partner. As a result, both of them get frustrated. Furthermore, the study that is written by Tiffany G. Renalds illustrates that this skill is very necessary for intercultural marriage couples especially Asian spouses. This is because Asians are likely to want their spouse knows or feel their desire. And also, they rely on nonverbal communication to tell what they want (Renalds, 2011, p. 47). This means that if their partner does not know the meaning of Asian's body language or facial expression, the spouses can not even understand what their partner want. To solve the situation, couples should express more obliviously what they want to or their will.

## Reference

Romano, D. (2008). *Intercultural marriage: Promises and pitfalls*. Boston: Intercultural Press.

Renalds, G,T. (2011). *Communication in Intercultural Marriages: Managing Cultural Differences and Conflict for Marital Satisfaction*. Retrieved from: (May, 5, 2012) DIGITAL@LIBERTY UNIVERSITY.

[Zebroski, S.A. (1999). Black-white intermarriages: The racial and gender dynamics of support and opposition. *Journal of Black Studies, 30*(1), 123–132.]

■ Version B: with feedback on line of argument and integration of source texts for Response Lesson 2: Training for Peer Review

Among intercultural marriages, the couples have more possibilities of having conflicts than monocultural couples have. It seems to that couples have to have special elements to overcome the various difficulties. Arguably, it has been suggested that the key elements that intercultural married couples should know to avoid the conflicts or overcome the conflicts by many interviews to intercultural couples. <u>The key elements are strong determination, flexibility, liking the other culture; sensitivity to each other's need and self-disclosure.</u> **You do a great job forecasting the structure of your argument here.**

The first of all, to be a successful couple, people should know that intercultural marriage brings various kinds of problems which are mentioned in the beginning part of this paper. In addition, Zebroski (1999) stated Marriage <u>across racial lines</u> is often perceived negatively by family, friends and community. This means that for <u>intercultural couples</u> usually difficult to get supports from their relatives or acquaintances. **The source talks about marriage across racial lines and you talk about intercultural marriage; these aren't exactly the same, so it's a little confusing. Could you add a clarification about this?** As a result, intercultural couples should understand the situation that the couples are difficult to get support from others and build <u>strong determination</u> to overcome the problems or conflicts to keep relationship with a partner before they get marriage. **I can see you renaming the first key element here, and it really helps me keep track of your line of argument.**

The second element is a being flexible. According to "Intercultural Marriage promises & pitfalls", flexibility is a necessary characteristics for intercultural couples. "Being flexible means being like a reed swaying in the wind, bending this way and that according to the circumstances" (Romano, 2008, p.180) In other words, flexibility is essential to adapt to rapid changes and different environments. In intercultural marriage, the couples are likely to face the sudden changes because of cultural differences and different nationalities. Sometimes, you have to move to your partner's country that has different lifestyles. To become confortable in another cultural environment, flexibility is a necessary element. **Wouldn't intercultural marriages also require people to be flexible in terms of their daily living habits, too, like whether or not you take your shoes off when you enter the house, or whether or not a parent and children greet each other immediately upon returning from work, etc.?**

The third element is "a liking for the other culture" (Romano, 2008, p.178). In case of intercultural couples, a couple should respect the culture that partner belongs to. This is because person can know about their partner through learning partner's culture such as how the partner educated, how the spouse is brought up. In other words, by knowing partner's culture, the person is able to know and understand their partner more. In addition, in case of intercultural marriage, one dislike one's partner's culture can mean that partner disrespect and dislike the partner because culture usually becomes a part of identity. In addition, if person likes his or her partner's culture, the person is highly motivated to learn partner's culture more. Future more, being familiar with partner culture, the person can adopt himself or herself easily when people move to their mate's native country. A liking partner's culture brings to intercultural couples a lot of benefits to their marriage life. **It's not clear to me if the reasons you list in this paragraph are your own ideas or come from Romano?**

The forth element is "sensitivity to each other's need." (Romano,2008, p.177) Sensitivity is one of the essential skills for successful marriage lives especially for intercultural marriages. Incidentally, What is a being sensitivity? According to Romano(2008), "Being sensitive means being able to feel or perceive and respond to out side stimuli" (Romano, 2008, p.177). In other words, partner should perceive or feel what their partner wants to do or hopes for and take an appropriate response to their desire. In addition, the book also stated "it also means learning to understand and tolerate (if not share) the other's values, beliefs and needs, and comprehending how the other interprets life."(Romano, 2008, p. 177) Being sensitive can be good opportunities to know more about partner's characteristics, desire and their culture. **This whole paragraph seems to rely only on Romano. You quote the source three times. Is it possible to quote less, or to bring in more of your own ideas? Also, by now I'm realizing that the last three elements are all taken from Romano; it makes it seem like you're just repeating Romano's argument.**

The fifth element is self-disclosure. If one of the partners hide his or her feeling, it is very hard for his or her spouse to know what to do for their partner. As a result, both of them get frustrated. Furthermore, the study that is written by Tiffany G. Renalds illustrates that this skill is very necessary for intercultural marriage couples especially Asian spouses. This is because Asians are likely to want their spouse knows or feel their desire. And also, they rely on nonverbal communication to tell what they want (Renalds, 2011, p.47). This means that if their partner does not know the meaning of Asian's body language or facial expression, the spouses can not even understand what their partner want. To solve the situation, couples should express more obliviously what they want to or their will. **In this paragraph, you specify Asian spouses, which seems a little odd since you didn't do it for the other elements.**

# Reference

Romano, D. (2008). *Intercultural marriage: Promises and pitfalls*. Boston: Intercultural Press.

Renalds, G,T. (2011). *Communication in Intercultural Marriages: Managing Cultural Differences and Conflict for Marital Satisfaction*. Retrieved from: (May, 5,2012) DIGITAL@LIBERTY UNIVERSITY.

[Zebroski, S.A. (1999). Black-white intermarriages: The racial and gender dynamics of support and opposition. *Journal of Black Studies, 30*(1), 123–132.]

■ Version C: with feedback on incorporation of quotes for Response Lesson 2: Training for Peer Review

Among intercultural marriages, the couples have more possibilities of having conflicts than monocultural couples have. It seems to that couples have to have special elements to overcome the various difficulties. Arguably, it has been suggested that the key elements that intercultural married couples should know to avoid the conflicts or overcome the conflicts by many interviews to intercultural couples. The key elements are strong determination, flexibility, liking the other culture; sensitivity to each other's need and self-disclosure.

The first of all, to be a successful couple, people should know that intercultural marriage brings various kinds of problems which are mentioned in the beginning part of this paper. In addition, Zebroski (1999) stated Marriage across racial lines is often perceived negatively by family, friends and community. This means that for intercultural couples usually difficult to get supports from their relatives or acquaintances. As a result, intercultural couples should understand the situation that the couples are difficult to get support from others and build strong determination to overcome the problems or conflicts to keep relationship with a partner before they get marriage.

The second element is a being flexible. According to "Intercultural Marriage promises & pitfalls", flexibility is a necessary characteristics for intercultural couples. "Being flexible means being like a reed swaying in the wind, bending this way and that according to the circumstances" (Romano, 2008, p.180) In other words, flexibility is essential to adapt to rapid changes and different environments. The sentence that begins "According to" introduces the quote nicely, but it needs a citation and doesn't have one. The sentence after the quote applies the idea to intercultural marriages, and helps us understand what you mean good work. In intercultural marriage, the couples are likely to face the sudden changes because of cultural differences and different nationalities. Sometimes, you have to move to your partner's country that has different lifestyles. To become confortable in another cultural environment, flexibility is a necessary element.

The third element is "a liking for the other culture" (Romano, 2008, p.178). In case of intercultural couples, a couple should respect the culture that partner belongs to. Here, you do a nice job paraphrasing the quote for us, although I'm not sure "like" and "respect" are really the same thing. This is because person can know about their partner through learning partner's culture such as how the partner educated, how the spouse is brought up. In other words, by knowing partner's culture, the person is able to know and understand their partner more. In addition, in case of intercultural marriage, one dislike one's partner's culture can mean that partner disrespect and dislike the partner because culture usually becomes a part of identity. In addition, if person likes his or her partner's culture, the person is highly motivated to learn partner's culture more. Future more, being familiar with partner culture, the person can adopt himself or herself easily when people move to their mate's native country. A liking partner's culture brings to intercultural couples a lot of benefits to their marriage life.

The forth element is "sensitivity to each other's need." (Romano,2008, p.177) Sensitivity is one of the essential skills for successful marriage lives especially for intercultural marriages. Incidentally, What is a being sensitivity? According to Romano(2008), "Being sensitive means being able to feel or perceive and respond to out side stimuli" (Romano, 2008, p.177). In other words, partner should perceive or feel what their partner wants to do or hopes for and take an appropriate response to their desire. **You have used two quotes before giving your own paraphrase explaining what "sensitivity" is and how it relates to intercultural marriage. Maybe you could use more of your own words here?** In addition, the book also stated "it also means learning to understand and tolerate (if not share) the other's values, beliefs and needs, and comprehending how the other interprets life."(Romano,2008, p.177) Being sensitive can be good opportunities to know more about partner's characteristics, desire and their culture. **Here, you use the word "know" but the source uses the words "tolerate" and "share," so I think your interpretation isn't quite accurate.**

The fifth element is self-disclosure. If one of the partners hide his or her feeling, it is very hard for his or her spouse to know what to do for their partner. As a result, both of them get frustrated. Furthermore, the study that is written by Tiffany G. Renalds illustrates that this skill is very necessary for intercultural marriage couples especially Asian spouses. This is because Asians are likely to want their spouse knows or feel their desire. And also, they rely on nonverbal communication to tell what they want (Renalds, 2011, p.47). This means that if their partner does not know the meaning of Asian's body language or facial expression, the spouses can not even understand what their partner want. To solve the situation, couples should express more obliviously what they want to or their will.

# Reference

Romano, D. (2008). *Intercultural marriage: Promises and pitfalls*. Boston: Intercultural Press.

Renalds, G,T. (2011). *Communication in Intercultural Marriages: Managing Cultural Differences and Conflict for Marital Satisfaction*. Retrieved from: (May, 5,2012) DIGITAL@LIBERTY UNIVERSITY.

[Zebroski, S.A. (1999). Black-white intermarriages: The racial and gender dynamics of support and opposition. *Journal of Black Studies, 30*(1), 123–132.]

# SAMPLE 5

## Excerpt from the Introduction to *The Lenses of Gender* by Sandra Lipsitz Bem (1993)

(Excerpt from pp. 1–2, three versions included)

- Version A: with notes for writing a summary for Process Lesson 4: Note-Taking Strategies for Different Writing Tasks

  Throughout the history of Western culture, three beliefs about women and men have prevailed; that they have fundamentally different psychological and sexual natures, that men are inherently the dominant or superior sex, and that both male-female difference and male dominance are natural. Until the mid-nineteenth century, this naturalness was typically conceived in religious terms, as part of God's grand creation. Since then, it has typically been conceived in scientific terms, as part of biology's --or evolution's-- grand creation.

  People in the West have always thought men and women are different and that men are superior, and that these things are natural.

  Consequently, most Americans did not see any inconsistency between commitment to **equality** and denial of **political rights** to women until the appearance of the women's **rights** movement in the mid-nineteenth century. The **first wave of feminist advocacy** not only established women's basic **political rights**; it also made the inconsistency between ideology and the treatment of women widely visible for the first time on U.S. history.

  The "first wave of feminist advocacy" (mid-19th c) was the first time Americans realized that women were treated unfairly.

  Beginning in the 1960s, the **second major wave of feminist advocacy** raised social consciousness still further by exposing --and naming-- the "sexism" in all policies and practices that explicitly **discriminate** on the basis of sex. This second feminist challenge gradually enabled people to see that restricting the number of women in professional schools or paying women less than men for **equal** work was not a natural requirement of a woman's biological and historical **role** as wife and mother but an illegitimate form of **discrimination** based on outmoded cultural stereotypes. Even political reactionaries began to espouse the principle of **equal** pay for **equal** work.

  The "second major wave of feminist advocacy" (1960s) was the time when people started seeing the treatment of women as discrimination; they invented the word "sexism" for discrimination based on sex.

  But as profound as the transformation of America's consciousness has been during the past 150 years, hidden assumptions about sex and gender remain embedded in cultural discourses, social institutions, and individual psyches that

<u>invisibly and systematically reproduce male power in generation after genera-tion</u>. Not only do these lenses shape how people perceive, conceive, and discuss reality, but because they are embedded in social institutions, they also shape the more material things --like **unequal** pay and inadequate day care-- that constitute social reality itself.

**Even though much has changed, Americans still have sexist beliefs and discrimination still exists.**

■ Version B: with notes for writing a personal response for Process Lesson 4: Note-Taking Strategies for Different Writing Tasks

Throughout the history of Western culture, three beliefs about women and men have prevailed; that they have fundamentally different psychological and sexual natures, that men are inherently the dominant or superior sex, and that both male-female difference and male dominance are natural. Until the mid-nineteenth century, this naturalness was typically conceived in religious terms, as part of God's grand creation. Since then, it has typically been conceived in scientific terms, as part of biology's --or evolution's-- grand creation. **That is so true. We think of men as stronger -- Are there ways in which women are stronger? Are men stronger as an outcome of evolution? Are men in fact stronger? Is dad stronger than mom? Are all men stronger than all women?**

Consequently, most Americans did not see any inconsistency between commitment to equality and denial of political rights to women until the appearance of the women's rights movement in the mid-nineteenth century. **What made them see the inconsistency between equality and treatment of women for the first time? How is it exactly that women always seemed to hold important positions in my country? Is it because we are a more secular society?** The first wave of feminist advocacy not only established women's basic political rights; it also made the inconsistency between ideology and the treatment of women widely visible for the first time on U.S. history.

Beginning in the 1960s, the second major wave of feminist advocacy raised social consciousness still further by exposing—and naming—the "sexism" in all policies and practices that explicitly discriminate on the basis of sex. **What policies and practices were named? I wonder what mom thought about this at the time…** This second feminist challenge gradually enabled people to see that <u>restricting the number of women in professional schools or paying women less than men for equal work was not a natural requirement of a woman's biological and historical roles as wife and mother</u> but an illegitimate form of discrimination based on outmoded cultural stereotypes. Even political reactionaries began to espouse the principle of equal pay for equal work. **It makes me so mad that pay discrimination still exists! Not to mention the glass ceiling…I wonder what younger women in the US think about this today? I wonder what my peers from different countries feel about this. Note to self--maybe I could do an informal survey?**

But as profound as the transformation of America's consciousness has been during the past 150 years, hidden assumptions about sex and gender remain embedded in cultural discourses, social institutions, and individual psyches I certainly know some people with sexist attitudes! that invisibly and systematically reproduce male power in generation after generation. Not only do these lenses shape how people perceive, conceive, and discuss reality, but because they are embedded in social institutions, they also shape the more material things --like unequal pay and inadequate day care-- that constitute social reality itself. **Wait--what does it mean for beliefs to be "embedded" in social institutions? How can beliefs "shape...reality itself"? What is meant by "material things"?**

■ Version C: with notes for writing an argument for Process Lesson 4: Note-Taking Strategies for Different Writing Tasks

Throughout the history of <u>Western culture, three beliefs</u> about women and men have prevailed; that they have fundamentally <u>different psychological and sexual natures,</u> **What about physical natures? Why does she leave this out?** that <u>men are</u> inherently the dominant or <u>superior</u> sex, and that both male-female <u>difference and male dominance are natural</u>. Until the mid-nineteenth century, this naturalness was typically conceived in <u>religious terms,</u> as part of God's grand creation. Since then, it has typically been conceived in <u>scientific terms,</u> as part of biology's --or evolution's-- grand creation. **I know people who still see these differences as religion-based.**

Consequently, most Americans did not see any inconsistency between commitment to equality and denial of political rights to women until the appearance of the women's rights movement in <u>the mid-nineteenth century</u>. **This seems true -- "All <u>men</u> are created equal."** The <u>first wave</u> of feminist advocacy not only established women's basic political rights; it also made the inconsistency between ideology and the treatment of women widely visible for the first time on U.S. history. **This seems true, too, since this is when women won the right to vote. She doesn't say it, though. Maybe she'll say it later; this is just the intro.**

Beginning in the <u>1960s, the second major wave</u> of feminist advocacy raised social consciousness still further by exposing --and naming-- the "sexism" in all policies and practices that explicitly discriminate on the basis of sex. **I doubt they covered "all" policies.** This second feminist challenge gradually enabled people to see that <u>restricting the number of women in professional schools or paying women less than men for equal work</u> was not a natural requirement of a woman's biological and historical roles as wife and mother but an illegitimate form of discrimination based on outmoded cultural stereotypes. Even political reactionaries began to espouse the principle of equal pay for equal work. **But if "outmoded cultural stereotypes" still exist, then why is this?**

But as profound as the transformation of America's consciousness has been during the past 150 years, hidden assumptions about sex and gender remain embedded in cultural discourses, social institutions, and individual psyches that invisibly and systematically reproduce male power in generation after generation. Not only do these lenses shape how people perceive, conceive, and discuss reality, but because they are embedded in social institutions, they also shape the more material things --like unequal pay <u>and inadequate day care</u>-- that constitute social reality itself.

Outline -- comparing U.S. to Danish women's rights

3 beliefs for both ("West"): (need to consider if this is true in both countries -- compare to my own experiences, maybe ask my roommate about the U.S.)

- Different natures (mental, sexual). ADD: physical (do some research on body size, etc.)

- Men are superior.

- It's natural for men to be considered superior.

- Used to be based on religion, now in science. (Maybe not true?)

<u>History of feminism</u> (compare timelines -- which country is ahead of which?)

US: 1st wave--mid-18th c; 2nd wave--1960s; 3rd wave--1990s

Need to do some research for Denmark.

<u>Today</u>:

US/Denmark: What is the wage discrepancy now? Do fewer women go to college? Grad school?

Is daycare really a women's issue, if both men and women get it? And if both get parental leave?

# SAMPLE 6

## "Planning: Strategies for countering procrastination and selecting sources"

(Excerpt from drafts of Chapter 5.)

- Version A: Early draft for Process Lesson 6: Revising to Integrate Source Ideas and Bring Out Your Own

Planning for source use includes setting aside sufficient time for the entire reading-thinking-writing process and selecting appropriate sources. We begin with setting aside time, as procrastination may lead to difficulty with producing effective writing from sources. 13.85 percent of L2 Chinese college students in Lowinger, He, Lin, and Chang's (2014) study and 35% of L2 Asian students in Kim, Alhaddab, Aquino, and Negi (2016) study reported that they procrastinate when completing academic tasks. In a study of L1 college student writers in the US, Roig and Detommaso (1995) found a correlation between self-reported procrastination and self-reported prototypical plagiarism. Given this connection, we see an opportunity for writing instructors to help students develop self-regulatory strategies effective in avoiding procrastination and keeping on track with extensive college-assignments such as source-based papers. These strategies include goal setting (e.g., Boice, 1989) and adhering to deadlines (Ariely &

Wertenbroch, 2002). Writing instructors can encourage students to set daily or weekly writing goals and keep track of the ways in which they attain these goals in a journal or a short debriefing session with a "paper buddy" at the beginning or end of each class. They can also break down assignments into manageable sub-products (e.g. reading notes, outline or a visual organizer, 1-2 pages of the paper draft) which students can be made accountable and rewarded for turning in for feedback by set deadlines (Ackerman & Gross, 2005).

- Version B: Revised draft, with sentences that form the backbone of the argument underlined, for Process Lesson 6: Revising to Integrate Source Ideas and Bring Out Your Own

<u>Many student writers become overwhelmed by the prospect of writing a paper from sources, but they react to the assignment in different ways.</u> Some may procrastinate until the last minute, while others dive in, spending hours and hours reading texts they do not understand and, if L2 writers, perhaps translating every word that they do not know. <u>Both behaviors may lead to issues with writing from sources that can be addressed by providing students with better strategies.</u>

<u>Anticipating students' tendency to procrastinate is necessary because procrastination has been associated with prototypical plagiarism</u> among L1 students (Roig & Detommaso, 1995). Procrastination has also been shown in research on L2 students (Kim, Alhaddab, Aquino, & Negi, 2016; Lowinger, He, Lin, & Chang, 2014). <u>One way to forestall procrastination is to promote students' engagement with the topic.</u> No matter whether you assign the topic or the students choose it themselves, students will need to narrow it down to fit the scope of their paper. Teachers should guide students through this process to ensure that students choose a topic that is engaging to them. For instance, instructors can ask students to read about topics in the popular press and on Wikipedia and freewrite about their own knowledge and experience with the topic. They can also take time in class to read an article on the general topic aloud to model how a single intriguing claim or statistic can lead to questions and then explain how these questions can lead to a literature search and eventually to a narrowed research topic.

<u>Another way to help students avoid procrastination and thus facilitate their writing from sources is to encourage self-regulatory practices, such as adhering to deadlines</u> (Ariely & Wertenbroch, 2002). Writing instructors can break down assignments into manageable subtasks such as taking notes on reading, producing an outline or visual organizer of ideas from source texts, or drafting a short section of the paper and set deadlines for them (Ackerman & Gross, 2005). Requiring and responding to intermediary products reinforce the message that teachers value all the tasks associated with the reading-thinking-writing process. <u>In addition, instructors can introduce the strategy of goal setting</u> (e.g., Boice, 1989) <u>to help students stay on track with source-based writing assignments.</u> Research has shown that even experienced writers benefit from setting goals and, specifically, from checking their source use against task guidelines (Plakans, 2009).

# Appendix 4: Idea Organizers

## Graphic Organizer

- Version 1: Based on prior knowledge and sources for Process Lesson 5: Idea Organizers: Tools for Digesting Content, Organizing Information, and Finding Connections (pp. 112–114)

*italics* = writer's own ideas

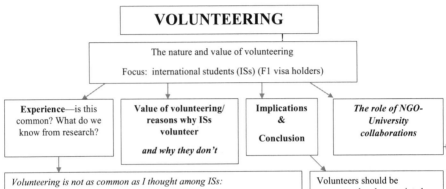

**VOLUNTEERING**

The nature and value of volunteering

Focus: international students (ISs) (F1 visa holders)

| **Experience**—is this common? What do we know from research? | **Value of volunteering/ reasons why ISs volunteer** *and why they don't* | **Implications & Conclusion** | *The role of NGO-University collaborations* |
|---|---|---|---|

*Volunteering is not as common as I thought among ISs:*

- Zhao, Kuhand, and Carini (2005) studied 3,000 undergraduate ISs at 317 US four-year colleges and universities. They found that both first-year and senior ISs volunteer less than their American counterparts.
- Dudley (2007): Only 8/55 ISs had volunteering experience
- Cruce and Moore (2007): ISs are less likely than other students to volunteer during the first year of college (only about 3% of first year ISs plan to volunteer.)

*But important to do!* Lee & Seong-Gin Moon (2011): "Having received formal education in the United States increases the likelihood of mainstream volunteering, not affecting the likelihood of ethnic volunteering (p. 823)".

**Reasons for volunteering/ Positives from volunteering:**

- Fostering feelings of inclusion and belonging, enhancement of social cohesion of diverse people, fostering feelings of self-validation, and attainment of social, cultural, and human capital (Manguvo et al. (2013)
- "Increased development of interpersonal and communication skills" and "increased self-confidence and knowledge of a subject area, along with access to career opportunities" (Dudley, 2007, p. 542)
- Benefits related to the development of English (Dudley, 2007, p. 542 & 547), "killing time, meeting people, professional experience" (p. 547)
- "involvement in volunteering helped to socialize and affiliate sojourners into the mainstream culture." (Ksienski, 2004, p.118, as cited in Mahguvo et al. 2013)
- Transition to college, benefits for domestic students (Cruce & Moore, 2007)

**Reasons for not volunteering among international students:**

- "Fear of not being understood, feelings of incompetence, and the cumbersome bureaucratic process in the application process deterred some participants from volunteering …" (Manguvo et al. 2013, p.117)
- Lack of opportunity and knowledge about volunteering, lack of time, limited language ability (Dudley, 2007, p. 546, p. 555)

Volunteers should be encouraged and appreciated (Manguvo et al., 2013), *but also trained?*

Increase students' awareness about volunteering (e.g., orientation sessions by local agencies) and create curricular opportunities that allow ISs to volunteer. Dudley (2007)

Reach out to career services (Cruce & Moore, 2007)

*Own ideas building on the sources:*

- *University/ESL program investment*
- *Buddy program so they can have someone to process/reflect on the experience with.*

*Many NGOs already train volunteers and have considerable experience placing people and reviewing placement. Institutions of Higher Ed need to find appropriate NGOs to collaborate with!*

*Idea: Interview 1-2 NGO directors with experience placing ISs.*

# Traditional Outline
# (for Process Lesson 5: Idea Organizers)

*italics* = writer's own ideas

**Tentative thesis**: This paper will examine the potential of volunteering for international students (ISs) and discuss implications for institutions of higher education, specifically focusing on the unexplored value of university-NGO partnerships.

1. **Volunteering among international students**

   a. Not common—Cruce & Moore (2007): ISs are less likely than other students to volunteer during the first year of college.

   b. Dudley (2007): Only 8/55 ISs had volunteering experience
   *But important to do!* Lee & Moon (2011): "Having received formal education in the United States increases the likelihood of mainstream volunteering, not affecting the likelihood of ethnic volunteering (p. 823)."

2. **Reasons for ISs' volunteering/Value of volunteering**

   a. *My ideas from brainstorming: learn English, gain job experience, meet people, emotional support, moral/religious reasons, university requirements*

   b. Fostering of feelings of inclusion and belonging (Manguvo et al., 2013)

   c. Enhancement of social cohesion of diverse people (Manguvo et al., 2013)

   d. Fostering of feelings of self-validation (Manguvo et al., 2013)

   e. Attainment of social, cultural, and human capital (Manguvo et al., 2013)

   f. Reasons for volunteering (8/55): Killing time, Improving English speaking skills, Meeting people, Gaining professional experience (Dudley, 2007) Note to self: Dudley lists additional research specifically focused on language related benefits on volunteering.

   g. Better transition to college for ISs and benefits for domestic students who interact with ISs during volunteering opportunities (Cruce & Moore, 2007)

3. **Reasons why ISs do not volunteer**

   a. "Other participants in this study felt inadequate, alienated, and devalued during the volunteer process. Fear of not being understood, feelings of incompetence, and the cumbersome bureaucratic process in the application process deterred some participants from volunteering …" (Manguvo et al., 2013, 117)

   b. 46/55 students said lack of opportunity and knowledge, lack of time, and limited language (Dudley, 2007)

   c. *Relate to own experience with a lack of volunteering as an IS?*

4. **Implications/Conclusions**

   a. Manguvo et al. (2013): Initial experience is key so there needs to be monitoring. Also they mention the importance of encouragement and appreciation of volunteers.

   b. Dudley (2007): Increase ISs' awareness about volunteering (e.g., orientation sessions by local agencies, including volunteering in the curriculum, and volunteer fairs)

   c. *Own idea: University/ESL program investment*

   d. *Own idea: Buddy program would allow ISs to process/reflect on the experience with.*

5. **The role of non-profits:** *Do university-NGOs partnerships have potential for meaningful collaboration?*

   a. *Many NGOs have experience placing and training volunteers, maybe even IS volunteers.*

   b. *Consider interviewing an NGO director about their experience with placing, monitoring IS volunteers?*

# Chart
# (for Process Lesson 5: Idea Organizers)

*italics* = writer's own ideas

| | Volunteering among International Students (study info, key findings, value of volunteering) | Reasons For and Against | Recommendations and Implications | Important Notes and Relevance to Own Argument |
|---|---|---|---|---|
| Dudley (2007): | A study of 55 international students<br><br>46/55 did not volunteer for English-speaking organizations (p.546)<br><br>87% would like to volunteer in future (p. 547) | -against p.546:<br>lack of opportunity or knowledge (where/how, inaccurate perceptions)<br>lack of time<br>limited lang. ability—listening (p. 547)<br>-for: help others, kill, time, improve English (oral fluency), meet people, prof. exp.<br>-seen as lang. learning strategy (p.550) & insight/ integration into culture (p.552) | type of placement & work must be controlled<br>-increase awareness about opportunities through presentations, training, and curriculum (p.555)<br><br>*ESL programs and institutions of higher education need to consider this seriously!* | **Relevance to my argument**: *The author calls for service-learning curriculum and collaborations with NGOs to increase volunteering opportunities for ISs.*<br><br>**Other notes:**<br>p.548—good quotes on social reasons for volunteering<br>p.549—table 2, shows type/range of services among 8 volunteers. |
| Manguvo et al. (2013) | 13 participants (African ISs) were interviewed about their volunteering experience<br><br>"most participants developed positive feelings during and after the process of volunteering that could potentially hasten their social integration and adaption to the host culture" (p. 125)<br><br>excerpts of positive/ valuable experiences (pp.121-123) | positive influence on social integration, inclusion, cohesion, self-validation (pp.121-22)<br><br>capital for social integration. -social, cultural, human (pp.122-23)<br><br>"volunteerism connected with language proficiency and perfecting language skills"—increased fluency, speaking strategies (p. 124)<br>"…learn norms and values and other codes of behavior that are appropriate for adaptation (p. 126)"—transferable to prof. development<br><br>Negative: social alienation, inadequacy & self-devaluation, failure to make connections (2/13 ISs).<br>Barriers: accent/ speaking, bureaucratic process | "The initial volunteering experience is crucial as it can have long-lasting effects on future involvements. There is a need, therefore, for volunteer agents and peer volunteers to regularly affirm the competency of new international volunteers through appreciation & encouragement." (p. 126) | **Relevance to my argument**: *In addition to encouragement and appreciation for volunteers (mentioned in the article), it is clear that volunteers need to be prepared for their volunteering placements (not discussed!)* |

| | Volunteering among International Students (study info, key findings, value of volunteering) | Reasons For and Against | Recommendations and Implications | Important Notes and Relevance to Own Argument |
|---|---|---|---|---|
| Handy et al. (2010) | Analyzed motivations to volunteer (MTV) across 12 countries; resume-building as an positive indicator for MTV—disproven, do not volunteer more<br><br>rates of volunteering higher & rising among younger students (p.502) | -resume-building (competitive pressure)<br>-social<br>-altruistic/value-based<br>-may have multiple/complex motives<br><br>explains motivators of North American cultures—often external, professional (pp.501-502) | Select volunteers with altruistic MTV rather than resume building MTV<br><br>-MTV impacts intensity | **Relevance to argument:** *Not sure yet—if altruistic reasons to volunteer are better predictors of meaningful volunteering experience should interested ISs be asked about their MTV?*<br><br>**Other**: interestingly India & China show higher rates—aspire to study/work in the US (p.518) |
| Cruce & Moore (2007) | 129,597 first-year students from 623 U.S. colleges and universities<br><br>Only 3.2% of ISs have made a decision to volunteer. 3.4% intend to volunteer during college (Compare to almost 85+% of domestic students) | Reasons why ISs do not volunteer: language & cultural barriers, feelings of isolation (p. 670)<br><br>Reasons to get them involved:<br><br>"Bringing community service initiatives… aid[s] in the students' college transition… gives both international and native students an opportunity to interact with diverse others, an important goal for higher education in today's climate (p. 670)" | Ss who come to college better prepared are more likely to volunteer, but Ss who are less well prepared need to volunteer more because it increases their academic efficacy and allows them to feel like experts in an educational setting (e.g. they can tutor high school students under supervision of upper classmen.)—This model could be implemented in remedial classes! (p. 668)<br><br>Tie volunteering with career planning services! This can help Ss explore career options, especially important for Ss who have not declared a major! (p. 669) | Ss with moderate workloads are better able to do extracurricular activities such as volunteering. (p. 670)<br>**Relevance to argument:** *Since ISs are not allowed to work off campus and are limited as to how many hours they can work on campus, they are well positioned to engage in volunteering.*<br><br>Ss who are members of sororities students who live on campus, and students with a declared major end up volunteering more. (p. 669) |

# Graphic Organizer Version 2: based on prior knowledge activation (for Process Lesson 5: Idea Organizers)

*italics* = writer's own ideas

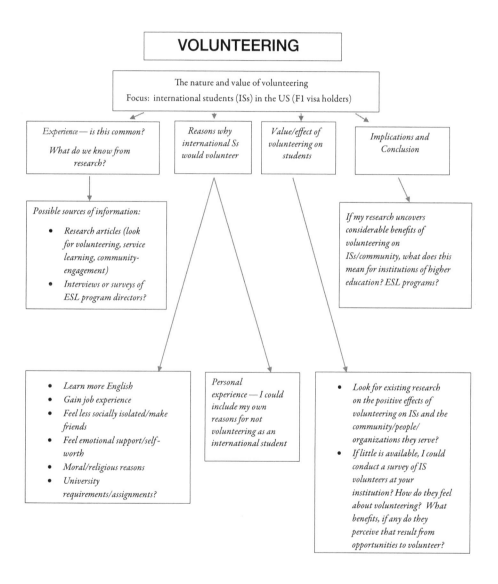

# References

Abasi, A. R., & Akbari, N. (2008). Are we encouraging patchwriting? Reconsidering the role of the pedagogical context in ESL student writers' transgressive intertextuality. *English for Specific Purposes, 27*, 267–284.

Abasi, A.R., Akbari, N., & Graves, B. (2006). Discourse appropriation, construction of identities, and the complex issue of plagiarism: ESL students writing in graduate school. *Journal of Second Language Writing, 15*(2), 102–117.

Ackerman, D. S., & Gross, B. (2005). My instructor made me do it: Task characteristics of procrastination. *Journal of Marketing Education, 27*(1), 5–13.

Angélil-Carter, S. (2000). *Stolen language? Plagiarism in writing.* New York: Longman.

Ariely, D., & Wertenbroch, K. (2002). Procrastination, deadlines, and performance: Self-control by precommitment. *Psychological Science, 13*(3), 219–224.

Asención, Y. (2004). *Validation of reading-to-write assessment tasks performed by second language learners:* Unpublished doctoral dissertation. Northern Arizona University, Flagstaff.

Bauerlein, M. (2011, Aug. 5). How to combat plagiarism. *The Chronicle of Higher Education.* Retrieved from http://chronicle.com/blogs/brainstorm/how-to-combat-plagiarism/37862

Bean, J. C. (2011). *Engaging ideas: The professor's guide to integrating writing, critical thinking, and active learning in the classroom.* San Francisco: Jossey-Bass.

Bem, S. L. (1993). *The lenses of gender.* New Haven, CT: Yale University Press.

Benesch, S. (1999). Rights analysis: Studying power relations in an academic setting. *English for Specific Purposes, 18*, 313–327.

Benesch, S. (2001). *Critical English for academic purposes: Theory, politics, and practice.* Mahwah, NJ: Lawrence Erlbaum.

Benesch, S. (2016, April). When institutional policies ignore student diversity: English language instructors' responses to a monolithic university plagiarism policy. Paper presented at the 50th Annual TESOL International Convention, Baltimore, Maryland.

Bereiter, C., & Scardamalia, M. (1987). *The psychology of written composition.* Hillsdale, NJ: Lawrence Erlbaum.

Berg, E.C. (1999). The effects of trained peer response on ESL students' revision types and writing quality. *Journal of Second Language Writing, 8*(3), 215–241.

Berkenkotter, C., & Huckin, T. N. (1995). *Genre knowledge in disciplinary communication.* Hillsdale, NJ: Lawrence Erlbaum.

Biddix, J. P., Chung, C. J., & Park, H. W. (2011). Convenience or credibility? A study of college student online research behaviors. *The Internet and Higher Education, 14*(3), 175–182. doi:10.1016/j.iheduc.2011.01.003

Bikowski, D. (2012). Exploring non-native English speaking students' use of technology to improve their paraphrasing skills and avoid plagiarism. In G. Kessler, A. Oskoz, & I. Elola (Eds.), *Technology across writing contexts and tasks* (pp. 255–276). San Marcos, TX: CALICO Monograph.

Bloch, J. (2012). *Plagiarism, intellectual property and the teaching of L2 writing*. Clevedon, U.K: Multilingual Matters.

Blum, S. D. (2009). *My word! Plagiarism and college culture*. Ithaca, NY: Cornell University Press.

Boice, R. (1989). Procrastination, busyness and bingeing. *Behaviour Research and Therapy, 27*(6), 605–611.

Borg, E. (2000). Citation practices in academic writing. In P. Thompson, (Ed.), *Patterns and perspectives: Insights into EAP writing practices* (pp. 27–45). Reading, U.K.: University of Reading.

Borg, E. (2009). Local plagiarisms. *Assessment & Evaluation in Higher Education, 34*, 415–426.

Briggs, R. (2003). Shameless! Reconceiving the problem of plagiarism. *Australian Universities Review, 46*(1), 19–23.

Burton, V. T., & Chadwick, S. A. (2000). Investigating the practices of student researchers: Patterns of use and criteria for use of internet and library sources. *Computers and Composition, 17*(3), 309–328. doi:10.1016/S8755-4615(00)00037-2

Cai, G. (1999). Texts and contexts: Understanding Chinese students' English compositions. In C.R. Cooper and L. Odell (Eds.), *Evaluating writing* (pp. 279–297). Urbana, IL: National Council of Teachers of English.

Campbell, C. (1990). Writing with others' words: Using background reading text in academic compositions. In B. Kroll (Ed.), *Second language writing: Research insights for the classroom* (pp. 211–230). Cambridge, U.K.: Cambridge University Press.

Canagarajah, A. S. (1997). Challenges in English literacy for African-American and Lankan Tamil learners: Towards a pedagogical paradigm for bidialectical and bilingual minority students. *Language and Education, 11*(1), 15–37.

Canagarajah, A. S. (2001). Addressing issues of power and difference in ESL academic writing. In Flowerdew & Peacock (Eds.), *Research perspectives on English for academic purposes* (pp. 117–131). Cambridge, U.K.: Cambridge University Press.

Canagarajah, A. S. (2002). Multilingual writers and the academic community: Towards a critical relationship. *Journal of English for Academic Purposes, 1*(1), 29–44.

Casanave, C.P. (2004). *Controversies in second language writing: Dilemmas and decisions in research and instruction*. Ann Arbor: University of Michigan Press.

Chandrasoma, R., Thompson, C., & Pennycook, A. (2004). Beyond plagiarism: Transgressive and nontransgressive intertextuality. *Journal of Language, Identity, and Education, 3*(3), 171–193.

Cisneros, S. (1984). *The house on Mango Street*. New York: Vintage.

Conzett, J., Martin, M., & Mitchell, M. (2010). Proactively addressing plagiarism and other academic honesty issues with second-language writers. *Writing and Pedagogy, 2*(2), 293–309.

Coxhead, A. (2000). A new academic word list. *TESOL Quarterly, 34*(2), 213–238.

Cruce, T. M., & Moore, J. V. (2007). First-year students' plans to volunteer: An examination of the predictors of community service participation. *Journal of College Student Development, 48*(6), 655–673. doi:10.1353/csd.2007.0063

Currie, P. (1998). Staying out of trouble: Apparent plagiarism and academic survival. *Journal of Second Language Writing, 7*(1), 1–18.

Dean, J. (2014, June 11). Being bored can fire up your creativity. *Psyblog—Understanding your mind*. Retrieved from www.spring.org.uk/2014/06/being-bored-can-fire-up-our-creativity.php.

Dong, Y.R. (1996). Learning how to use citations for knowledge-transformation: Nonnative doctoral students' dissertation writing in science. *Research in the Teaching of English, 30*(4), 428–457.

Dudley, L. (2007). Integrating volunteering into the adult immigrant second language experience. *Canadian Modern Language Review-Revue Canadienne Des Langues Vivantes, 63*(4), 539–561. doi:10.3138/cmlr.63.4.539

Durst, R. K. (1987). Cognitive and linguistic demands of analytic writing. *Research in the teaching of English, 21*(4), 347–376.

Eighner, L. (1993). *Travels with Lizbeth*. New York: St. Martin's.

Ennis, R. H. (1991). Critical thinking: A streamlined conception. *Teaching Philosophy, 14*(1), 5–25.

Farhang, K. (2014, Oct. 8). For some international students, 'plagiarism' is a foreign word. Retrieved from http://www.mprnews.org/story/2014/10/08/international-students-cheating

Ferris, D. (2003). *Response to student writing: Implications for second language students*. Mahwah, NJ: Lawrence Erlbaum.

Ferris, D. (2007). Preparing teachers to respond to student writing. *Journal of Second Language Writing, 16*, 165–193.

Ferris, D. (2014). Responding to student writing: Teachers' philosophies and practices. *Assessing Writing, 19*, 6–23.

Ferris, D.R., Liu, H., & Rabie, B. (2011). "The job of teaching writing": Teacher views on responding to student writing. *Writing and Pedagogy, 3*(1), 39–77.

Flaherty, C. (2014, May 13). New book, new allegations. *Inside Higher Ed*. Retrieved from https://www.insidehighered.com/news/2014/05/13/arizona-state-professor-accused-plagiarism-second-time

Flint, A., Clegg, S., & Macdonald, R. (2006). Exploring staff perceptions of student plagiarism. *Journal of Further and Higher Education, 30*(2), 145–156.

Flowerdew, J., & Li, Y. (2007). Language re-use among Chinese apprentice scientist writing for publication. *Applied Linguistics, 28*(3), 440–465.

Folse, K. (2008). Myth 1: Teaching vocabulary is not the writing teacher's job. In J. Reid (Ed.), *Writing myths: Applying second language research to classroom teaching* (pp. 1–17). Ann Arbor: University of Michigan Press.

Foster, A.L. (2002, May 17). Plagiarism-detection tool creates legal quandary. *The Chronicle of Higher Education*. Retrieved from http://chronicle.com/article/Plagiarism-Detection-Tool/29885

Fountain, T.K., & Fitzgerald, L. (2008). "Thou shalt not plagiarize"? Appeals to textual authority and community at religiously affiliated and secular colleges. In R.M. Howard & A.E. Robillard, (Eds.), *Pluralizing plagiarism: Identities, contexts, pedagogies* (pp. 101–123). Portsmouth, NH: Boynton/Cook Heinemann.

Garrett, M. (2008). *College Cheating Story*. Retrieved from https://www.youtube.com/watch?v=gpPnjWP59MU

Gilbert, N. G. (1977). Referencing as persuasion. *Social Studies of Science, 7*, 113–122.

Gladwell, M. (2004, Nov. 22). Something borrowed: Should a charge of plagiarism ruin your life? *The New Yorker*. Retrieved from http://www.newyorker.com/magazine/2004/11/22/something-borrowed

Goldstein, L. (2006). Feedback and revision in second language writing: Contextual, teacher, and student variables. In K. Hyland & F. Hyland (Eds.), *Response to student writing: Implications for second language students* (pp. 185–205). Cambridge, U.K.: Cambridge University Press.

Gulla, A. (2010). *Creating values in life: Personal, moral, spiritual, family, and social values*. Bloomington, IN: AuthorHouse.

Grabe, W., & Zhang, C. (2013). Second language reading-writing relations. In A. S. Horning & E. W. Kraemer (Eds.), *Reconnecting reading and writing*. Fort Collins, CO: The WAC Clearinghouse and Parlor Press. Retrieved from http://wac.colostate.edu/books/reconnecting/

Gu, Q., & Brooks, J. (2008). Beyond the accusation of plagiarism. *System, 36*, 337–352.

Handy, F., Cnaan, R. A., Hustinx, L., Kang, C., Brudney, J. L., Haski-Leventhal, D., & Zrinscak, S. (2010). A cross-cultural examination of student volunteering: Is it all about résumé building? *Nonprofit and Voluntary Sector Quarterly, 39*(3), 498–523. doi:10.1177/0899764009344353

Harwood, N. (2009). An interview-based study of the functions of citations in academic writing across two disciplines. *Journal of Pragmatics, 41*, 497–518.

He, L., and Shi, L. (2008). ESL students' perceptions and experiences of standardized English writing tests. *Assessing Writing, 13*, 130–149.

Hinds, J. (1983). Contrastive rhetoric: Japanese and English. *Text, 3*(2), 183–195.

Hinkel, E. (2005). Hedging, inflating, and persuading in L2 academic writing. *Applied Language Learning, 15*(1 & 2), 29–53. Retrieved from http://www.cs.columbia.edu/~prokofieva/CandidacyPapers/Hinkel_Hedging.pdf

Hinkel, E. (2016). Practical grammar teaching: Grammar constructions and their relatives. In E. Hinkel, (Ed.), *Teaching English grammar to speakers of other languages* (pp. 171–199). New York: Routledge.

Hirvela, A. (2016). *Connecting reading and writing in second language writing instruction (2nd ed.)* Ann Arbor: University of Michigan Press.

Hirvela, A., & Du, Q. (2013). "Why am I paraphrasing?": Undergraduate ESL writers' engagement with source-based academic writing and reading. *Journal of English for Academic Purposes, 12*(2), 87–98.

Ho, I. (1998). Relationship between motivation/attitude, effort, English proficiency, and socio-cultural educational factors and Taiwan technological university/institute students' English learning strategy use. Unpublished doctoral dissertation, Auburn University, AL.

Holtzman, A. (2009). Original misunderstanding. *Knowledge Quest, 37*(3), 62–64.

Howard, R. M. (1992). A plagiarism pentimento. *Journal of Teaching Writing, 11*(2), 233–245.

Howard, R. M. (1995). Plagiarisms, authorships, and the academic death penalty. *College English, 57*(7), 788–806.

Howard, R. M. (1999). *Standing in the shadow of giants: Plagiarists, authors, collaborators*. Stanford, CT: Ablex.

Howard, R. M. (2007). Understanding "Internet plagiarism." *Computers and Composition, 24*, 3–15. doi: 10.1016/j.compcom.2006.12.005

Howard, R. M., & Davies, L. J. (2009). Plagiarism in the internet age. *Educational Leadership, 66*(6), 64–67.

Hsu, A.Y. (2003). *Patterns of Plagiarism Behavior in the ESL Classroom and the Effectiveness of Instruction in Appropriate Use of Sources*. PhD Dissertation. University of Illinois at Urbana–Champaign.

Hu, G., & Sun, X. (2015, Mar.). What do Chinese university English language teachers know about plagiarism? Paper presented at the TESOL International Convention, Toronto, Canada.

Huang, A., & Han. X. (2008). 'The academic style construction committee is by no means an ornament.' *Chinese Education and Society, 40*(6), 31–34.

Hunt, R. (2002). Four reasons to be happy about internet plagiarism. Retrieved from http://www.stthomasu.ca/~hunt/4reaons.htm

Hyland, F. (2001). Dealing with plagiarism when giving feedback. *ELT Journal, 55*(4), 375–381.

Hyland, K. (1999). Disciplinary discourses: Writer stance in research articles. In C. N. Candlin and K. Hyland, (Eds.), *Writing: Texts, processes and practices* (pp. 99–121). London: Longman.

Hyland, K. (2002). Specificity revisited: How far should we go now? *English for Specific Purposes, 21*(4), 385–395.

Hyland, K. (2004). *Disciplinary discourses: Social interactions in academic writing*. Ann Arbor: University of Michigan Press.

Hyland, K. (2011). Disciplines and discourses: Social interactions in the construction of knowledge. In D. Starke-Meyerring, A. Paré, N. Artemeva, M. Horne, & L. Yousoubova (Eds.), *Writing in the knowledge society* (pp. 193–214). West Lafayette, IN: Parlor Press and The WAC Clearinghouse.

Hyland, K. (2015, Mar.). Undergraduate understandings: Stance and engagement in L2 undergraduate writing. Paper presented at the TESOL International Convention, Toronto, Canada.

Johns, A., & Mayes, P. (1990) An analysis of summary protocols of university ESL students. *Applied Linguistics, 11*(3), 253–271. doi: 10.1093/applin/11.3.253

Joy, A. (2000). *Crossing borders: An international reader*. Fort Worth, TX: Harcourt.

Kaplan, R. (1966). Cultural thought patterns in intercultural education. *Language Learning, 16*, 1–20.

Kaplan, R.B. (1987). Cultural thought patterns revisited. In U. Connor & R.B. Kaplan, (Eds.), *Writing across languages: Analysis of L2 Text* (pp. 9–21). Reading, MA: Addison-Wesley.

Keck, C. (2006). The use of paraphrase in summary writing: A comparison of L1 and L2 writers. *Journal of Second Language Writing, 15*, 261–278.

Keck, C. (2010). How do university students attempt to avoid plagiarism? A grammatical analysis of undergraduate paraphrasing strategies. *Writing & Pedagogy, 2*(2), 193–222. doi: 10.1558/wap.v2i2.193

Keith-Spiegel, P. (1972). Early conceptions of humor: Varieties and issues. In J. H. Goldstein & McGhee, (Eds.), *The psychology of humor: Theoretical perspectives and empirical issues* (pp. 3–39). New York: Academic Press.

Kim, E., Alhaddab, T.A., Aquino, K. C., & Negi, R. (2016). Delaying academic tasks? Predictors of academic procrastination of Asian international students. *Journal of International Students, 6*(3), 817–824.

Kincaid, J. (1990). *Lucy*. New York: Plume.

Kirkpatrick, D.D. (2002, Jan. 5). 2 Accuse Stephen Ambrose, popular historian, of plagiarism. *The New York Times*. Retrieved from http://www.nytimes.com/2002/01/05/national/05AMBR.html

Knoblauch, C.H., & Brannon, L. (2006). Teacher commentary on student writing: The state of the art. In R. Staub, (Ed.), *Key works on teacher response: An anthology* (pp. 69–76). Portsmouth, NH: Boynton/Cook Heineman.

Kostka, I., & Eisenstein Ebsworth, M. (2014). Using Turnitin to support students' understandings of textual borrowing in academic writing: A case study. In S. Li & P. Swanson (Eds.), *Engaging language learners through technology integration* (pp. 44–67). Hershey, PA: IGI Global.

Ksienski, H. (2004). Enhancing volunteer participation with the ethno-cultural community. Retrieved from https://www.muttart.org/wp-content/uploads/2014/12/Enhancing-Volunteer-Participation-Hadassah-Ksienski-2004

Lee, M.S. (2004). Effects of video game violence on prosocial and antisocial behaviors. *Journal of Young Investigators, 11*(2). Retrieved from http://legacy.jyi.org/volumes/volume11/issue2/articles/lee.html

Lee, Y., & Moon, S. (2011). Mainstream and ethnic volunteering by Korean immigrants in the United States. *Voluntas: International Journal of Voluntary and Nonprofit Organizations, 22*(4), 811–830. doi:10.1007/s11266-010-9176-y

Lei, J., & Hu, G. (2014). Chinese ESOL lecturers' stance on plagiarism: Does knowledge matter? *ELT Journal, 68*(1), 41–51.

Leki, I. (1995). Coping strategies of ESL students in writing tasks across the curriculum. *TESOL Quarterly, 29*, 325–360.

Leki, I. (2003). Living through college literacy—Nursing in a second language. *Written Communication, 20*, 81–98.

Leopold, T. (2014, Aug. 8). 'True Detective' writer accused of plagiarism. Retrieved from http://www.cnn.com/2014/08/08/showbiz/tv/true-detective-pizzolatto-plagiarism/

LexTutor Vocabulary Profiler. (n.d.). Retrieved from http://www.lextutor.ca/vp/eng/

Li, Y., & Casanave, C. P. (2012). Two first-year students' strategies for writing from sources: Patchwriting or plagiarism? *Journal of Second Language Writing, 21*(2), 165–180. doi:10.1016/j.jslw.2012.03.002

Liu, D. (2005). Plagiarism in ESOL students: Is cultural conditioning truly the major culprit? *ELT Journal, 59*(3), 234–241.

Liu, J., & Hansen, J. G. (2002). *Peer response in second language writing classrooms.* Ann Arbor: University of Michigan Press.

Lowinger, R. J., He, Z., Lin, M., & Chang, M. (2014). The impact of academic self-efficacy, acculturation difficulties, and language abilities on procrastination behavior in Chinese international students. *College Student Journal, 48*(1), 141–152.

Lu, M.-Z. (1987). From silence to words: Writing as struggle. *College English, 4*, 437–448.

Lundstrom, K., & Baker, W. (2009). To give is better than to receive: The benefits of peer review to the reviewer's own writing. *Journal of Second Language Writing, 18*, 30–43.

Lunsford, A.A., & Ede, L. (1994). Collaborative authorship and the teaching of writing. In M. Woodmansee & P. Jaszi (Eds.), *The construction of authorship: Textual appropriation in law and literature* (pp. 417–438). Durham, NC: Duke University Press.

Lunsford, R.F., & Straub, R. (2006). Twelve readers reading: A survey of contemporary teachers' commenting strategies. In R. Staub, (Ed.), *Key works on teacher response: An anthology* (pp. 159–189). Portsmouth, NH: Boynton/Cook Heineman.

Manguvo, A., Whitney, S., & Chareka, O. (2013). The role of volunteerism on social integration and adaptation of African students at a mid-western university in the United States. *Journal of International Students, 3*(2), 117.

Marsh, B. (2004). Turnitin.com and the scriptual enterprise of plagiarism detection. *Computers and Composition, 21*, 427–438.

Marshall, S., & Garry, M. (2006). NESB and ESB students' attitudes and perceptions of plagiarism. *International Journal of Educational Integrity, 2*(1), 26–37.

Matsuda, P.K. (2001). Voice in Japanese written discourse: Implications for second language writing. *Journal of Second Language Writing, 10*, 35–53.

Matsuda, P.K., & Tardy, C.M. (2007). Voice in academic writing: The rhetorical construction of author identity in blind manuscript review. *English for Specific Purposes, 26*, 235–249.

Merriam-Webster. (2017). Stimulate. Retrieved from http://www.merriam-webster.com/dictionary/stimulate

Moon, Y. (2002). Korean university students' awareness of plagiarism in summary writings. *Language Research, 38*(4), 1349–1365.

Moore, T. (1997). From test to note: Cultural variation in summarization practices. *Prospect, 12*, 54–63.

Moore, V. (2002, Aug. 15). Playing dirty in the war on plagiarism. *The Chronicle of Higher Education.* Retrieved from http://chronicle.com/article/Playing-Dirty-in-the-War-on/46035/

Mott-Smith, J.A. (2011). Establishing textual authority and separating voices: A new approach to teaching referencing. *English Teaching Forum, 49*(2), 16–25.

Mott-Smith, J.A. (2013). Viewing student behavior through the lenses of culture and globalization: Two narratives from a US college writing class. *Teaching in Higher Education.* doi: 10.1080/13562517.2012.725222

Mott-Smith, J.A. (2016). Ideological English: A theme for college composition. In C. Hastings & L. Jacob, (Eds.), *Social Justice in English Language Teaching* (pp. 95–104). Alexandria, VA: TESOL International.

Mullin, B. (2014, September 16). Is it original? *An editor's guide to identifying plagiarism.* Retrieved from http://www.poynter.org/2014/is-it-original-an-editors-guide-to-identifying-plagiarism/269273/

Murdoch University of Dubai. (2011). *Plagiarism.* Retrieved from https://www.youtube.com/watch?v=7lmp3-0UIFM

Myers, G. (1990). *Writing biology: Texts in the social construction of scientific knowledge.* Madison: University of Wisconsin Press.

Norton, B. (1997). Language, identity, and the ownership of English. *TESOL Quarterly, 31*(3), 409–429.

Nussbaum, E. M. (2008). Collaborative discourse, argumentation, and learning: Preface and literature review. *Contemporary Educational Psychology, 33*(3), 345–359.

Nussbaum, E. M., & Schraw, G. (2007). Promoting argument-counterargument integration in students› writing. *The Journal of Experimental Education, 76*(1), 59–92.

Paul, R., & Elder, L. (2009). *The miniature guide to critical thinking concepts and tools.* Dillon Beach, CA: Foundation for Critical Thinking Press.

Pecorari, D. (2001). Plagiarism and international students: How the English-speaking university responds. In D. Belcher & A. Hirvela, (Eds.), *Linking literacies: Perspectives on L2 reading-writing connections* (pp. 229–245). Ann Arbor: University of Michigan Press.

Pecorari, D. (2003). Good and original: Plagiarism and patchwriting in academic second-language writing. *Journal of Second Language Writing, 12*, 317–345. doi: 10.1016/j.jslw.2003.08.004

Pecorari, D. (2006). Visible and occluded citation features in postgraduate second-language writing. *English for Specific Purposes, 25*, 4–19. doi: 10.1016/j.esp.2005.04.004

Pecorari, D. (2013). *Teaching to avoid plagiarism: How to promote good source use.* Berkshire, U.K.: Open University Press.

Pecorari, D. (2015). Plagiarism in second language writing: Is It time to close the case? *Journal of Second Language Writing.* http://dx.doi.org/10.1016/j.jslw.2015.08.003

Pecorari, D., & Petrić, B. (2014). Plagiarism in second-language writing. *Language Teaching, 47*(3), 269–302.

Pecorari, D., & Shaw, P. (2012). Types of student intertextuality and faculty attitudes. *Journal of Second Language Writing, 21*, 149–164.

Pennycook, A. (1996). Borrowing others' words: Text, ownership, memory, and plagiarism. *TESOL Quarterly, 30*(2), 201–230.

Petrić, B. (2004). A pedagogical perspective on plagiarism. *NovELTy, 11*(1), 4–18.

Petrić, B. (2007). Rhetorical functions of citations in high- and low-rated master's theses. *Journal of English for Academic Purposes, 6*, 238–253.

Petrić, B. (2012). Legitimate textual borrowing: Direct quotation in L2 student writing. *Journal of Second Language Writing, 21*(2), 102–117. doi: 10.1016/j.jslw.2012.03.005.

Petrić, B. (2015). What next for research on plagiarism? Continuing the dialogue. *Journal of Second Language Writing.* http://dx.doi.org/10.1016/j.jslw.2015.08.007

Plakans, L. M. (2009). The role of reading in integrated L2 writing tasks. *Journal of English for Academic Purposes, 8*(4), 252–266.

Popova, M. (2012, June 12). Combinatorial creativity and the myth of originality: The power of the synthesizing mind and the building blocks of combinatorial creativity. *The Smithsonian.* Retrieved from http://www.smithsonianmag.com/innovation/combinatorial-creativity-and-the-myth-of-originality-114843098/?no-ist

Pratt, M. L. (1991). Arts of the contact zone. *Profession, 91*, 33–40.

Price, M. (2002). Beyond "Gotcha!": Situating plagiarism in policy and pedagogy. *College Composition and Communication, 54*(1), 88–111.

Primo. (2016). Peer-Reviewed Instructional Materials Online Database. Retrieved from http://primodb.org

Prior, P. (2001). Voices in text, mind, and society: Sociohistoric accounts of discourse acquisition and use. *Journal of Second Language Writing, 10*(1-2), 55–81.

Purdue University. (2016). OWL Purdue Online Writing Lab. Retrieved from https://owl.english.purdue.edu/owl/

Purdy, J. (2005). Calling off the hounds: Technology and the visibility of plagiarism. *Pedagogy, 5*(2), 275–296.

Qin, J., & Karabacak, E. (2010). The analysis of Toulmin elements in Chinese EFL university argumentative writing. *System, 38*(3), 444–456.

Radia, P., & Stapleton, P. (2008). Unconventional internet genres and their impact on second language undergraduate students' writing process. *The Internet and Higher Education, 11*(1), 9–17.

Ramanathan, V., & Atkinson, D. (1999). Individualism, academic writing, and ESL writers. *Journal of Second Language Writing, 8*(1), 45–75.

Reinking, J.A. & von der Osten, R. (2005). *Strategies for successful writing* (7th ed.). Upper Saddle River, NJ: Pearson Prentice Hall.

Robertson, I. (1994). Values. In M. L. Fjeldstad (Ed.), *The thoughtful reader: A whole language approach to college reading* (pp. 46–48). Orlando, FL: Harcourt Brace.

Robillard, A. E. (2006). Young scholars affecting composition: A challenge to disciplinary citation practices. *College English, 68*(3), 253–270.

Robillard, A. E. (2008). Situating plagiarism as a form of authorship: The politics of writing in a first-year writing course. In R. M. Howard & A. E. Robillard, (Eds.), *Pluralizing plagiarism: Identities, contexts, pedagogies* (pp. 27–42). Portsmouth, NH: Boynton/Cook Heineman.

Roig, M. (1999). When college students' attempts at paraphrasing become instances of potential plagiarism. *Psychological Reports, 84*(3), 973–982.

Roig, M. (2001). Plagiarism and paraphrasing criteria of college and university professors. *Ethics & Behavior, 11*(3), 307–323.

Roig, M., & Detommaso, L. (1995). Are college cheating and plagiarism related to academic procrastination? *Psychological Reports, 77*(2), 691–698.

Rollinson, P. (2005). Using peer feedback in the ESL writing class. *ELT Journal, 59*(1), 23–30.

Ryssdal, K., & Hill, A. (2015, Aug. 24). Joke stealing is no laughing matter. Retrieved from http://www.marketplace.org/2015/08/24/life/joke-stealing-no-laughing-matter

Salvatori, M. (1996). Conversations with texts: Reading in the teaching of composition. *College English, 58*(4), 440–454.

Schlosser, E. (2001). *Fast food nation: The dark side of the all-American meal.* New York: Houghton-Mifflin.

Scollon, R. (1994). As a matter of fact: The changing ideology of authorship and responsibility in discourse. *World Englishes, 13*, 33–46.

Segev-Miller, R. (2004). Writing from sources: The effect of explicit instruction on college students' processes and products. *L1–Educational Studies in Language and Literature, 4*(1), 5–33.

Shi, L. (2004). Textual borrowing in second-language writing. *Written Communication, 21*(2), 171–200. doi: 10.1177/0741088303262846.

Shi, L. (2006). Cultural backgrounds and textual appropriation. *Language Awareness, 15*(4), 264–282.

Shi, L. (2010). Textual appropriation and citing behaviors of university undergraduates. *Applied Linguistics, 31*(1), 1–24. doi: 10.1093/applin/amn045.

Shi, L. (2011). Common knowledge, learning, and citation practices in university writing. *Research in the Teaching of English, 45*(3), 308–334.

Shi, L. (2012). Rewriting and paraphrasing source texts in second language writing. *Journal of Second Language Writing, 21*, 134–148. doi: 10.1016/j.jslw.2012.03.003

Slaouti, D. (2002). The world wide web for academic purposes: Old study skills for new? *English for Specific Purposes, 21*(2), 105–124.

Song-Turner, H. (2008). Plagiarism: Academic dishonesty or "blind spot" of multicultural education? *Australian Universities' Review, 50*(2), 39–50.

Spack, R. (1997). The acquisition of academic literacy in a second language: A longitudinal case study. *Written Communication, 14*(1), 3–62.

Spivey, N. N. (1990). Transforming texts: Constructive processes in reading and writing. *Written Communication, 7*(2), 256–287.

Stapleton, P. (2005). Using the web as a research source: Implications for L2 academic writing. *Modern Language Journal, 89*(2), 177–189.

Starfield, S. (2002). "I'm a second-language English speaker": Negotiating writer identity and authority in Sociology One. *Journal of Language, Identity, and Education, 1*(2), 121–140.

Stern, L.A. & Solomon, A. (2006). Effective faculty feedback: The road less traveled. *Assessing Writing, 11*(1), 22–41.

Sutherland-Smith, W. (2005). Pandora's box: Academic perceptions of student plagiarism in writing. *Journal of English for Academic Purposes, 4*(1), 83–95.

Sutherland-Smith, W. (2008). *Plagiarism, the Internet, and student learning: Improving academic integrity*. New York: Routledge.

Swales, J. M. (1990). *Genre analysis: English in academic and research settings*. New York: Cambridge University Press.

Swales, J. M., & Feak, C. B. (2012). *Academic writing for graduate students: Essential tasks and skills* (3rd ed.). Ann Arbor: University of Michigan Press.

Tan, S. (2001, July). Originality and creativity. Paper presented at the Joint National Conference of the Australian Association for the Teaching of English and the Australian Literacy Educators' Association, Hobart, Tasmania, Australia. ERIC: ED 458582

Tang, R., & John, S. (1999). The 'I' in identity: Exploring writer identity in student academic writing through the first person pronoun. *English for Specific Purposes, 18*, S23–S39.

Text Fixer. Retrieved from http://www.textfixer.com/tools/online-word-counter.php

Thompson, C. (2005). "Authority is everything": A study of the politics of textual ownership and knowledge in the formation of student writer identities. *International Journal for Educational Integrity, 1*(1). doi: http://doc.doi.org/10.21913/IJEI.vlil_18

Tomaš, Z. (2010). Addressing pedagogy on textual borrowing: Focus on instructional resources. *Writing and Pedagogy 2*(2), 223–250.

Tomaš, Z. (2011). *Textual borrowing across academic assignments: Examining undergraduate second-language writers' implementation of writing instruction*. Unpublished dissertation. University of Utah, Salt Lake City.

Tomaš, Z., & Marino, B. (Developers). (2014). *Departing from punishing plagiarism: Toward addressing ineffective source use pedagogically*. Retrieved from https://www.youtube.com/watch?v=tEskWSfrwzo&feature=youtu.be (18 min., 33 sec.)

Tomaš, Z., Marino, B., and Pantelides, K. (Developers). (2015a). *Describe an assignment in which you had to use and cite outside sources.* Retrieved from https://youtu.be/_mwaHic YZmY. (2 min., 33 sec.).

Tomaš, Z., Marino, B., and Pantelides, K. (Developers). (2015b). *Describe your process for completing research-based assignments.* Retrieved from https://youtu.be/BjsTWCAm0_k. (2 min., 48 sec.).

Tomaš, Z., Marino, B., and Pantelides, K. (Developers). (2015c). *How do you choose and refine a topic?* Retrieved from https://youtu.be/bEOxnWbbgvA. (1 min., 20 sec.).

Tomaš, Z., Marino, B., and Pantelides, K. (Developers). (2015d). *How do you find and evaluate sources?* Retrieved from https://youtu.be/vGKRhBtq_GA. (3 min., 7 sec.).

Tomaš, Z., Marino, B., and Pantelides, K. (Developers). (2015e). *How do you manage your time when you are challenged with an extensive assignment?* Retrieved from https://youtu.be/ Fi9BgRH0aVg. (2 min., 11 sec.).

Tomaš, Z., Marino, B., and Pantelides, K. (Developers). (2015f). *How do you track information from different sources?* Retrieved from https://youtu.be/_0rF0jWRTJ8. (1 min., 37 sec.).

Tomaš, Z., Marino, B., and Pantelides, K. (Developers). (2015g). *What are your strengths and challenges as a writer?* Retrieved from https://youtu.be/brNr_pzLrc4. (2 min., 6 sec.).

Tomaš, Z., Marino, B., and Pantelides, K. (Developers). (2015h). *What resources do you use when writing a paper?* Retrieved from https://youtu.be/iFo2okhyCp8. (3 min., 12 sec.).

Tomaš, Z., Marino, B., and Pantelides, K. (Developers). (2015i). *What strategies do you find useful when completing research?* Retrieved from https://youtu.be/mmgHArN8TiY. (1 min., 53 sec.).

Tomaš, Z., Marino, B., and Pantelides, K. (Developers). (2015j). *What writing advice would you give a less experienced university student?* Retrieved from https://youtu.be/5rI5FYW10KY. (2 min., 6 sec.).

Toor, R. (2011, June 20). Unconscious plagiarism. *The Chronicle of Higher Education.* Retrieved from http://chronicle.com/article/Unconscious-Plagiarism/127928/

Turnitin. (n.d.) Aiming for integrity: How well do you know plagiarism? Retrieved from http://turnitin.com/assets/en_us/media/plagiarism-quiz/

Valentine, K. (2006). Plagiarism as literacy practice: Recognizing and rethinking ethical binaries. *College Composition and Communication, 58*(1), 89–109.

Vanacker, B. (2011). Returning students' right to access, choice and notice: a proposed code of ethics for instructors using *Turnitin. Ethics and Information Technology, 13*(4), 327–338.

Walling, D.R. (2009). The creativity continuum. *TechTrends, 53*(4), 26–27.

Wette, R. (2010). Evaluating student learning in a university-level EAP unit on writing using sources. *Journal of Second Language Writing, 19*, 158–177.

White, H.D. (2004). Citation analysis and discourse analysis revisited. *Applied Linguistics, 25*(1), 89–116.

Williams, H. (2010). Implicit attribution. *Journal of Pragmatics, 42*(3), 617–636. doi: 10.1016/j.pragma.2009.07.013

Williams, H. (2015). Are citation standards a function of learner skill level? Paper presented at the TESOL International Convention, Toronto, Canada, March 25–28.

Woodmansee, M. (1994). On the author effect: Recovering collectivity. In M. Woodmansee & P. Jaszi, (Eds.), *The construction of authorship: Textual appropriation in law and literature* (pp. 15–28). Durham, NC: Duke University Press.

Word and Phrase. Retrieved from http://www.wordandphrase.info/analyzeText.asp

Yamada, K. (2003). What prevents ESL/EFL writers from avoiding plagiarism?: Analyses of 10 North-American college websites. *System, 31,* 247–258.

Zhao, C-M., Kuh, G. D., & Carini, R. M. (2005). A comparison of international student and American student engagement in effective educational practices. *Journal of Higher Education, 76*(2): 209–232.

Zhu, W. (2005). Source articles as scaffolds in reading to write: The case of a Chinese student writing in English. *Journal of Asian Pacific Communication, 15*(1), 129–152.

Zhu, Y. (2008). The Pan Zhichang incident. *Chinese Education and Society, 40*(6), 20–30.

Zwagerman, S. (2008). The scarlet *P*: Plagiarism, panopticism, and the rhetoric of academic integrity. *College Composition and Communication, 59(*4), 676–710.